Dedication

To my husband
My dreams came true because of you.

ISBN 978-0-9788952-2-8

Published by Agri Marketing magazine
c/o Henderson Communications L.L.C.
P.O. Box 396
Adel, IA 50003
515-954-8381
www.AgriMarketing.com
www.AgriManners.com
Twitter.com/AgriManners

Graphics provided by FLM+
www.wideopenthinking.com

Printed in the United States of America

To order copies of *Agri Manners*, go to: www.AgriMarketing.com. From the top navigation bar access the "Bookstore" tab.

Table of Contents

Chapter One

Agri Manners – Essential Etiquette for Professional Success

"Let us not forget that the cultivation of the earth is the most important labor of man. When tillage begins, the other acts will follow. The farmers, therefore, are the founders of our civilization."
- *Daniel Webster*

I am proud to be the daughter of a farmer.

Throughout his career as an agricultural banker and farmer, my father always used the mantra, "Treat people better than they deserve. It's the kindest thing to do."

When a farmer would call the bank to discuss their credit and insurance needs, Dad would strap on his four-buckle overshoes, pull a pair of bib overalls over his dress shirt and tie, then drive the gravel road to the farmstead to meet with the farmer in person. Together they would walk the edge of the farm field. Dad would listen as long as the farmer wanted to talk about his crops. And he listened. And listened. And listened.

One of Dad's favorite clients was a pair of bachelor brother farmers. Maurice and Chester lived south of town on several hundred acres of prime farmland they owned and operated. Chester would call the bank on his rotary dial, black wall phone, asking for Dad. During his lunchtime, Dad would drive the gravel road to Chester and Maurice's farm. Chester would often ask for a ride back to town when he needed groceries, and Dad would oblige him. Chester was not a big man and, sitting in the front car seat, he had to strain to see over the dashboard of the car. His wire-rimmed eyeglasses would move slightly as he crinkled his eyes to see out. Off they would go to our small grocery store. Dad would wait in the car, while Chester went inside the market to shop. Out Chester would come, a small paper bag in hand.

"What did you get?" Dad would inquire. "Chocolate marshmallow cookies," Chester humbly replied, his seed corn cap pulled down to his very old eyes. It was always chocolate marshmallow cookies for Chester. Never fruit or vegetables or steak. He explained to Dad that he and his brother "Grew all of that on the farm. Don't need to buy it from someone else."

Once, early in the friendship, Dad came back to the bank with a bulging shoebox. "I guess they trusted me," Dad said quietly. He opened the shoebox to reveal a large amount of cash, neatly tied in bundles. He set up accounts for his new friends, including depositing the cash. "Trust and respect is everything. Treat people better than they deserve. Follow through on your word. Your word is your bond." The friendly relationship between Dad and the bachelor farmers continued for several years.

The core belief to treat people with respect has stayed with me. Throughout my career, I have made every attempt to accept people, treat them well and always respect them, despite sometimes differing viewpoints. It hasn't always been easy, but I always came away from the interaction knowing that I gave it my best shot.

In recent years, I've noticed the pendulum has swung a bit too far towards intolerance, indifference and ill-mannered quips that pass as tolerance. We can do better and we must. I have a couple of basic beliefs that spurred me into writing this book.

The first: My belief in the fact that agriculture and its related industries are fundamental to all of us. I grew up on a farm. The changes that have taken place over the years are nothing short of phenomenal. We have the task of feeding and clothing an ever-growing population, as well as providing fuel. Every year, every season, every harvest, we do it a little bit better than the year before. We have cutting-edge technology in our machinery. There are exciting developments in biology, chemistry, nutrition, anthropology, psychology, genetics and sociology; all of which benefit agriculture and its related businesses. It is astonishing.

The second: It is very easy to get bogged down in the busyness of our day. The food/fiber/biofuel chain can be complicated and sometimes cumbersome. We need to remember the huge beneficial impact we in agriculture have on the lives of people everywhere. I am proud to be a member of an industry that has been around since nearly the beginning of time. I welcome new and exciting changes, so we can continue to face the challenges of today.

When we peel away the layers of stress and busyness, we will always find that people have certain basic needs. I have long been interested in human behavior. Why do people act the way they do? Some might say that I am almost compulsive about understanding behavior and the inter-relationships among people. Every action, reaction and response makes sense once the observer comprehends the motivation of an individual. One basic need is that all people need to be treated with respect and dignity, as well as equal rights and protections. As Jim Autry, a seasoned Fortune 500 executive, writes in his book, "Love and Profit," "Management is a part of life, and life is largely a matter of paying attention. Listen and act on what you hear. Be attentive to personal needs and accomplishments as well as professional ones … then write a personal note."

Good manners today require more than just saying "please" and "thank you," though these are still the gold standard. It may be dinner with the boss, planning and conducting training for new employees or leading the problem-solving team in the office. It may mean the task of telling the new hires their slovenly look is not appropriate.

On the business of relationships, Autry writes, "The way to do business with people is to do business with *people* … business, like art and science, has been revealed and conceived through the intellect and imagination of people, and develops or declines because of the intellect and imagination of people … in fact, there is no business; there are only people. Business exists only *among* people and *for* people."

It is easy to talk about treating people well in business but much harder to do in real life. Relationships among people are fundamental to the sales and profit a business makes. For managers, the single most important factor is to motivate and care for people. If a manager does not motivate and care for people, the business will suffer. According to Autry: "No matter what anyone tells you, when you lose business, [when people leave your employ], it's almost *always* a relationship problem."

Management guru Peter Drucker has emphasized that "Management always lives, works and practices in and for an institution. And an institution is a human community held together by the bond that, next to the tie of family, is the most powerful human bond: the work bond."

No other justification is needed. We need to treat each other like human beings, with kindness, courtesy and respect. It seems like Manners 101, but how many among us can respond to this statement with a resounding "yes?" *"I love my work. I love my boss. I wish I could spend more time at work, because I feel needed and appreciated there. I am truly making a difference. I can't wait to go back to work tomorrow. In fact, I love my work so much, I would almost do it without getting paid."* For those with a deep passion and motivation for their work, it is not inconceivable for them to want to spend more time at work.

I envision workplaces where everyone is treated with dignity, respect, courtesy, honor and love. Yes, love. If we care enough about the business we are in, then treating people with honesty, trust and love will help to weather the tough times when the business is not going well. Presenting yourself with dignity, respect and aplomb is key to achieving and keeping success, despite the obstacles life may present to you. Good manners are a big part of success. Standards of civility, cooperative behavior, attitude and actions are the seeds of good manners.

With a clear vision of purpose and a passion for the herculean task ahead, are your manners and etiquette in line to move you to the next level?

Whether you work in:

- Ad/PR agencies
- Ag retailing or distribution
- Agribusiness management and marketing
- Ag credit
- Agricultural research and engineering
- Animal health, nutrition and genetics
- Biofuels
- Crop consulting
- Crop protection
- Crop or livestock production
- Education
- Energy
- Farmstead structures
- Feed
- Fertilizer
- Food science

- Government
- Insurance
- Law
- Livestock nutritionists
- Machinery and equipment
- Media
- Processing and retailing
- Professional farm management
- Real estate
- Seed/traits
- Trade associations or checkoffs
- Transportation and logistics
- Veterinarian
- Water management
- Professions such as:
  - Architects
  - Attorneys
  - Banking

You have an enormous impact on the health and well-being of our nation in terms of the food supply. I encourage you to do your work to the best of your ability each day. Treat people better than they deserve. Respect, courtesy and civility should be at the forefront of each day, both for yourself and for those around you.

Though the world has changed, the fundamental truths remain:

- Agriculture's history, economic, social and environment concerns are of significance to all of us.
- Enhanced knowledge of the role of agriculture in our lives will assist in making more informed choices about our food supply.
- The great leadership and dedication to land stewardship by people in the agricultural industry has never been greater or more important.
- Global security, in large part, depends on a safe and reliable food supply making its way to consumers.

Those who work in agriculture and its related businesses are making an impact on the economy and the environment that has never been greater or more positive. That is why *Agri Manners – Essential Etiquette for Professional Success* is important. Agriculture and its related businesses are leading the way to a brighter future for all of us, and we need to do so in the most civilized, well-mannered way possible.

Agriculture: Bigger than you think and more important than you know. Manners and civility: the refinement and cultivation of people who manage and nourish the advancement of our culture through agriculture and its related businesses.

Ready, set, time to say please and thank you again.

Chapter Two

History of Etiquette

A family of four could live 10 years off the bread produced by one acre of wheat ... cracker's main ingredient is unbleached flour from soft red or soft white wheat.
Source: Washington Wheat Growers Association

Pinkies up! Or not? For many folks, the word "etiquette" suggests white gloves, finger bowls and children curtsying. All of these decorous manners were once the hallmark of proper and genteel behavior. The actual definition of etiquette by my trusty Oxford Universal dictionary:

(e'tiket). 1750. a. The prescribed ceremonial of a court; the usages of diplomatic intercourse. b. The order of procedure established by custom in the army and navy, in parliament, etc. c. The conventional rules of behavior and ceremonies observed in polite society. d. The unwritten code of honor that discountenances certain practices in some of the professions.

The actual definition of etiquette is a system of conventional rules regulating social behavior. Many of today's etiquette rules came from the 17th century French Royal court and were adopted by other societies in Europe and around the world. The etymology of the French word "etiquette" means a "ticket" or a "card," which refers to the bygone custom of the French monarch making ceremonial rules for members of his court. The card or ticket would designate the proper dress code, expected impeccable behavior and specific dining instructions for all who attended court. While these elaborate court rituals have come and gone, today's etiquette remains traditional and constant.

The French culture and population have certainly changed over the years, but French society still has a degree of formality about everything it does, from dress to dining. Some French manners are harder to perceive. While in public, the French tend to keep the noise level low. Outrageous laughter at the table would receive disdainful looks from adjoining tables.

All cultures and periods throughout time had rules for proper etiquette. Some of the rules, like covering your mouth while yawning to avoid swallowing flies, have health-related origins. Others were used to distinguish between classes or prevent social conflicts.

Since the beginning of civilization social skills, manners and rules had to be created so societies could cooperate and survive. During this early effort of people trying to get along with one another, we developed ways to make life easier and more pleasant. This led to certain practices for all aspects of life.

In Germany, Adolph Franz Friedrich Ludwig Knigge wrote a seminal book on human relations in 1788. Knigge (pronounced with a hard 'K' and a long 'E') is best remembered for his book "Über den Umgang mit Menschen"

("On Human Relations"), a treatise on the fundamental principles of human relations that has the reputation of being the authoritative guide to behavior, politeness and etiquette. The work is more of a sociological and philosophical treatise on the subject of human relations than a how-to guide on etiquette, but the German word "Knigge" has come to mean "good manners." Nothing else matters more to Germans than hierarchy and credentials, which are used to establish trustworthiness.

Table manners were most likely low on a list of priorities, as the chief focus was sustenance for sheer survival. Implements and utensils used for eating evolved out of necessity, not fashion. After fire was used to cook foods, burned fingers surely motivated man to use sticks, shells, animal bones and whatever else was handy for bringing food to one's mouth. These early utensils often did not last long and were eventually replaced with more durable utensils made of copper and other pliable materials. There is evidence that forks were used throughout early history and during the Roman Empire.

The Dark Ages in Europe brought about many changes, including the abandonment of forks and spoons for dining and were replaced with double-edged knives, and fingers and cupped hands throughout Western Europe along with hallowed-out trenchers, which were an early form of a plate made of dried bread. Forks remained in use in the Middle East and Africa, though more commonly for serving purposes along with spoons. Chopsticks were favored by Asian cultures.

Dining with one's hands, however, remained a popular method among the more primitive of societies. Soups and broths were drunk from saucers and bowls. With time, bread trenchers were replaced by wood, pewter and porcelain tableware depending on the household and family budget. While eating, the little finger and other fingers were extended and kept away from greasy food so the index finger and thumb could be used for dipping into exotic and expensive sauces. Because the food was very hot, keeping a few of the fingers extended, including the pinky, saved one from having burned fingers.

In 1533, Catherine de' Medici of Italy brought several dozen small dining forks with her when she arrived in France to marry Henry II. She was believed to be the first prominent person to have used forks in Western Europe. Though considered an oddity at first, the fork slowly became popularized in European courts. Over time, silver utensils of all sorts, along with Chinese inspired tableware, were created for wealthy Europeans. Table manners began to evolve throughout Europe. Along with more foods, larger and more extensive sets of silver were created for the table. By the mid-1800s, silver electroplating made utensils affordable for the growing middle class of Europe and America.

In the 19th century Victorian era in the United States, etiquette was a way for the social classes to separate themselves and, before the American Civil War, exclude non-whites, immigrants and children from the table. During the Victorian era, hosts and hostesses were fond of exclusive and ornately decorated flatware. There were numerous styles of ice-cream forks, corn scrapers, orange spoons and mango forks. Instruments were specifically designed for serving olives, peas, baked potatoes, berries, and for tinned fish such as sardines and herring.

Bread was served with a specially designed fork. Even crackers had their own scoop-like serving spoon. Pickled foods had lavishly adorned forks, spears and tongs, and flamboyant pickle casters. Table manners and proper protocol brought on by the Victorian era swept through Europe and, soon after, beautiful dresses and properly set tables began to be seen in American dining rooms.

First lady Dolley Madison loved the European look, from fine draperies to a properly set table with linen tablecloths and the finest silver. The first lady liked to dress up in imported French dresses with very low necklines. She also wore turbans adorned with feathers. Her wardrobe raised many an eyebrow, but her manner was so warm and unpretentious that nearly everyone who met the first lady liked her.

This was in contrast to President Madison's general demeanor, which was that of a bashful man. He was the principal author of the U.S. Constitution, but was uncomfortable making small talk at parties. He was happiest at his desk, among his books and papers.

In an effort to improve the American image, Dolley Madison took it upon herself to completely redecorate the White House. She invited congressmen from both political parties to have tea at the White House. When they arrived, she took them on tours of the mansion, then charmed them through the finely set tea table. Mrs. Madison's grace and manners were exquisite. She believed she was setting the example for the new nation.

Sure enough, Mrs. Madison's charisma worked. A majority of the congressmen appropriated funds for the renovation of the White House. The first lady hired an architect and the two of them began to choose furnishings, including $2,150 for three mirrors, $556 for new china, $220 for silverware and $458 for a new piano. Mrs. Madison wanted velvet curtains for the drawing room. The architect deemed the velvet drapes as gaudy and inappropriate; tasteless, even. A well-mannered hostess always had a refined and lovely place to entertain. The first lady persisted and the curtains were ordered.

Mrs. Madison became alarmed in 1813 when she learned British sympathizers and spies in Washington, D.C., intended to set fire to the White House. The first lady began sleeping with a saber beneath her bed in the event someone tried to climb into her bedroom window. In the summer of 1813, the British began marching toward Washington. President Madison, saying that he needed to be with the troops to encourage them, asked his wife if she was afraid to stay in the White House alone. Of course, she wouldn't be afraid, if only for her husband's welfare and the welfare of the army.

The situation deteriorated over the next few days. Dolley Madison went to the roof of the White House with a spyglass, hoping to see her husband returning from the battlefield. Instead, she saw groups of American soldiers running back toward Washington without their weapons.

Dolley knew she had to flee the White House for her safety. She ordered a carriage, grabbed her precious velvet curtains, a small clock, some books and some silver, then departed for Virginia. She spent a restless night with friends, concerned about her husband and her beloved White House.

The next day, President Madison joined his wife in Virginia, much to her relief, but Dolley was upset to learn that British troops had burned both the Capitol and the White House before marching back to their ships.

Dolley Madison was told that British troops had done no damage to private property in the city and that they had been "perfectly polite" to the citizens. Nevertheless, she expressed the opinion that only insensate barbarians could have committed such a hideous act of vandalism as the burning of the White House. Their acts were "churlish and uncivilized."

After World War I, the invention and mass production of the automobile and the dawn of the suburban family led to etiquette rules becoming more relaxed, though Sunday dinner – the noon meal – continued to be a prominent tradition in American households in the years following World War II. The table was set with a tablecloth that had been starched and pressed, and the best silver and china was used for this formal family meal. Father sat at the head of the table. Mother sat at the other end of the table. As they engaged in polite conversation, children were taught table manners by their parents.

Fast forward to today, where the general stance on etiquette in America is to treat others equally and politely. However, in this fast-paced world where many families have two parents who work outside the home, general civility and manners have taken a hit. Meals are often picked up at the fast food restaurant on the way home or retrieved from the supermarket deli section. Stressed parents pick up the children from basketball practice, dance practice and so on, and the meal is an effort to continue on with duties, while feeling the exhaustion of the day. Then, of course, parenting has to take place: homework, music lessons and getting the children to bed on time.

Then, the next day it repeats.

Even at a time when our lives are overflowing with activities, distractions and pressures, each of us need to strive to make room in the mix for everyday good manners and civilized behavior. Doing so doesn't add to the complexity, but rather elevates us and gives our lives deeper meaning and fulfillment amid all the static and demands of our contemporary existence.

Chapter Three

Enforcing the Unenforceable

The Clydesdale is a breed of draught horse derived from the region of Clydesdale, Scotland in 1826. Originally one of the smaller breeds of draught horses, it is now a tall breed. The breed was originally used for agriculture and haulage, and is still used for draught purposes today. Some of the most famous Clydesdales are the Budweiser Clydesdales. Other members of the breed are used as drum horses by the British Household Cavalry. They have also been used to create and improve other draught breeds.
Source: Wikipedia

Nearly 100 years ago, an esteemed British judge, The Right Honorable Lord Moulton, delivered an impromptu speech at the Author's Club in London. Lord Moulton served as first baron and Minister of Munitions for Great Britain at the outbreak of World War I.

He also was a noted judge, an esteemed parliamentarian and administrator, and spent much of his career as a commissioner. In his role as commissioner, Lord Moulton worked with individuals who had offended the law. As a result, he frequently found himself interpreting the written law and whether the law would apply to a defendant, "You must do this," or (regretfully) I had to say "I must leave it to you."

All of the circumstances surrounding the individual's decisions made it difficult to subject the defendant to all things rigidly prescribed by the law. There were some things the law could not enforce, such as the individual's poor choices.

In a land of freedom of action, Lord Moulton knew that the freedoms inherently present in society also brought with it a personal responsibility. To that end, Lord Moulton described the three domains of human action.

The first domain is positive law, where our actions and behaviors are ordered by laws that we can and must obey. If someone takes something that does not belong to them, this action breaks the rule of law, and the individual is brought before the law to correct the wrong. Positive law is the law of the land, as it were, prescribing to us the framework within which we live. These are the things we may do. Phillip K. Howard, in his book "The Collapse of the Common Good," stated, "Between can do and may do exists the whole realm that recognizes the sway of duty, fairness, sympathy, taste and all the other things that make life beautiful and society possible."

The second domain is that of free choice, which includes all of those actions in which we enjoy complete and utter freedom. If we want to take a walk in the park, then we take a walk in the park. The domain of free choice is where spontaneity, originality and energy are born. The domain of free choice is where businesses are created, grow and thrive because of the creative people involved in those businesses.

The Three Domains of Human Behavior

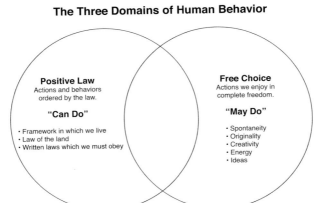

Positive Law
Actions and behaviors
ordered by the law.

"Can Do"

• Framework in which we live
• Law of the land
• Written laws which we must obey

Free Choice
Actions we enjoy in
complete freedom.

"May Do"

• Spontaneity
• Originality
• Creativity
• Energy
• Ideas

It is between the realms of positive law and free choice that Lord Moulton recognized a third domain, large and extensive in its scope and depth. This third domain is an important domain in which there is neither positive law nor free choice. There is no written law that determines our course of action, yet we may feel we are not free to choose as we would like.

This third domain varies in every case and by each individual. It comes from a consciousness of a sense of duty that is very strong. Some might call this the domain of duty, another the domain of public spirit, another might call it the domain of good form. Still others may refer to it as "doing the right thing." Still others refer to it as "the honorable thing to do."

Manners is the civil area between positive law and free choice. This area is not legislated, and yet individuals behave in a way that is mindful of how their actions and choices affect the overall dynamic. "Manners" is a term broader than duty and morals, but might include both. Manners are not enforceable by law, but include all the things a person would impose upon themselves.

However, Lord Moulton called it "obedience to the unenforceable." The obedience is the obedience of the person to that which the person cannot be forced to obey. It goes from a consciousness of duty nearly as strong as positive law, to a feeling that the matter is all but a question of personal choice.

This domain between positive law and free choice, obedience to the unenforceable, he called manners. While this may include moral duty, social responsibility and appropriate behavior, it extends beyond them to cover "all cases of doing right where there is no one to make you do it but yourself." In other words, it is the unofficial code of duty to goodness.

When we are polite, we confer regard. The original meaning of "to regard" is "to look," "to notice" and to "keep in view." People who are rude disregard the unenforceable. To disregard is to look elsewhere, to withdraw attention and, with it, respect and consideration. Rudeness is disregard. It diminishes and demeans.

How does etiquette differ from manners? Etiquette describes definable situations and gives rules and specific behaviors for those occasions. Manners are more ambiguous. Manners refer to those situations in which no law determines our course and yet we feel we are not free to choose as we would.

The Three Domains of Human Behavior

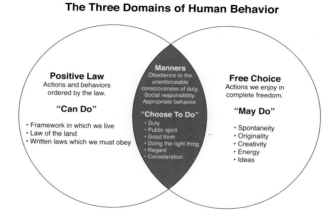

Positive Law
Actions and behaviors ordered by the law.

"Can Do"

• Framework in which we live
• Law of the land
• Written laws which we must obey

Manners
Obedience to the unenforceable consciousness of duty. Social responsibility. Appropriate behavior.

"Choose To Do"

• Duty
• Public spirit
• Good form
• Doing the right thing
• Regard
• Consideration

Free Choice
Actions we enjoy in complete freedom.

"May Do"

• Spontaneity
• Originality
• Creativity
• Energy
• Ideas

The domains of positive law and free choice currently threaten to infringe upon the middle domain of manners. Moulton's central point is that, "The real greatness of a nation, its true civilization, is measured by the extent of this land of obedience to the unenforceable. It measures the extent to which the nation trusts its citizens, and its area testifies to the way they behave in response to that trust." (The New Criterion, retrieved October 7, 2014)

Today in America, the domains of positive law and free choice have corroded the domain of manners. There are people among us who do whatever they want to do, whatever "it" is. They deem "it" right, if nothing more than "it" feels good or "I want to, so I will."

This type of behavior not only diminishes the sphere of manners and morals, it also puts a strain on our positive law, not to mention the general public's required financial support of the law. Diminishing the central domain of the obedience to the unenforceable also results in a weakening of the authority and effectiveness of the law, simply because there are those among us who choose to overstep their boundaries of free choice. As a result, these individuals fall into this middle domain of manners or lack thereof.

Rudeness can be defined as "focused" or "unfocused." Focused rudeness is often caused by anger and is usually mean spirited. Ongoing, continued focused rudeness can qualify as bullying or harassment if it is continual and consistent over a period of time. Examples of focused rudeness include gossiping in a malicious way about someone in the office, or someone interrupting you, hoping to impress the boss.

Unfocused rudeness is generic and mindless. It is usually not hostile or malicious. Oftentimes, people just don't notice or realize what they are doing. Some examples of unfocused rudeness include doors slamming in someone's face or littering.

Consider a recent listing of titles for television programming: "Criminal Minds," "Cold Case," "Dude, You're Screwed," "Cutthroat Kitchen," "Your Worst Nightmare," "Drugs Inc.," "American Horror Story: Freak Show," "Love the Way You Lie," "Sex Sent Me to the ER" and "Naked and Afraid." Have we really dumbed ourselves down that much? Have we become desensitized to the crude and rude violence going on all around us? Has the coarse and vulgar language become too commonplace?

It is not surprising that with 300+ channels to watch on our televisions, there are but a handful of programs that are tasteful and refined enough to consider watching, for those of us who prefer entertainment that is true entertainment, without shocking violent scenes and boorish language.

We live in a deeply flawed society in which indecent shock value, obscenity and savagery seem to be everywhere. Whether we are on our smartphones, laptops, tablets or watching the evening news, we are surrounded by raw and rough scenes that hammer our sense and our sensibilities daily. Part of this is because 24-hour news sources can bring the violence into our living rooms in a nanosecond. This does not mean, however, that we need to imitate the violence and vulgarity we are witnessing.

Philosopher Thomas Hobbes described a state of the nature of human beings this way: "No arts; no letters; no society; and which is worst of all, continual fear and danger of violent death; and the life of man, solitary, poor, nasty, brutish and short." Surely we don't want to live this way?

How do we end this state of offensive violence and restore the art of living humanely? It will not work to just get tougher on crime, or build more jails, or call for capital punishment. It will not work to raise taxes on the general public. Both Lord Moulton and Hobbes observed that a civilized society cannot establish its authority by force alone. Civil order and respect for authority depend in large measure on the consent of those governed. In other words, obedience to the unenforceable.

The domain of positive law depends on the voluntary, conscious support of its citizens for law and order. The rule of the law is contingent upon the morality of people, and, disappointingly, the morality of too many people is on a very slippery slope. People tend to forget that freedom was given to them in trust to help build, not destroy, a community, a town, or a nation.

The real greatness of a nation and its true civilization is measured by the breadth and extent of obedience to the unenforceable. Just abiding by the law is good, but that alone does not make a nation great.

The true test of a great nation is when its citizens can be trusted to follow and obey self-imposed law, including following and supporting the law's spirit and representation on a day-to-day basis, even in the most common and mundane of tasks.

How did the social ills of our society and other societies come to be so prevalent? Unfortunately, there is no single cause, for the root causes are complex and complicated. Why are we spending more money building jails and prisons than funding our schools? What if families had not split apart, if churches and synagogues had not lost some of their influence? What if there had not been an emphasis on materialism and money, money, money?

What if people in leadership positions were really leaders and not so susceptible to character failings? What if drugs had not become easily available? What if weapons had not become easily available? What if 24-hour television, the Internet and social media had not exposed us to the violence and underbelly of the world and at home?

Let's be clear: Television and social media bring us many good and wonderful things. Prior to television and the disintegration of the family, parents often tried to preserve and enhance the observances of innocence and family time by Sunday dinners around the dining room table and spending time together as a family. Board games were popular. Spending time together was a given. Inviting Grandpa and Grandma over for dinner was a regular event. How quaint it now seems.

These days, children are exposed to filthy language, premature exposure to sex and indiscriminate violence 24/7. By the age of 4 or 5, too many children can speak the language of the gutter, teenagers engage in sexual activity on the first date and perpetrate violent acts against others.

In many of our great cities, we see teenagers, modeling what they have seen on television, movies and the Internet, engage in horrendous acts of violence, blowing away parents, classmates or strangers with a malicious, amoral, psychopathological indifference to the feelings or suffering of others with guns that are readily available to them. Even if the majority of youths do not imitate the violent acts they have witnessed, their sensibilities are numbed to the abomination.

The natural reactions to violence – revulsion and repugnance – are suppressed. They've become desensitized to the fact that violence need not be a part of our society.

When young people do not have a good relationship with their parents, they will look for a relationship elsewhere. When children do not have a healthy relationship with their family, they will look for a mentoring, family-type relationship through social media or street gangs. This is often not a conscious decision, but rather a behavioral need.

We are all hard wired to belong. This sense of belonging is innate to our sense of self. The problem with a young person having a social media friend is that the relationship is often one sided. There is not a dialogue of support, but rather a one-way communication where the listener or the young person is passive. For young minds at a very vulnerable time – the human brain is not fully developed until about age 24 – the messages are soaked into their young brain, often changing behavior in an instant.

"One advantage of free speech is that you can recognize the idiots more easily."
— *Unknown.*

Thankfully, there are children in our society who come from strong homes, who attend weekly church activities, who develop sound and healthy study habits and who love books and people. They are leaders in their school settings. They volunteer in the community. These are children who have developed a moral core to guide their choices. These are also children who have a sense of individual obedience to the unenforceable on which manners and morals and, ultimately, the law depends.

Within the realm of obedience to the unenforceable are many of the things we hold dear in this life. We all want the right to decide whom we should marry or which religion we should follow. We all want the right to live where we would choose to live. We love our freedom of speech and our rights to have a difference of opinion with our elected leaders.

There is time for self-correction of the social ills we witness. Those in positions of responsibility, whether in media, social media, parenting or other leadership positions, need to understand that we cannot continue to beat down our own sensibilities and our children's sensibilities and have our society survive. The crisis we face will not be solved by higher taxes, increased governance, more welfare, larger military budgets, Medicaid or building more prisons.

When we have the wherewithal to regain control over individual selves, we will have regained our capacity for self-government. It is then we will not only survive, we will thrive, and we will have the capacity within us for obedience to the unenforceable.

W. Edwards Deming, well-known management consultant, once remarked, "You don't have to do it. Survival is not compulsory."

As individuals, we have been given the gift of making our own choices. It is vital that we realize, consciously, that the future of our society is in our hands. We need to regain control over our behavior and take personal responsibility for the actions we exhibit to the world each day.

Between our "can-do" spirit and "may-do" behavior exists the entire realm of duty, fairness, empathy, good taste, refinement and all the other things that make life beautiful and society promising and full of hope.

The great principle known as obedience to the unenforceable is not an idyllic pipe dream. The opportunity to experience obedience to the unenforceable is strong in the hearts of all except those who are most depraved.

For an example of how strong we can be, consider the account of the Titanic disaster. The men were at the edge of death as the great ship was sinking. "Ladies and children first."

Why was that? The law did not require it. Force would not have compelled it even in the face of certain death. It was an expression of good manners in the sense of obedience to the unenforceable. As terrible as that moment was, if the people could look back, they would have wished to behave this way.

For those among us who become aware enough to understand and embrace obedience to the unenforceable, the power that comes from having a wider outlook has taught us that the obligation we have as free citizens is to do the right thing.

It is time to exercise patience and let people grow until their positive life experience teaches them to better appreciate their true and rightful position. With grace, they will behave as worthy and honorable people would behave. The future of our country and our future happiness for our children depends in large part whether we as individuals and as a people consistently practice obedience to the unenforceable.

Who deserves respect? Everyone. Even those you encounter in a walkway or while passing through a door. Those with whom you work, and those with whom you live. The time to start is now.

The Right Honorable Lord Moulton stated, "Now I must tell you why I chose the title 'Law and Manners.' It must be evident to you that Manners must include all things which a man should impose upon himself, from duty to good taste.

"I have borne in mind the great motto of William of Wykeham— Manners Makyth Man. It is in this sense—loyalty to the rule of Obedience to the Unenforceable, throughout the whole realm of personal action—that we should use the word 'Manners' if we would truly say that 'Manners Makyth Man.'" (*The Atlantic Monthly*, July, 1924, Retrieved October 8, 2014).

Chapter Four

The Anatomy of Manners

Approximately one third of all the food Americans eat is directly or indirectly derived from honey bee pollination. During its six to eight week lifespan, a worker bee will fly the equivalent of 1 $\frac{1}{2}$ times the circumference of the earth and will make $\frac{1}{12}$ of a teaspoon of honey.
Source: American Beekeeping Federation

Photo courtesy of Bayer CropScience. www.bayercropscience.com

The realm of manners, etiquette, courtesy and civility has been around for a very long while.

Oxford Universal Dictionary:

Courtesy – origin 1645. The customary expression of respect by action or gesture. Manners – origin 1579. The modes of life, conditions of society prevailing in people. Good customs or way of living. Etiquette – origin 1750. The conventional rules of behaviour and ceremonies observed in a polite society. The unwritten code of honor. Civilize – origin 1601. To make civil; to bring out of a state of barbarism; to instruct in the arts of life; to enlighten and refine.

In Arthur Schlesinger's delightful book "Learning How to Behave," he writes, "From the 1820s on... an incomplete enumeration shows that, aside from frequent revisions and new editions, 28 different manuals on manners appeared in the 1830s, 36 in the 1840s and 38 more in the 1850s – an average of over three new ones annually in the pre-Civil War decades."

The conduct books during this time were of two general kinds: one upholding the time-honored conception of manners as "character in action." The Earl of Chesterfield wrote extensively on a new distinction between morals and manners in England.

The second type were American conduct books elaborating the view held by Chesterfield that manners were a set of rules to be learned.

As reported by Schlesinger, George W. Harvey, in "The Principles of Courtesy," excused himself for touching on such trivia by the need to counteract the many handbooks that "appealed to unworthy motives, and taught a heartless and selfish system of politeness." On the other hand, T.S. Arthur warned against drawing room usages based on self-seeking and vanity, and urged his readers to study etiquette manuals for their own sake.

With the flurry of etiquette books during this time period knowing no end, Schlesinger wrote about the well-born Miss Sedgwick saying, "I have seen it gravely stated by some writer on manners that 'It takes three generations to make a gentleman.'" She continued, "This is too slow a process in these days of accelerated movement ... you have it in your power to fit yourselves by the cultivation of your minds, and the refinement of your manners for [social] intercourse, on equal terms, with the best society in the land."

In today's world, manners books continue to be abundant, but we live in a world that moves at breakneck speed. We all have invisible walls built around us by iPods and cellphones. Even in public places, we are working through our cellular devices. We walk on the street and nearly bump into folks because we are staring at the small smartphone in our hands.

It is not just a public irritation, it is a cultural crisis. There is an inherent yearning in human beings to interact with one another, but we barely take time away from our electronic devices to say hello. No one is paying attention to where they are going. When we're on the telephone, we talk so quickly the words are hard to understand. At the risk of revealing my generational age, it reminds me of a 45 record playing at 78 RPMs. Too fast.

We are in danger of becoming a society of hyper-connected, thumb-frenzied hermit crabs with only one thought: Is my smartphone charged up or where is my charging cord?

Before we bury ourselves in the cloud any further, let's explore further the anatomy of manners for today's busy world.

Intellectual Manners

Intellectual: belonging to the intellect or understanding; possessing a high degree of understanding.

Most people believe that having good manners or being civilized and/or cordial to others is the right thing to do. People lament good manners have gone out of style.

I often do not hear "Thank you" after purchasing an item. Any item.

One incident remains burned in my memory. I rented a movie and handed the young man my money. He handed me the change, then stared at me, as if to say, "Move out of the way. Someone is behind you."

I stood there, looking at him. Quietly, I said, "I didn't hear thank you." The young man bristled, then stated boldly, "We don't say thank you here." I was stunned. I never returned to that store.

Other examples of rude behavior abound. People cut others off in traffic, or another driver takes the parking space for which you were signaling. The clerk in the convenience store cheerfully states, "Have a nice day." There is nothing wrong with the phrase "Have a nice day," but the words "Thank you" need to precede it, as in, "Thank you for shopping with us. Have a nice day."

Why "No Problem" should not replace "Thank you" or "You're welcome."

Are people in your organization saying "Thank you" to customers or clients? The phrase "No problem" indicates that you, as the client or customer, have intruded upon the individuals who are providing you with a service for which you are paying. "No problem" is a self-centered blow off. This buzzword indicates the customer is secondary to the need of the person providing the service.

"You're welcome" signals to the customer their business and time is appreciated. Customers are the lifeblood of any business.

How many times have we waited in line, and waited and waited, at the computer store or convenience store, etc., paid money to the clerk, then said "Thank you" to the clerk? To which the clerk replied, "No problem."

It **is** a problem. We've just paid money to obtain something. Money that allows them stay in business.

The appropriate sequence is this: Joe purchases a soda at the store. Joe hands the money to the clerk. The clerk returns change to Joe, then says to Joe, "Thank you. Have a great day." Joe responds, "You're welcome." Manners and civility are the bedrock of our society. Unfortunately, "Thank you" seems to be absent too much of the time. We are in such a hurry that we don't take the time to correct the situation.

Intellectual manners means that people don't think consciously about what is taking place. We are either preoccupied with the project at hand, the unreasonable boss, or the kids' soccer practice, or the fundraisers at the nonprofit we promised to do. Oh, and our friend is in the hospital so flowers need to be sent. Oh, and the lawn needs to be mowed. Did the birthday card get sent out?

A recent study reported the average mom in America completes an average of 47 tasks per day. More than half of those tasks are before 9 a.m. Humanity is not always a pretty sight, but it is real. No wonder we are strung out. We push ourselves to the limit. We are tired, hungry and exhausted. Bing. A new text arrives. We push on.

Another way to think of intellectual manners: People are not aware or in the moment. We are busy trying to keep up within this fast, speedy world in which we live.

Tips for practicing intellectual manners:

- Find ways each day to rejuvenate yourself: take a brief walk, do some stretches.
- Get plenty of good sleep each night.
- Nourish yourself with healthy food and thank the farmers who grow it for you.
- Do something for yourself, something that feeds your soul. If you don't have time to practice the piano, play one song.
- Remember the lessons from yesterday, plan for tomorrow and live for today.

Being fully present will help you to have good intellectual manners, and, you'll just feel better.

Intellectual manners: Thinking of the right thing to do and doing it.

Emotional Manners

People like to talk about psychological terms without really understanding the full meaning and scope of the terminology. "Don't go manic on me." "Oh, don't deal with him. He is a psycho." "She is schizo most of the time." "I'm feeling depressed." "She is going postal."

The truth is this: We all have feelings, and sometimes those feelings get hurt. For those among us who appear to be tough on the outside, sometimes those are the folks with the most tender feelings.

There is nothing wrong with this. Feelings, after all, are just feelings.

Emotional manners are this: You are a feeling person, and you've felt the sting of being wronged. One side of your brain wants to lash out through hurtful words or actions. The other side of your brain says, "No, don't do that. It will not help things and may make things worse."

The rational, emotional side of you thinks, "It was wrong. I am hurt by it, but I cannot help the situation, therefore, I'm going to let it go." Be mature enough to think, "They wronged me, and it hurts, but I am mature enough to grow beyond this, and I realize that I will never treat someone that way."

Sometimes it takes a little time before you can come to realize this. You have enough self-respect to realize that you don't have to treat someone else this way. It is important to learn from this, so you do not grow up to do the same thing to someone else.

If you are able to say to yourself, "I did the best I could do," then that is all you can do at this particular time for this particular situation.

Then you need to practice letting it go. This does not mean you need to forget about it. Not at all. Rather, it means that you are putting it aside in your memory and remembering the lessons you have learned from it.

"Let it go" is one of the most helpful phrases in human behavior. Grow from it. Learn the lessons. If you grow from the situation and remember the lessons, you will be fine. Emotional manners involve the realization that not everything is going to go your way in this world. Darn it all, but it is true, and accepting this will bring you contentment, a much-needed commodity in today's busy world.

Emotional manners: Be emotionally strong and take the time to believe in yourself. Even when no one is watching. Especially when no one is watching.

If you have trouble believing in yourself, then think about those folks who want you to fail. Show them to be wrong. This can be a great motivator.

Behavioral Manners

Oxford Universal Dictionary:
 "Behave" is a word coined in 1440. "To bear, comport or conduct oneself."
How many of us think of our behavior when it comes to manners?

The other day, while at the office supply store, I stood behind a young woman whose summer top revealed the entire back of her undergarments. She seemed oblivious to the fact the world was witnessing something private. The No. 1 faux pas in behavioral manners is viewer discomfort. I was suffering from huge viewer discomfort. The young lady had no idea.

I live in a small town with a beautiful courthouse in the center of the square. One day, I saw a person dressed in black-and-white striped prison clothes walking with a deputy into the courthouse. His arms and legs were shackled in steel cuffs with heavy chains. It brought to mind a tethered, rabid animal. It makes me wonder what behavior he did that was wrong, and I wonder if he has any shame or embarrassment at being caught doing something illegal. Is there no shame anymore? It made me feel embarrassed to watch him, not to mention the money it takes to house and feed him.

I once asked a police chief about the prisoners he attended. "Wouldn't our lives be much easier if people were just nicer to each other?" I asked the chief. "If someone made a mistake, if they just admitted to the mistake, apologized and agreed to correct the mistake, wouldn't it be easier for all of us?" The chief gave me a wry smile and said, "It would change everything for the better." However, human behavior, alas, is not that simple.

Does your behavior—public or private—make other people uncomfortable? Keep in mind that most folks are going to be too nice to say anything. We also have the little things called individual rights and freedom of speech.

In the spirit of individualism, people have invented new and colorful ways to outfit themselves. We see hats in restaurants, elbows on the table, too many vulgar words and overall bad behavior too much of the time.

Have we dumbed ourselves down? Why has the way we present ourselves to the world become so slovenly? Whether we realize it or not, our behavior affects all of those around us. Check your behavioral manners. Are your respecting yourself and the world around you?

Behavioral manners: Put one foot in front of the other and be true to your word and respectful of yourself. Follow through.

One final thought: When you are weary or tired, either physically or emotionally, your body is trying to tell you to rest. If you are physically weary, taking a break from your activity for a few minutes will often revive you, and you'll be ready to go again.

However, if you are emotionally or mentally weary, the only thing that will help you to feel better is a good night's sleep. Things always look a bit brighter in the morning.

Chapter Five

How Does Your Personality Fit In?

**One pound of wool can make 10 miles of yarn.
There are 150 yards of wool yarn in a baseball.**
Source: www.farmersfeedus.org

P ersonality helps us to understand why people behave the way they do. When dealing with people, have you ever wondered:
- Why is that person so rude?
- Why are they dressed in such a sloppy way?
- Why did she get the promotion?
- Why are they always winning?
- Why doesn't the boss ever ask me to help out?
- Why do they ignore me?

Belief: a specific statement that we hold to be true.
Value: culturally defined standards by which people assess desirability, goodness and beauty; serves as broad, social guideline for living.

We tend to see and accept what we have already chosen to believe.

Do you sometimes feel as though you are one of the few well-mannered people in your office, at social gatherings, on your daily commute, at the supermarket or at a restaurant?

The manners pendulum has taken a deep swing over the past several years in the wrong direction. People have become so casual the word slovenly comes to mind. Perhaps casual has been taken to an extreme, from comfortable to grubby garden clothes, which are perfect for the garden, of course, but not so for church services.

In traffic congestion, some people remain calm and collected. Others become irate. Still others may become so outraged they are a menace to those around them. How people handle their frustrations is one part of their personality. How well mannered they are is another part of their personality.

First things first. What is the core reason why people behave as they do? Are ill-mannered people born that way? Is being borderline rude and unrefined a learned skill? Our personalities tend to characterize who we are and who we become as an adult. Are we trusting? Are we skeptical? Are we hard-driven or impulsive?

Some psychologists think our evolutionary roots are the main factor in how we connect and get along with other people. Men look for women who are attractive because it implies a healthy fertility, assuring men their DNA will carry on to endure another generation. Of course, what is attractive varies by the person.

Women look for a similar thing, but in a different way. Women look for providers to guarantee their children will be cared for and secure. These primal needs are with us throughout our life, and nothing else trumps them. This is part of evolutionary psychology.

Personality reflects the consistent patterns of thinking, feeling and behaving that make you different from some folks and, in some ways, similar to others. Some personalities may be more suitable to work construction, while other personalities are better fitted to a desk job. Some personalities would rather work with people. Others are more suited to work with things, such as computers or machinery.

Personality typing as we know it now can be traced back to the 19th century and the work of British scientist Sir Francis Galton. Sir Galton was one of the first to talk about emotional reactivity, which is the idea that we all respond to the world in different ways, and these different ways can be quantified and measured.

Emotional reactivity is a way to distinguish introverts – people who are quieter, more solitary and more easily emotionally aroused – from extroverts – people who are louder, more outgoing and less reactive.

Within North American cultures, there are gender differences in the development of self-esteem and personality. Females tend to show an interdependent self-system where their sense of self and self-esteem comes from attachments to others. On the other hand, men develop self-esteem in relation to achievement, which is more in keeping with an independent self-system (Cross & Madson, 1997).

We humans differ in countless ways, but many of us can be characterized by whether we voluntarily turn toward the world or toward ourselves. Are we introverts or extroverts? Are we internal or external? The thing we don't want to do is try to pigeonhole people.

Those folks will prove us wrong every time, because human behavior is not an exact science.

How does personality fit into the equation?

The Structure and Development of Personality

The Psychodynamic Approach

Dr. Sigmund Freud, an Austrian neurologist, is known as the father of psychoanalysis. Dr. Freud developed one of the most influential personality theories ever proposed. His ideas shaped Western thinking from medicine to religion. Freud's psychodynamic therapies introduced the use of personality assessments as we know them today.

According to Freud, personality develops out of the individual's struggle to satisfy needs for food, water, air, sex and aggression. The personality is then reflected in how each person goes about satisfying these needs.

The personality is composed of three parts: the id, the ego and the superego.

The **id** operates according to the pleasure principle, and contains the life and death instincts. The id is pure pleasure. If one is fond of ice cream, and the doctor discourages your partaking of the treat because it is not good for your blood sugar level or overall health, it matters not according to your id.

When you drive past a shop serving ice cream, of course you have to stop. The sights, the sounds, the smells of the tasty sweet treat pull you in. You think not of what your doctor has recommended. All you know is that you are hungry for the real ice cream, and you justify it, thinking to yourself, "I'll help all of the dairy farmers out there." This is your id coming into play. It is pure pleasure, and, man, does it feel good.

The **ego** operates according to the reality principle. This means that your ego is going to try to temper your id when it wants soft-serve ice cream or some other temptation, while trying to obey society's rules.

The ego is going to find ways for the person to get what they want in the real world, as opposed to the fantasy world of the id. Because it operates on the reality principle, the ego is going to make compromises between the id's unreasonable demands for immediate satisfaction and the more practical limit bestowed by society.

You are on your drive home after a long day at work. You know dinner will be later on this particular evening, and the upcoming fast-food place looks mighty tempting. You pull into the parking lot of the fast-food restaurant, but your ego wins out as you think of dinner with the family in two hours. You decide to wait for dinner and forego purchasing a snack.

You pull out of the fast-food place and continue the drive home. Your ego has scored a victory over your id, as your decision to not have a fast food snack lost out to your reasoning that waiting for a nutritious dinner later is the better option.

As children grow and develop, they learn about society's rules and values, and tend to adopt them. The children also adopt their parents' cultural values by taking those values on as their own. This is what helps to shape the personality as we know it.

This is called the **superego**, and it tells us what we should and should not do. It is like our moral compass. The superego has a strong effect on our personality, an effect that lasts well into adulthood.

As a young adult, I spent summers working as a bank teller in the small town bank in which my father worked. As an 18-year-old, I walked into the vault for the first time and was amazed. I had never seen so much cash in one place. Piles of paper money were neatly stacked, as well as shelves of gold bars and rolls of new coins. Everything was neat and tidy. With his hand sweeping a gesture, Dad quietly said, "This money belongs to other people. It is our job to take care of it for them." At the end of each day, the heavy steel door of the vault closed, and its huge outside wheel turned to click the locks into place.

For the next four years, I worked at the bank in the summer while on break from college. I was responsible for the money drawer at the drive-through teller window. Each afternoon, as I counted back the money from the drawer, I knew it had to balance with the amount I had started to the penny. To take care of peoples' money was a privilege and a responsibility, and I learned to get it right every time.

I didn't realize it at the time, but Dad had taught my superego the right thing to do with regards to other people's money. It was a great lesson that I still practice today even though I've not been in a bank vault lately.

The id, the ego and the superego are all part of our personality.

Why We All Want and Need to Belong

It is a fundamental, basic human need to want to belong. It is innate to all of us who profess to be human beings. We are hard wired for this particular need.

Through the development of our personality, we come to form our own view of the world. The authority figures in our lives – parents, clergy, teachers, supervisors, etc. – help to shape our personality through covert and overt (modeling) ways.

Some theorists say this is the unconscious part of us and others say it is the conscious part of us. Still other theorists will say it is a combination of the unconscious and conscious part of our personality.

Self-defense strategies, commonly called defense mechanisms, are a series of coping mechanisms designed to assist us in coping. Sometimes the strategies are used before actions are carried out, hence, insulating us against possible disappointments or failures. Other strategies are invoked after failure or other esteem-threatening consequences.

Whether self-defense strategies are used before or after, all are designed in helping us to adapt to life's difficult situations.

According to Freud, defense mechanisms help us to deflect anxiety and stress in the short term, but may deplete our energy. These defense mechanisms are beneficial in that they help us to adapt and cope with life on a daily basis. In other words, sometimes defense mechanisms are good because they help us, but defense mechanisms are not a substitute for dealing with the core issue of your problem.

As human beings, we use defense mechanisms a lot. Why? Because they help us out in the short term. They are effective. They work.

Ego Defense Mechanisms
1. **Repression** – Unconsciously pushing threatening thoughts, memories, urges or ideas from our awareness. If we remembered all of the negative things that happened to us over the years, it may be difficult for us to even function as a human being. Our mind tends to repress things as a way to help us cope and get up in the morning to carry on.
2. **Rationalization** – An attempt to make actions or mistakes seem reasonable. "I didn't get the sale yesterday because the price was too high, and my boss wouldn't let me cut it further." This sounds rational, but price is just one of the reasons for purchase decisions.
3. **Projection** – Unconsciously ascribing one's own unpleasant thoughts or impulses to another person. Instead of recognizing that Rob talks too

much about himself during the lunch break, it is really you who may talk too much, much of the time.

4. **Reaction Formation** – Defending against unacceptable impulses by acting opposite to them. "I could never date anyone I work with" actually may mean the person is somewhat interested in dating her co-worker.

5. **Sublimation** – Changing unacceptable impulses into socially acceptable actions and perhaps expressing those thoughts symbolically: aggressive or dominant desires may show themselves in the company symbol of an African lion. Many companies today have a mammal or bird as their corporate symbol, giving psychological reference to the characteristics of the mammal or bird that the company takes as its own.

6. **Displacement** – Deflecting an impulse from its original target to a less threatening one. After a rough day at work, Linda comes home and yells at her kids. Her yelling has nothing to do with the kids. She is still feeling frustrated from work.

7. **Denial** – Dismissing the existence of threatening impulses. A small business owner has known that one of her employees has stolen merchandise from the store. The business owner says, "She was going through a rough patch at the time and needed some help."

8. **Compensation** – Working to make up for unconscious fears, needs or impulses. A top executive works until 9 p.m. each day in an effort to be successful, because while growing up, his mother did not compliment him. He is emotionally starved for attention and positive "strokes."

Keep in mind that we often don't think consciously about the defense mechanisms we use on any given day, but most of us use them nonetheless. Be mindful that if defense mechanisms we use become habitual or harmful, then we may need to revisit them.

How Defense Strategies Manifest in Real Life

Two of the most common self-defense strategies using a combination of ego defense mechanisms are:

- **OK/Not OK** – Some people, when needing to feel superior or better than someone else, may use the strategy of "OK/Not OK." This means that Jane, who is the new supervisor, may purposely put other people down through words or actions. In effect, Jane is making someone else feel less okay so she can feel more okay. The OK/Not OK tends to rise from out-of-control ego by the perpetrator.

- **Learned Helplessness** – A behavior in which people seem forced to endure adverse, unpleasant situations and may become unwilling or unable to avoid such situations, even if they are escapable. It is presumed the individual has learned the situation cannot be controlled and, therefore, no action is taken to avoid the situation.

Psychologist Dr. Martin Seligman tested learned helplessness in 1967 at the University of Pennsylvania as an extension of his interest in depression. Dr. Seligman's groundbreaking research discovered that learned helplessness did not account for varying reactions to situations that caused learned helplessness. The research showed that learned helplessness sometimes is specific to one situation, but at other times can be generalized across situations.

People with a pessimistic type of personality – who see events as permanent (this will never change), personal (it's my fault; it's always my fault), and pervasive (once again, I cannot do anything right; why me, why is it always me?) – are most likely to suffer from learned helplessness and depression.

Regardless of origin, people who view events as uncontrollable often suffer from a disruption of emotions, aggressions or physiology. They often have difficulties with problem-solving tasks. The helpless experiences may show themselves as passive and uncontrollable. This results in poor thinking skills, ultimately jeopardizing peoples' physical and mental well-being.

For all of the jokes we hear about Freudian slips, Dr. Freud did make an important contribution to theories of personality. He believed that humans are driven mainly by instincts and the unconscious ignores the role of conscious motivations and learning in determining behavior.

The Trait Approach

If you were to describe someone, it may sound something like this: Tina is caring, conscientious, extroverted and would help you with any project. Yet sometimes she overextends herself and doesn't get anything done. She says yes to everyone because she wants to be liked and accepted.

In other words, we tend to describe others by the characteristics we see in them (extroverted and conscientious), to the thoughts, feelings and actions that are most typical of them (caring, overextends herself, doesn't get anything done) and to their needs (wants to be liked and accepted by them).

People like Tina tend to come to work to get their personal needs met, rather than coming to work to work. People like this are often pleasant to be around, but they undermine the work process. Not as much work gets done, because folks like Tina are too busy getting their own needs met.

Together, these statements describe personality traits: the tendencies or inclinations that help direct how a person usually thinks and/or behaves (Carver & Sheier, 2004; Pervin & John, 2001). Trait theorists believe that many personality characteristics are present in everyone, just in differing amounts.

The **trait** approach to personality makes three basic assumptions:

1. Personality traits are relatively stable and therefore predictable over time. A gently mannered person tends to stay that way day after day, year after year (Costa & McCrae, 2002).

2. Personality traits are relatively stable across situations, and they can explain why people act in predictable ways in many different situations. A person who is competitive at work will probably also be competitive on the golf course.

3. People differ in how much of a particular personality trait they possess. No two people are exactly alike on all traits. The result is that we have a wonderful, endless mix of truly unique human personalities. Aren't we lucky?

The Big Five Model of Personality

More recently, trait theorists have sufficient research to believe that personality is organized around only five basic factors (McCrae & Costa, 2004). This seemingly robust model identified five cross-cultural factors called the Big Five or five-factor model around which personality is formed.

OCEAN is the acronym for the Big Five personality traits: Openness, Conscientiousness, Extroversion, Agreeableness and Neuroticism.

The components of this Big Five model of personality are:

Dimension	Defining Descriptors
Openness to Experience	Artistic, curious, imaginative, insightful, original Wide interests, unusual thought processes, intellectual interests
Conscientiousness	Efficient, organized, planful, reliable, thorough Dependable, ethical, productive, thoughtful
Extraversion	Active, assertive, energetic, outgoing, talkative Gesturally expressive, gregarious, excitable
Agreeableness	Appreciative, forgiving, generous, kind, trusting Noncritical, warm, compassionate, considerate, straightforward
Neuroticism	Anxious, self-pitying, tense, emotionally unstable Impulsive, vulnerable, touchy, worrisome

Some version of the Big Five model of personality is present and has been studied in many countries and cultures, including Canada, China, the Czech Republic, Germany, Finland, India, Japan, Korea, the Philippines, Poland and Turkey (Allik & McCrae, 2004; Ashton et al., 2004; McCrae et al, 2004). This provides further evidence that a few dimensions may indeed represent the core components of human personality for both the Western culture and cross-cultural populations.

Many trait theorists believe that the Big Five model of personality represents a major breakthrough in understanding the personalities of people who come from different backgrounds, may differ in age, or may live in different parts of the world. Many psychologists postulate that working relationships with a healthy amount of the first four traits and hardly any of the fifth trait fare the best.

However, a good dose of neuroticism always helps a bit. Don't we love a male macho sports star who shows his vulnerable side every now and again, and don't we love the female sports star who wins against the guys?

British psychologist Hans Eysenck studied the structure of personality that helped to lay the groundwork for the Big Five model of personality. Eysenck stated that personality traits could be described using two basic dimensions: introversion-extraversion and emotionality-stability (Eysenck 1990a, 1990b):

1. Introversion-extraversion – Extroverts are sociable and outgoing, enjoy parties and other group activities, take risks and love

excitement and change. Introverts tend to be quiet, thoughtful and reserved, enjoying solitary activities and avoiding excitement and social involvement.

2. Emotionality-stability – People at one end of the emotionality-stability dimension may display characteristics such as moodiness, restlessness, worry, anxiety and other negative emotions. Those people at the other extreme are calm, even-tempered, relaxed and emotionally stable. This dimension is also called neuroticism.

Eysenck suggested the differences in personality characteristics in people can be traced to differences in their nervous systems, especially in the brain. What this means is that people are hard wired to behave in a certain way. For someone who has a nervous system that usually operates below the optimum arousal level, they will constantly be on the lookout for energetic, exciting things to increase their arousal level. They are often called extroverts.

On the other hand, for an individual whose nervous system is usually over aroused, they will avoid excitement, social contact and variation in their life. Think of having to calm down in the evening in order to get a good night's sleep. These types of people could be called introverts.

What about the emotional-stability component? Eysenck suggested that people who lean toward the stability side have nervous systems that are relatively insensitive to stress and its symptoms. Those who are more emotional tend to have nervous systems that are more vulnerable to stress.

The Social-Cognitive Approach

The social-cognitive approach differs from the psychodynamic and trait approaches in two important ways:

1. Social-cognitive theorists look to conscious thoughts and emotions for clues to how people differ from one another and what guides their behavior.

2. The social-cognitive approach did not come out of clinical cases or descriptions of people's personalities. It was instead based on the principles of animal and human learning. Personality consists mainly of the thoughts and actions we learn through observing and interacting with parents and others in social situations.

Modeling or imitation can be a very powerful tool.

The social-cognitive approach to personality is an approach in which the personality is viewed as the patterns of thinking and behavior that a person learns over time. According to Dr. Walter Mischel, an American psychologist, social-cognitive theorists study conscious thoughts and emotions for clues to how people differ (Mischel, 2004).

Dr. Burrhus Frederic (B.F.) Skinner was an American psychologist, behaviorist, author, inventor and social philosopher. B. F. Skinner tried to understand behavior in terms of the function it serves in obtaining rewards or avoiding punishments. The principles of classical and operant conditioning launched a social learning approach, but because the classical and operant conditioning focused on observable behavior, they were somewhat limited in terms of exploring how thoughts guide behavior.

Yet, moving toward pleasure or obtaining rewards or avoiding punishment does contribute to understanding how our learned thought patterns and feelings contribute to behavior, and how behavior and its consequences alter our cognitive activity, hence our future actions.

Think of the most recent thing you purchased. Was it a package of chewing gum, a candy bar, fast-food meal, a soda or a new shirt?

When thinking of the most recent thing you purchased, answer this question: Did you purchase the item to move toward pleasure or move away from pain? Let's say you purchased a candy bar. You didn't have time for lunch. You were hungry. You remembered you have an early dinner after work. You knew the candy would satisfy you, if only for a short while.

If you purchased the candy bar for this reason, then you purchased it to move away from pain. You knew the candy bar would settle your grumbling stomach as you rushed to the next meeting.

However, let's say you purchased the candy bar because you saw it on the shelf, and said to yourself, "I haven't had one of those for years, and it looks good." You are not necessarily hungry.

You're not satisfying any physical need. You are purchasing it just because you enjoy it. It brings back good memories from your childhood. You moved toward pleasure by having the candy bar.

The social-cognitive theorists rely solely on operant and classical conditioning to explain behavior and how patterns of thoughts and feelings contribute to behavior. The behavior then alters cognitive activity as well as future actions.

Police officers, in doing their very important jobs, always run a background check on individuals they are investigating. This could be called a social-cognitive approach, as the officer needs to learn if the offender has past actions i.e., a record that could influence current or future actions or put the general public at risk. The best predictor of future behavior is past behavior.

Personality is shaped by the way in which our thoughts, behavior and the environment interact and influence one another. Like a well-woven tapestry, our DNA-based biology and environmental, sociological threads make each of our personalities richly different.

Reciprocal Determinism

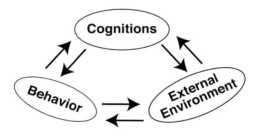

B = Behavior
E = External environment
P = Cognitions: Personal factors such as thoughts, feelings, biological events

Social cognitive therapist Dr. Albert Bandura saw personality as being shaped by the interactions between thoughts, behavior and the environment. He said whether people get rewards or punishment for their behavior, they learn through this direct experience.

People also learn through what Bandura called observational learning. The changes that take place affect how the individual thinks, and the thinking then affects their behavior.

If a child grows up in a home where hostility is a daily occurrence – name calling, put-downs, rude behavior, violence – then the child will learn this type of behavior must be the norm. As the child grows into adulthood, the hostile thoughts they have grown up with stay with them. The hostile thoughts may lead to hostile behavior, which leads to even more hostile thoughts, leading to more hostile behavior.

At the same time, this individual's hostile behavior may offend other people. As increasingly negative thoughts affect the way the person is thinking, the environment seems more threatening than ever.

An especially important cognitive element in the social-cognitive field is the influence perceived as self-efficacy i.e., the learned expectation of success. What we do and what we try to do is largely controlled by our perceptions or beliefs about our chances of success at a particular task or problem. The higher our perceived self-efficacy with regard to the task or event, the greater our actual accomplishments will be.

It is the self-efficacy that will determine our emotions and behavior (I think I can, I think I can, I know I can). In other words, some people just have it in them to succeed.

The Humanistic Approach

The humanistic approach to personality focuses on the mental capabilities that set human beings apart from other animals: self-awareness, creativity, decision-making, planning and responsibility. This approach defines personality as the distinctive way in which each individual views the world. The primary motivator is an innate drive toward growth that influences all human behavior.

Dr. Carl Rogers was an influential American psychologist and among the founders of the humanistic or client-centered approach to psychology. Dr. Rogers called this client-centered approach an actualizing tendency. The self is what people identify as I or me. The development of the self concept depends on evaluation of self and the positive regard shown by others.

If there are incongruities between self-evaluations and others' evaluations, this can cause anxiety, stress and other problems. Whenever people are evaluated, conditions of worth are created.

According to Rogers, the conditions of worth are the feelings an individual is experiencing, rather than their actual behavior. Therefore, people come to believe they are worthy only under certain conditions, which are those conditions in which rewarded behaviors are on display.

This also explains why – no matter our age, educational degrees or high rank in the working world – when we are with our parents, we feel like a child again.

Abraham Harold Maslow was an American psychologist best known for creating Maslow's hierarchy of needs, a theory of psychological health predicated on fulfilling innate human needs in priority, culminating in self-actualization. Through his development of growth theory or hierarchy of needs, Maslow saw personality as the tendency to grow toward self-actualization.

In fact, Maslow believed that self-actualization, in addition to being a human capacity, was also a human need. He placed self-actualization as the highest in the hierarchy of motives or needs.

According to Maslow, people often get sidetracked from becoming fully self-actualized because they tend to focus on needs that are lower in the hierarchy. In other words, personality is formed by focusing on what we have, not on what we don't have or on what we've lost.

The humanistic approach to personality believes human behavior is motivated by an innate drive toward growth that prompts people to fulfill their unique potential. Humanistic psychologists believe that to explain people's actions in a particular situation, it is more important to understand the individual's view of the world or their feelings rather than their instincts, traits or learning experiences.

The major approaches to personality can help to facilitate an understanding of why people behave the way they do. By observing the way people behave, we can understand why an individual may be less than well mannered or perhaps they set the standard for good manners and civility.

A gentle reminder: Understanding does not imply agreement. It simply means that we understand where the person is coming from and whether their mannered or ill-mannered ways fit into our world. Here is an overall summary of the main approaches to understanding the human personality.

REVIEW: Major Approaches to Personality

Approach	Basic Assumptions About Behavior
Psychodynamic	Determined largely by unconscious conflicts
Trait	Determined by traits or needs
Social cognitive	Determined by learning, cognitive factors and individual situations
Humanistic	Determined by innate growth Tendency and the individual's perception of reality

Over the years, some therapists have revised Freud's psychodynamic ideas. Others have developed and researched new therapies based on the humanistic approach to personality. The humanistic psychologists, sometimes called phenomenologists, accentuate the way in which people tend to interpret the events in their lives. They view people as being able to consciously control their own actions and take personal responsibility for their actions.

The humanistic psychologists believe human behavior is not motivated by sexual or aggressive tendencies, but rather an innate drive toward growth. This growth is guided by the day-to-day actions of the individual. Disordered behavior by individuals, according to the humanists, reflects a blockage of natural growth caused by distorted perceptions or lack of awareness of feelings.

When individuals are fully accepted and supported as human beings, no matter how undesirable their behavior, including their manners, they will grow and develop as human beings.

Carl Rogers called this unconditional positive regard. This means treating the individual as a valued person, no matter what.

One does not have to approve of everything a person does or says, but if unconditional positive regard, genuineness and empathy (understanding, responsiveness) is shown to the individual, then acceptance of the individual's view of the world helps the individual to grow and develop. Growth and continued growth is a choice, of course.

"Dogs love their friends and bite their enemies; quite unlike people, who are incapable of pure love and always have to mix love and hate."

—Sigmund Freud

Chapter Six

Men and Women: What's the Difference?

Land, water and vegetation are just that dependent on one another. Without these three primary elements in natural balance, we can have neither fish nor game, wild flowers nor trees, labor nor capital, nor sustaining habitat for humans. – "Ding" Darling–award winning cartoonist for the Des Moines Register newspaper and noted conservationist.
Source: www.americasfarmers.com

Gender Roles

What makes us who we are? Why we are the way we are? What helps us get along? Are women and men really different?

Men and women have co-existed on the planet for a very long time. The discussion about how men and women interact with each other is a constant source of conversation. Are women and men really different? If so, does this affect how we work with each other in the workplace?

Women now outnumber men in many veterinary colleges. Women are presidents of advertising agencies and CEOs of large corporations. Female entrepreneurs are adding to the economy through their growing businesses. There are female agronomists working in the fields. At agricultural equipment dealerships, women take on the sales roles. The World Food Prize recipient from 2013 was a female with a chemistry Ph.D. For the first time, women are viable candidates for the U.S. presidency.

Among men, we have college-educated executive assistants, stay-at-home dads, male nurses and a plethora of other professions.

This is all a very good thing. Differences do remain between women and men. It is important to understand what those differences are.

In his popular relationship book, "Men are from Mars, Women are from Venus," author John Gray says the same communication difficulties we struggle with in our personal lives also play out in the office and work setting.

Gray and gender intelligence specialist Barbara Annis conducted interviews with more than 100,000 male and female executives. They argue that innate differences between how men and women respond to situations in the workplace and understanding what they are and why they exist cannot only facilitate better communication but can result in a happier and more productive work environment.

More than 50 percent of the women surveyed said they didn't feel included in the workplace, whether in business social events, casual meetings or conversation. Meanwhile, 90 percent of men surveyed believed women had equal opportunities and didn't believe they excluded women.

Men are typically linear in their thought processes and narrower in their focus, so they are able to dissect a problem into different parts and solve it, according to Annis. Women more often see the problem holistically and are able to come up with an understanding of the situation without needing to know what the different parts are. Women leaders score significantly higher than male leaders in persuasiveness and assertiveness. They are able to read situations accurately and take information from all sides. A willingness to see all sides of the problem enhances persuasive ability. When it comes to problem solving in the workplace, both female and male perspectives are needed.

Gender characteristics do exist and play an influential role in today's workplace. An important aspect of understanding other people and being socially skilled is knowing about social roles, including gender roles. Gender roles are the general patterns of work, appearance and behavior associated with being a man or a woman in a given society.

Gender roles are in every culture, but are more pronounced in which there are greater differences in the male-female interactions in terms of social status. One survey of gender roles in 25 countries found children learn these roles earliest in Muslim countries, where gender roles are perhaps the most extreme. Gender roles persist because they are deeply rooted in both nature and nurture.

Gender differences in the workplace usually come from social factors or the socialization process. Social factors have an effect on the behaviors of both men and women. There are some workplaces where gender diversity is welcomed and encouraged of both sexes in terms of decision-making and promotional opportunities. With most companies, gender diversity adds value and important perspectives to the organization, in addition to being more representative of the society in which we live.

In his book "The Social Psychology of Work," Michael Argyle reported men and women tend to seek different things in their work. Men want to have a job that pays them well, is secure and provides prestige. They are quite happy working with things rather than people and do not mind risk.

Women are more concerned with self-expression and creativity, want to work with people rather than things and to be helpful to others. As a result, women tend to seek different occupations. Women often choose to be a nurse, teacher, social worker or administrative assistant. Men want to be managers, builders, farmers, scientists and lawyers.

These sex differences in occupation can be partly accounted for by the traditional roles played by mothers and fathers in families. Often, the mother has a nurturing, socio-economic, people-oriented role, while the father is more concerned with the economic support of the family and looking after the physical aspects of the home.

Thankfully, these gender-oriented roles have gradually been shifting to where we see more women in what might be considered a nontraditional role such as engineering and veterinary medicine, ag sales or leading companies, and we see more men choosing a nontraditional role such as secretary, nurse or stay-at-home dad.

Physical and behavioral differences between the sexes are evident early on and tend to increase over the years. Gender differences involve physical, psychological and emotional factors. Girls write and speak earlier than boys and tend to be better at grammar and spelling. Boys tend to be better at manipulating objects. Girls are more likely to play in pairs, boys are more likely to play in groups.

How does this happen? There are three basic ways to look at the differences between men and women: biological, social and cognitive.

Biological Factors

We are all hardwired through our biology. The biological contribution to male-female differences is clear. Studies show gender differences exist in anatomy, hormones, plus brain organization and functioning (Ruble & Martin, 1998; Geary, 1999). Also, cross-cultural research shows consistent gender patterns even in the face of differing socialization practices (Simpson & Kenrick, 1997).

Finally, research done with nonhuman primates has found sex differences that parallel those seen in human children. One study showed young female animals preferred playing with dolls and young males preferred playing with a toy car (Alexander & Hines, 2002).

Of course, our biology determines who births the babies. It is the women who have the natural characteristics needed to carry a baby for nine months and then deliver the baby. Though it takes a male and a female to set the biology in motion, a question never exists about who carries the baby to term. We always know who the birth mother is. Each and every birth is always a miracle.

Social Factors

The socialization process has an enormous effect on influencing our gender roles, in part by exaggerating gender differences that may already exist.

From the moment they are born, boys and girls are treated differently. Boys have blue blankets; girls have pink blankets. Forward-thinking parents or grandparents purchase green or yellow blankets for the new baby.

Adults have a tendency to play more gently and talk more softly to babies they believe are girls. Girls are showered with dolls and doll clothes. Boys are presented with trucks, tools and footballs. Boys are encouraged to achieve, compete, explore, control their feelings, act independently and assume personal responsibility. Girls are encouraged to be reflective, dependent, domestic, obedient and unselfish (Ruble & Martin, 1998).

In these and countless other ways, parents, teachers and media consciously or unintentionally model their ideas about appropriate behavior for boys and girls. In sixth grade, boys and girls show equal interest in science and earn the same grades. Yet parents underestimate their daughters' interest in science, believe that science is difficult for them and are less likely to give them scientific explanations when working on a physics task (Tennebaum & Leaper, 2003).

Children also pick up clues of what is gender-appropriate behavior from their peers (Martin & Fabes, 2001). As an example, boys tend to be better than girls at computer and video games according to Greenfield (1994). Part of the reason is because boys encourage and reward each other for the high level of performance at these games more than girls do (Law, Pellegrino, & Hunt, 1993).

Finally, children are more likely to play with other children of the same sex and to act in gender-typical ways when they are on the playground more so than when they are at home or in the classroom. These children grow up to be adults in the working world.

Cognitive Factors

Most children are born wanting to be innately loved and accepted. As they grow older, they want to be accepted by their peers. Martin and Ruble found that children, in essence, will become "gender detectives" and look for clues about who should do what, who can play with whom, and in what ways boys and girls are different (Martin & Ruble, 2004).

During this process, children will develop something called a gender schema, simplifications about what toys and activities are appropriate for boys vs. girls and what jobs are meant for men vs. women (Fagot, 1995). By the age of 3, children believe that dolls are for girls and trucks are for boys.

Once the gender schemas are developed, children know themselves to be male or female and then tend to choose activities, toys and behaviors that are appropriate for their own gender (Ruble & Martin, 1998). Children begin to develop feminine or masculine attributes they believe are consistent with their self-image of being a female or male. By the age of 8 or 9, children become a bit more flexible about what is okay for girls to do and okay for boys to do, but most say they wouldn't be friends with a boy who wore lipstick or a girl who played football (Levy, Taylor, & Gelman, 1995).

In summation, the socialization process by adults, peers, social media and TV, along with the child's own cognizance about the world, tends to reinforce and magnify any biological predispositions that differentiate boys and girls.

Cognitive bias can be a difficult challenge. Attitudes that are hardwired into the minds of men and women are very difficult to change. The characteristics admired in alpha male executives – boldness, decisiveness, passion and intensity – are not necessarily valued in female executives. Conflicting notions about the importance of a mother's role in raising children can complicate a woman's career in many ways that many men may not even think about.

Social and Emotional Growth of Human Beings and How it Relates to Manners

Age	Relationship w/Parent	Relationship with other children	Social Understanding	Manners
Birth-2	Infants form attachment to primary care giver.	Play focus on toys, not other children.	Infant responds to emotional expression of others.	Please and thank you modeled by parents.
2-4 yrs.	Children become more autonomous; no longer need parents' unceasing attention.	Toys are a means of getting responses from other children.	Children can recognize emotions of others.	Can say please, thank you; basic introduction.
4-10 yrs.	Parents actively socialize with their children.	Child can cooperate, compete, play games, understand rules.	Children learn social rules, like how to be polite and form friendships with children outside of family unit. They learn the roles of being a boy or a girl.	Hold fork correctly, chew with mouth closed, say please, thank you, excuse me, sit up correctly, "please pass...", don't say something disgusting.

My ophthalmologist is a brilliant eye doctor; caring, compassionate and highly skilled. She completed medical school as a single woman and started her career. Her practice was booming. She married and now has two beautiful children under the age of 5. When asked about completing further training to become an eye surgeon, she confidently said, "My priority now is my two children. I would rather be home with them than hitting the books, only to work harder and have less time with them. No way. I choose my children over longer hours at work."

It is beautiful that she has choices.

Stress and Gender

Women and men may also differ in their reactions to stress. In a review of 200 studies of stress responses and coping methods, Taylor and her colleagues found that males under stress had a tendency to get angry, avoid stressors, or both, while females were more likely to help others and tap into their social support networks (Taylor et al., 2000).

This was shown to be a significant difference statistically. Why?

The gender-role learning taking place which was discussed earlier certainly has an impact, but Taylor puts forth the proposal that women have a "tend and befriend" style that differs from the "fight or flight" so often seen in men because of how gender differences and hormones play out when under stress.

Hans Selye, M.D., a pioneer in the study of stress, introduced the concept in 1936. Since then, the original definition of stress has progressed to differentiate between stress and stressor. As Selye traveled the world, he discovered words such as dommage, aggression, tension and detresse did not fit the phenomenon he was trying to describe.

Dr. Selye coined the word "stress" and it amused him to think the languages of the world would be enriched by this new word. "Stress is essentially reflected by the rate of all the wear and tear caused by life," Selye observed.

It is important to note that early studies on stress were done only on men. Seyle's observation that people vary in their perceptions of stressors was reflected in the belief that the stressors themselves were less dangerous to health than people's maladaptive responses to them.

Since Seyle's groundbreaking work on stress, more than 150,000 articles and books have been written on stress. This author's doctoral dissertation was titled "Sources and Effects of Stress in the Workplace." Seyle's work on stress is now known as the general adaptation syndrome, or GAS. It is a term to describe the body's short-term and long-term reactions to stress.

GAS is not an official diagnostic category but rather a descriptive term. Stressors in human beings may be physical stressors such as not having enough food to eat, being in an automobile accident, or getting caught in severe weather. Stressors can also be mental or emotional such as the death of the loved one, the inability to find a job or working with a difficult boss.

We all experience GAS, but in different ways. For both men and women, hormones will combine differently under stress. As an example, oxytocin, a hormone released in both sexes under stress as part of GAS, will amplify in men's physical stress and reduce in women's physical stress. This difference could be responsible for men's responses being more intense emotional and behavioral actions. In women, this could be an explanation of why women in North America live an average of 7.5 years longer than men.

It is important to note that stress is not a purely negative phenomenon and not necessarily bad for you. It can be the spice of life because any emotion or activity is going to cause stress. Later researchers have coined the term "eustress" or pleasant stress to reflect the fact that pleasant and happy life experiences such as a wedding, vacation and finishing a college degree are also stressful.

Your physical body cannot tell the difference between a positive stressful event and an unpleasant stressful event. This could explain why people are exhausted following a fun family vacation and are happy to get back to work.

Do Men or Women Make Better Leaders?

It depends. The more data-oriented answer comes from research done on men and women's leadership styles. Overall, it has been found that both men and women can be equally capable leaders.

The data revealed that men tend to be more effective when successful completion required a more task-oriented leader.

Women were shown to be more effective leaders when success required a more person-oriented leader (Eagly & Johnson, 1990; Eagly, Karau, & Makhijani, 1995). In other words, it appears that people of a specific gender tended to be most effective as leaders when they are acting in a manner consistent with gender role traditions (Eagly & Karau, 1991; Eagly et al., 1995). This may signal to us that folks tend to like a leader who is acting in a way consistent with their gender, rather than a woman who is taking on male characteristics in an effort to be successful.

Research has also found that women with a transformational/collaborative leadership style tend to be more encouraging than males with a transactional leadership style. In other words, transactional female leaders tend to focus on using rewards rather than punishments to modify and change group behaviors.

Do men or women make better leaders? It depends on the task at hand.

Is there a task that needs to be completed? Ask a man to be the leader.

Do you need to bring people together to complete a task? Then a woman might be the best choice.

Better yet, we need to understand, appreciate and respect the differences between men and women, and respond appropriately to them. After all, we need both men and women.

Motivational Differences in Men and Women

Because of the way human beings are hardwired, we tend to respond to motivational clues differently. It is not always clear whether these differences are the same in both men and women.

Financial Rewards: For employers who use money to motivate employees, the differences between men and women are very small. Though money is a short-term motivator, people respond positively to it.

Noticing/Acknowledgment: Women tend to be motivated by written and verbal forms of acknowledgment and will post the notes in their cubicles. Encouragement and hearing "Thank you" from the boss affects the working behavior of both men and women, even if people are simply doing their jobs. In fact, doing one's job is a great reason to say "Thank you."

Educational Opportunities/Training: Educational and training opportunities geared to advancing careers are always a good thing. One of the keys to good training is to conduct the training during working time, so more women can take advantage of the opportunity. Many women still serve as the primary caretakers of children and elderly parents. Therefore, it would be more difficult for those women to partake in training activities if the training took place outside of work time.

Respect: Showing respect in the workplace is a workplace motivator, not only because it enhances the dignity of the individual, but it also enhances overall morale. Showing genuine respect for both men and women and the work they do can only help increase their overall job satisfaction. If people feel valued for the work they do, they will be unstoppable in terms of excellent work.

Women and men: We are hardwired differently, but hopefully, respect and honor will rule the day, and we can all get along in a reasonably good and productive way.

Chapter Seven

The Proper Greeting and Introduction

Conservation methods have reduced wind and water erosion on American crop land by more than a third in the last 20 years even as yields have more than quadrupled.

Source: U.S. Department of Agriculture

Photo courtesy of AgriLife Studios. www.agrilifestudios.com

Introductions for today's agribusiness executive

Business etiquette rules for introducing people in a business setting are not much different from the accepted customs of personal introductions in a social setting. Unfortunately, the rules of introduction are not so straightforward and simple as one might think. The person you introduce first does matter.

In most social settings in the United States and worldwide, it is still considered customary and preferred for women to be introduced to men instead of men being introduced to women.

Situations Where Social and Business Introduction Rules Are Similar

In both business and social situations, generally, you should always introduce:
- Younger people to older people,
- Junior ranking professionals to senior ranking professionals,
- Business contacts and staff to clients,
- Personal acquaintances and family members to business professionals when attending a business function,
- Guests to their hosts.

In other words, as a sign of respect, introduce those of a lower status to those of a higher status whether it means a social or professional status. As archaic and unfair as this may sound, this protocol for introducing people is still considered socially acceptable and often expected in the United States and many other countries.

Differences Based on Discriminatory Practices are not Social Status Indicators

It is important to note that under no circumstances should you use introduction rules to socially define people of another race, color, religion, or sexual preference or as someone of a lower social status. This is just not okay and, in some cases, it is illegal. To do so would be essentially inappropriate and discriminatory.

The purpose of intended introductions is to demonstrate respect for presumed social order based on position or accomplishment and not to demean or categorize other people as anything other than respected and honored individuals.

The Etiquette of Introductions

How many times have you met someone only to immediately forget their name? The nature of our human brain is such that this happens to all of us at one time or another. Not to worry. Following are some suggestions.

An introduction is a social plan for placing two or more people on a friendly basis. There are correct forms for introductions, and they need to be learned as a first step in making introductions. More so, the person who is making the introduction should be able to direct the two people they are introducing into a pleasant conversation.

This is entirely possible if the person making the introduction will focus quickly on the backgrounds of the two people being introduced. Suppose you are introducing Ralph Smith to an older man, Dr. Jones. Dr. Jones is the potential supervisor of Mr. Smith in a new job situation. You think quickly that Mr. Smith has studied crop genetics at a prestigious university because you knew him while in college. Dr. Jones is an accomplished crop geneticist. You know both people. However, Ralph Smith does not know Dr. Jones. Because Dr. Jones is the senior of the two men, you will say his name first.

"Dr. Jones, it is my pleasure to introduce you to Mr. Ralph Smith."

You can use your hands to gesture from Dr. Jones to Mr. Smith. "Ralph, please meet Dr. Jones." Dr. Jones and Mr. Smith then shake hands, while you say, "Ralph has studied crop genetics at ABC University. Dr. Jones. I've heard there are some exciting things happening in the genetics of corn."

Notice that both names are being presented during the introduction. Make a mental note about Dr. Jones: maybe it is something he is wearing, for example, a red bowtie, and then mentally pair Dr. Jones with red bowtie. Later, while in your room, write down "Dr. Jones—red bowtie" in a place where you can remember it e.g., on the back of Dr. Jones' business card or in your contact file. Also, add any other details that will help you to remember Dr. Jones and others you have met.

Under no circumstances should you write these hints down while in the presence of Dr. Jones. Wait until you are in a private place. These notes are meant for your eyes only.

Other ideas to help you remember names and faces:
• Name of event,
• Date of event,
• A significant fact the person being introduced shares with you,
• Follow up action,
• What the next step in the relationship is.

Correct Forms

The simplest form of introduction is always the best. Call the two names when you introduce the two people whom you know quite well. Say, "Ms. Carter, please meet Mr. Jones."

A woman is always introduced to a man, which means the woman's name is called first. A younger man is presented to an older man; a younger woman is presented to an older woman, unless the younger woman is a bride. A newly married woman is considered a bride until she has been married one year.

If someone in the introduction is of higher stature, such as governor, president of a company, matriarch of the family, etc., their name is always stated first. "Mr. President, please meet my friend, Mr. Caleb Turner;" "Caleb, please meet the President of the United States." Caleb will then shake hands with the president while saying, "I'm pleased to meet you, Mr. President."

Including the person's name at the end of "I'm pleased to meet you [name]" will help you to remember the person's name. Try to say the new person's name at least three times in the first two minutes you meet. This will help to register the person's name in your brain so you can remember it later.

Do not use Mr., Ms. or Miss when introducing members of your family, if you can possibly avoid doing so. A wife, husband, son, daughter, sister or brother should always be spoken of as such. A man introducing his wife says, "Mr. Jones, please meet Katherine, my wife." A young man introducing a friend to his mother says, "Mother, please meet John. He and I are on the research team together. John, please meet my mother, Sheila."

Giving a bit of information about John e.g., "He and I are on the research team together" will allow your mother to begin a meaningful conversation with John. "How do you think the research is going, John?"

It is always good manners to be interested in what someone else is doing. Even if you are not the least bit interested in the particular topic, feign your interest. Why? Because the topic is utterly important to the new person you are meeting, and it demonstrates respect for you to be interested.

Appropriate Responses in Introductions

"Hello. I am pleased to meet you, Sharon" spoken as graciously as possible, or repeating the name of the person to whom you are being presented, is the correct way to accept an introduction. Always look in the eyes of the person to whom you are being presented, while you shake hands.

"How do you do, Simon?" is another popular phrase to use when meeting someone for the first time. Be sure to speak each word carefully and be sure to finish your words.

If you have difficulty remembering names, or if the name is difficult to pronounce, ask to have it repeated. It is also fine to practice the difficult name by checking it out with the individual. Say, "[Kee-shawn]. Am I saying it correctly? Good. I'm pleased to meet you, Keeshaun." Repeating the name helps your brain to remember it.

Continue to give your full attention to the exchange. Pick up on clues Keeshaun is saying so you can continue to ask questions and move the conversation to a deeper level. Use Keeshaun's name as much as possible in a sincere way. Don't become so repetitive with the name it becomes annoying.

At all cost, try to avoid the phrase "Hello. How are you? I am fine." This is known as phatic communication, to be used in acknowledging someone while in passing. It is not meant to be used as an invitation for conversation and, therefore, it is not appropriate for business communication.

Rather, say, "Hello. I am pleased to meet you, Ms. Christian." Then STOP and let Ms. Christian respond. It is at this point you become a listener.

Do take care to not shortchange your choice of words. Another way to say this is to speak the full words as they should be pronounced, rather than using a contraction. As an example, you would say, "I am pleased to meet you," rather than "I'm pleased to meet you."

Also, take care to finish each of your words by saying the ending of each word, rather than dropping the ends of your words into pronunciation purgatory. It has often been said that we are the way we speak. Choose sophistication rather than slovenly. It will serve you well in business. This also works well with the written word.

Shaking Hands

Men and women shake hands when introduced to others. Grasp the other's hand with a firm, cordial hold for two or three seconds. Never engage in a pump-handle or a bone-crusher shake. Rather, the curve of both hands between the thumb and the index finger should meet in a mutual way.

Your body language should be open and accepting of the other person. Shoulders need to be squared and your eyes should meet the face of the person you are meeting. Your handshake will speak volumes about who you are as a human being in just a few seconds.

It really is true: You rarely get a second chance to make a first impression. Seize the moment and make the best of it.

When To Rise

When a man is presented to a woman, he always rises and remains standing until the woman is seated. When a man is seated and another man is brought to him to be introduced, the man who is seated rises unless he is seated at a banquet table or some other place where it would be impossible.

A woman rises when she is introduced to an older woman, or to a woman of position, or when an older woman who is standing makes the introduction. A woman of position could be someone who is president of a company, a senator or congress woman or some other high ranking official.

A woman does not rise when introduced to a man unless he is a much older man, or a man of high position.

When a woman rises on leaving a group of men and women, the men rise and remain standing until she has left the room. The women in the room rise if she is an elderly woman, or if she is a woman of position. If they rise, they remain standing until she has left the room.

When a man leaves the room, all men and women, with the exception of the host and hostess, remain seated unless he is an elderly man or a man of position. If he is either of these, everyone stands.

Taking Leave

When you have stated that you must leave, do so at once. It is considered poor taste to keep the host and hostess, and perhaps others, engaged. Do not exit in a rude manner, but leave as quickly as you can courteously do. Don't forget to thank your host before you leave. Say goodbye to the folks nearest the door as well.

Group Introductions

Never lead a person around a room at a large gathering introducing them to everyone present. This puts undue pressure on the guest. Introduce them only to those who are nearest the door, or the place where the guest will be seated, at the time they enter the room. Make further introductions later, when it is more convenient.

It is in good taste to introduce oneself to others who are present at a party arranged by a mutual friend, or to talk with others without an introduction.

If the group is small, each guest may be introduced individually to each person present. If a new person arrives after the meeting has started, it is best to take a brief pause in the meeting and introduce the individual to the group.

Hugging

When meeting and greeting someone, be very careful about hugging them. If you have an established, platonic relationship with the person, then it might be okay. Here are some tips to consider:
- Hugging and touching someone in a business setting is a very slippery slope and can be easily misinterpreted.
- When you touch someone, don't take. "Don't take" means to not touch someone in an inappropriate way, ie: personal or private space such as the lower back, breast area or derriere area.
- Follow the three-second rule…any longer and it begins to be uncomfortable for everyone: the doer, the recipient and

the general public.

- Don't assume the other person wants you that close, even for three seconds.
- Always respect the other person's personal space.
- If you are unsure, then don't hug.
- If the other person initiates the hug, then it is probably okay.
- If someone reaches out for you, then respond to them.
- If you are a man, do not initiate a hug.

Chapter Eight

Specifics for Women in Agriculture

USDA reports that women are one of the most rapidly growing segments in the nation's agricultural landscape. The number of woman-operated farms more than doubled between 1982 and 2012 totaling nearly one million.

Source: United Soybean Board

My great aunt was an agricultural banker beginning in the 1930's. Some say she may have been the first female vice president in an Iowa bank. Aunt Thelma – we called her "Aunty" for short – was a whiz at balancing the books. She came from a farm background and could talk corn, cattle, tractors or the profits and margins of each and all with grace and aplomb.

Early in her banking career, Aunty told me of being on the receiving end of a bank robbery. The would-be robber approached the teller cage where Aunty was performing her bank teller duties. According to Aunty, the robber, with a scarf tied around his mouth, stated, "Hand me your money. Now!"

Aunty, with her quiet, steel reserve of courage, looked into the robber's eyes and stated very calmly, "Tell me your demands." While speaking to the robber, her right foot calmly stepped on the alarm button implanted into the floor. Within minutes, the police arrived and arrested the would-be robber.

Years later, she would retell the story while adding, "He was not going to take any of the money from my stack. My books would not have balanced at the end of the day. Besides, he was disheveled, unkempt and did not say please." We would roar with laughter at her courage and bravery.

When it came to women in agriculture, Aunty was one of my main role models during my growing up years. She dressed up every day and often wore her work shoes and stockings with her night duster coat, which she insisted was the most comfortable, in the evening at home.

I once asked her what the most important things were in business for women to know. She squared her shoulders, thought for a moment and then said, "A woman doesn't have to act like a man to be successful in business. Women have great minds, and we need to use them." "But, don't go out of the house without your earrings." Smile.

Wow. I thought about what she had just said. A women doesn't have to act like a man to succeed in business. In my 17-year-old mind, it struck me like a thunderbolt. The thought would always stay with me.

In today's world, women in agriculture have made great strides, thanks to the early pioneers of women in agricultural business like Aunty. We are grateful to them for paving the way.

What does it take for a woman to be successful in agricultural business today? Sometimes, it takes steel-toed boots and tough selvedge jeans to do the job. Other times, it might take a business skirt and jacket with the appropriate blouse and shoes, and earrings are part of the mix. Let's take a look at how women's clothing has historically led us to where we are today.

The Rise and Fall of the Power Suit

Can a power suit really give women real power? After all, it is just clothing, but in the workplace, a clever, well-fitting matching suit and jacket with a perfect shirt or blouse underneath screams confidence. Wearing the right shoes finishes off the package.

In the 1920's, a classic French woman named Coco Chanel freed all of us from the suffocating corset and actually gave women some room to breathe. Time to exhale. Thankfully.

The original Chanel power suit was a knitted wool cardigan paired with a matching skirt. This was paired with a string of pearls and came to be known as the Chanel suit. It was known as "the woman's new uniform." The Chanel suit could be seen everywhere in the United States.

By 1931, the first wide-shouldered suit for women made its appearance. The house of Rocha introduced this marvel, stating its silhouette was based on the costumes worn by Balinese dancers. It was said the wide shoulders would illuminate a woman's body in a way that would be very attractive.

1942: All hail Katharine! The iconic Katharine Hepburn showed us that a man's suit could be quite striking on a female. Her film "Woman of the Year" made this gorgeous tomboy a role model for millions of women with her slouchy new suit look. We are grateful, Katharine.

1966: The suit goes sexy. Designer Yves Saint Laurent introduces le smoking, the "first male-inspired couture evening suit with [optional] pants for women." While very attractive, this suit was not appropriate for work because of its tight, form-fitting design and above-the-knee skirt.

1978-1985: Shoulder pads ahoy. Suits with extreme shoulder width became the fashion rage. The bigger the better. Who can forget Carol Burnett's take on "Gone with the Wind" when she fashioned a gown out of a curtain rod? Hilarious. Other over-the-top shoulder pads? The television show "Dynasty." Those were shoulder pads on steroids.

Shoulder pads were all about power, and powerful they were in the late

70's and early 80's.

1980s: Power dressing. The '80s represented a decade of high-power clothes for women. Influential designers all embraced the new look: Giorgio Armani, Ralph Lauren, Anne Klein and others made classic clothes that were comfortable, yet fashionable, to wear. These were clothes that made a woman, well, look like a woman in a very smart way.

In the film "Working Girl," '80's power dressing was front and center. Actress Melanie Griffith stars as a smart but undereducated secretary who could not get ahead. She had big hair, big shoulder pads and made big mistakes. When she realizes that her boss is stealing her ideas, Melanie responds by stealing the boss's wardrobe that includes power suits. She cuts her big hair and in the end, lands a great job and Harrison Ford. Lucky girl.

Donna Karan and other designers began producing softer suits at the end of the 1980s, which paired a power blazer with a skirt instead of pants or trousers. The gigantic shoulder pads were giving way to a softer shoulder line. Who doesn't love a great skirt?

1990s: The softer side. Who can forget Madonna's "Blond Ambition" tour featuring her wearing a pinstriped suit paired with a lacy camisole and that famous cone-shaped bra? Wow! Suddenly, women started putting lacy camisoles and floral silk shells with the pants and skirt suits.

Casual wear Fridays were introduced into the workplace, and *Vogue* declared it the end of the power dressing era, as long, flowing dresses and leggings became fashionable. One designer was quoted as saying, "There is not only a change in fashion going on, but a change of mind."

2000s: Skirting the issue. 1997 introduced the television character Ally McBeal, a somewhat neurotic, yet talented attorney who wore a power suit blazer with a micro mini skirt. The lack of length on her skirt brought national attention including a cover on *Time* magazine with the blaring headline, "Is Feminism Dead?" Power dressing seemingly was over.

2012: The power suit is dead. Women, who were now at executive levels, had the confidence and power to embrace a more integrated and creative look. The new power look included soft colors such as pinks and blues, prints, patterns and feminine tailoring. No longer did women have to fit into the rigid, male-influenced power suit. Women had come into their own.

2014 and beyond. Women can now wear any color they want in the workplace. They can wear lace and florals, and flat, comfortable shoes instead of heels. Flat shoes are now sleek enough to be paired with feminine tailored suits, dresses and eveningwear, or, if women choose to wear high heels, go for it. Women no longer have to dress to be tough, because women are tough in their own right. Thankfully, it is not necessary for a woman to act or dress like a man anymore to be successful in the workplace.

Giorgio Armani, who made the power suit famous, was recently quoted as saying, "Women no longer need to wear powerful-looking clothes in order to earn respect from their peers in the workplace." Thank you, Mr. Armani. Women have edged out their unique place in the world. Today, they don't have to wear a suit jacket to show their authority.

Rules for Building your Workplace Wardrobe

Ladies, whether your workplace is strict or relaxed, in the corporate boardroom or the farm field, there is a certain level of refinement and finesse that should always be maintained and things you should simply never do.

For the ladies working in ag-related industries, the day might start off with a business suit and high heels, but midway through the day, a trip to the farm field or the barn is in order. This upcoming visit away from the office may require a change in clothing. Stiletto heels may not be the best choice of shoes for walking in the field or feeding the horses in the barn. And you may need a jacket that repels insects and thorny weeds.

Be sure to have a hat to protect you from the harmful rays of the sun. Leather work gloves will allow you to do the tough jobs with a good grip while protecting your hands.

The key is to have a change of clothes at the ready should you need them. Be practical and think of your clothes as part of your tool chest to help you do the job well.

For all of the agronomists, veterinarians and farm women: flannel shirts, jeans or long skirts and rigorous shoes will serve you well. One does not want to be distracted on the job by clothing that does not support your job. You need to be able to do the job well, and have the clothing you wear protect you while you are performing your duties.

Here are some ideas when building your workplace wardrobe.

1. Obey the rules, whether you agree with them or not. Follow the dress code in the company handbook. If your company does not have a handbook, ask your boss. Dressing against office dictates won't impress your boss or your co-workers. It is time to let go of your preconceived notions about office dressing and follow the norm of your office setting. Once you become the boss or the owner, you can set your own rules.

2. Never show your skin. Wear shirts and blouses of a proper length. Tuck the shirt in if needed. Be conservative about leaving open buttons at the top of your shirt. Open buttons on the shirt should never reveal (or almost reveal) your breasts. No amount of skin should show on your midriff. Save this for the beach. Do not wear pants that ride too low (think of bending over the file). Modesty is key.

3. Avoid revealing too much cleavage or show no cleavage at all. You are in the workplace for your good brain, work skills and work ethic. Focus on your cognitive abilities, not your physical attributes and others will see you for the great work you are capable of doing. Then, of course, do your best work.

4. Keep your straps under wraps. Never, ever let your bra show front or back, and make sure your shirt is buttoned up properly. If you are wearing a knitted shirt or sweater, the shirt/sweater needs to fit comfortably, not skin tight. Even if you have a drop-dead beautiful figure, the workplace is not the place to show it off unless you are a stripper in a night lounge. Keep in mind that images seen on television and Internet are not always the best examples of how to dress in the workplace.

5. Don't wear anything see-through in the workplace. Ever.

6. Keep your hemlines in check. Even if you have great legs, super-short skirts should be saved for evenings out or weekends. Knee length is the shortest you should go, if you want to move up in the company. Keep in mind that your hemline will move up when you are sitting.

7. Save your flip-flops for the beach and your sneakers for the gym. Wear a pair of simple flats for your commute instead. Be cautious of stiletto

heels while at work. After an hour or so, they will hurt your feet, and doctors caution us that in the long run, they may hurt the legs, too. For those of us in agriculture, sometimes good steel-toed boots are best, or a great pair of cowboy boots. The key is to wear the footwear designed for the work you do on a daily basis.

8. Use your best judgment. Save slinkier styles, like lacy camisoles, halter tops and strapless dresses, for evening and formal wear. Err on the side of being a little more conservative in your dress. Once you have been at the job for a while, you will come to know what is okay and not okay to wear to work.

9. Be aware of too tight. The office isn't the right place to display every curve and bump in the road. It is hard enough to navigate the roadway of your career. Don't make it harder on yourself by promoting the parts of your anatomy that usually do not enhance the bottom line of the company.

10. Don't get too wacky or weird. It is fine to express your individual style, but keep it refined. Crazy hats, over-the-top makeup, wild colored hair, big dangly earrings, noisy bracelets and raucous patterns or colors will make you seem too funky and far out. Get comfortable in your workplace before trying anything outrageous, or, better yet, save it for Halloween.

11. When in doubt, it is always safe to wear a shirt with your company's logo. One woman told me, "It's more than a job. It's a wardrobe."

Ten Sartorial Tips For Your Professional Working Wardrobe

Sometimes it seems as if men have all the fun and ease of a professional working wardrobe. A wardrobe that travels well, washes well and continues working in a classic way. Trousers, shirt, jacket, socks and shoes and men are ready to go. Mix and match – ta-da! Not to worry. Women can also have a sartorial working wardrobe that will work well, accessorized with jewelry and even fun scarves.

Fit: My hope is that we are past the "everyone needs to be a size 6" mentality. Given that, it is important that clothes fit the body of the woman who is wearing them. I know women who may be considered large sized, and when they wear their clothes, they look wonderful and professional. When you are wearing sweaters, avoid skin-tight sweaters. Buy a size up if you need to. Always wear undergarments.

Your goal in the workplace is to be respected for your good mind, good work skills and work ethic. Attention on any portion of your physical body is just not appropriate. By choosing clothes that fit your body style, you will be able to focus on the good work you are doing, as will those folks around you.

Quality: One can never go wrong by buying a nice quality of clothing. The cut of the clothing, the nice fabric used and the overall comfort of the clothing makes a big difference in helping your day go more smoothly. Be very careful of trends and fads. They come and go very quickly. There may be one brand name that you prefer. This is fine. If your funds are running short, visit your favorite brand outlet store. Buy the best quality you can afford. It will serve you well. Early in your career, it may be better to save up and purchase a couple of nice key pieces, then start building around those key pieces; a professional skirt and a blazer, for example.

Classic and Timeless: Classic and timeless means that clothes will still be in style years down the road, and if the clothes are made well, they will also still look good, even after several cleanings. Be cautious of trendy colors. If the new color does not suit you, then don't buy anything in that color. Choose colors that fit your eye color and your natural hair color. You may find that classic clothing will work better for you in the workplace, too. A nice sweater will keep you warm when the office air conditioning is running high in the summer. A classic skirt in a black or dark brown is a great start. A classic white shirt or blouse is a must-have. Try to buy clothes that will go with different pieces you already own. Continue to build your wardrobe as you are able to afford it. My favorite skirt is 20 years old. It is a classic pleated sweater skirt, and it looks as good today as the day I bought it. It goes with blazers, sweaters and shirts, and it has saved me on many a cross-Atlantic plane flight. It is fantastic. I step off the plane at Heathrow and, though I'm jet lagged, my skirt looks fresh and new.

Jeans: When you enter the workforce, it is time to put away the distressed jeans you wore in college. You know the ones with the holes in (ahem) different places. Get yourself a pair of nice selvedge jeans or dress jeans that can be worn on casual Fridays. The jeans should fit you well, with no part of your skin showing. Professional dress jeans can be dressed up or down, depending on what you need them for. A nice pair of jeans can be fantastic with a classic white shirt or blazer. You may also want to invest in a nice pair of khaki trousers. Khakis come in pleated or nonpleated styles. They can be worn with or without a belt. You can tuck your shirt in or let it out, but don't let the shirt go down to your knees as it tends to be too much of a distraction. Be cautious of leggings, the skin-hugging tights that are very popular. Leggings may or may not work in your workplace, depending on the office policy.

Shoes & Boots: Your shoe wardrobe can be as basic as a few key pairs or as elaborate as a famous movie star's shoes with a closet of their own. Workplace starter shoes should match almost anything you are going to wear. Flat skimmers in black or dark brown are a great starter pair of shoes. Heels are beautiful and wonderful, but can take a toll on your legs and feet if you try to wear them all day at work. Maybe consider saving your high heels for special occasions in the evening. At work, stick to your basic shoes. Invest in the best shoe you can buy. You don't want to be distracted during the work day by shoes that are pinching your toes.

For women working in agriculture, the shoe wear is varied depending on the job that needs to be done. For a female farmer, boots that will carry her to the cattle lot and the barn will be needed. Steel-toed boots will protect one's tootsies while keeping your feet warm. For the female executive working in agribusiness, flat skimmers or other professional shoes will fill the ticket. For the female scientist walking the research fields, pick the shoes that will fit best for this purpose, and it is usually not flip-flops. The key is to wear the footwear that fits the job you are to be doing.

Boots: They are so fun. Short boots, tall boots; all are wonderful. Depending on the area of the country you live in, choose boots that will fit your lifestyle. If your part of the country gets heaps of snow in the winter, choose boots that will work in the snow. Save your good shoes in a bag while you traipse through the office parking lot on a snowy day. Let your boots do the work.

As a small child, we experienced winters where several feet of snow would pile up. Cars would disappear as the snow covered them. With four children in our family, we couldn't afford fancy zippered boots, even when the Montgomery Ward catalog had them on sale. Mother got the idea to get each of us four-buckle overshoes. The rubber overshoes fit nicely over our regular school shoes, and Mother would deftly snap the buckles together all the way to the top of the boot. With a quick pull on our stocking hats, she would cheerfully say, "Off you go now. Have a great day at school!"

I was embarrassed to wear the rubber overshoes. They squeaked in the snow, and snow would clog the buckles, making them difficult to undo once we arrived at school. One day, I noticed a large tree on the way to school and thought, "I could leave the overshoes there and then pick them up after school. Mother will never know."

That's what happened. Every day, I undid my four-buckle overshoes and slipped them off, leaving them rolled up next to the snowy tree inside of a plastic bag. After school, I made my way to the tree to retrieve the boots and buckle them back on to my feet for my walk home. Mother did not learn of my trick until many years later. We had a good laugh about it. Today, four-buckle overshoes are still around. Believe it or not, I'd like to have a pair. They are homely, very basic and fantastic because they do the job perfectly. Are they the best or what?

Coats: Depending on the area of the country you live in, a winter coat may be a necessity. Your best bet is to go with a coat that is warm and will fit over winter clothing like heavy sweaters. A nice leather or wool coat is a good investment. Make sure the coat will hang past the level of your skirt. Black or dark brown color is a good start.

Wrap: Wool challis scarves are a wonderful investment. The wool challis is lightweight, yet very warm. The scarves are usually large in size so they can be wrapped on the outside of your coat, or wrapped around your neck under the coat. Scarves will change your look in an instant and are great for travel. The colors are magnificent. Silk scarves are also wonderful and warm. If you live in a warm area of the country, you will still need a light jacket or coat for cool days and evenings. Pick a coat in your favorite color. It will serve you well.

Speaking of warm and cozy, be sure to get a nice pair of gloves with a matching stocking hat or other dress wool hat. During cold winters, nothing is better. For dress gloves, I recommend leather gloves lined in silk. They fit like a second skin, and are wonderful and warm. You can also maneuver your life – driving, opening the umbrella, door, etc. – with leather gloves because they are very useful.

Blazers and Suits: Thankfully, women's clothing has taken a dramatic turn from the power suits of the 1980s. Be that as it may, a nice suit is a great investment. Choose a well-made suit in a color that will go with many things in your closet: dark green or chocolate brown, tweed, textured, navy blue or black. The suit topper of your first suit can come in all shapes, styles and colors, allowing you to express your personal style while maintaining a professional look. The shape could be closely cut or buttonless (open front), boyfriend style (relaxed cut, more boxy), cropped or double breasted. Whatever you choose should also be able to stand alone as a blazer to wear with trousers or other skirts. It should also be able to pair with your jeans and khakis. If possible, choose a blazer that will go with many things in your wardrobe.

The skirt of your suit should also be able to pair easily with shirts and/ or cardigan sweaters. The skirt should be of a nice professional length i.e., no shorter that the knee. If your skirt is chosen carefully in terms of color and style, you will be able to wear it with other things, making it more versatile.

Stockings or not? Hosiery or pantyhose are one of the great inventions of the century. Were women consulted as to the fit and design of the pantyhose? I wonder. Remember the television show "Desperate Housewives," from 2004-2012? During one episode, one desperate housewife, played by Felicity Huffman, rushed to another desperate housewife's house in a dramatic scene that promised exciting actions. Actress Marcia Cross suddenly had second thoughts about the scheme she had dreamed up. "But I put on pantyhose," deadpanned Felicity Huffman. Both Huffman and Cross looked at each other with a knowing stare, eyes wide open. With that statement, the scheme went on as scheduled. It was hilarious.

What woman cannot identify with the pantyhose part? Pantyhose, for all of their great qualities, can be a difficult thing to manage. Have you ever taken a pair of new pantyhose out of the package and, as you held them up, it appeared they would fit a child? Sigh. A secret for pantyhose is this: Buy at least one size bigger than you need. Better yet, buy tights. Especially in the winter time, nothing beats a nice pair of regular tights. They come in lots of colors and often fit better than pantyhose. Now if we could just do something about the seam running across the toes. The question we all want answered: Does one wear panties with pantyhose? It is true that the word "panty" is associated with the word "hose," but what does one do? The answer: It is a personal preference. I know some women who are religious about wearing panties under their pantyhose. For others, the "panty" in the hose serves them just fine. What about no pantyhose at all? There seems to be a trend lately for women to go bare legged with their skirts and dresses. Paired with a nice heel, it looks fabulous. Bare legged is fine, but if you choose to go this route, don't go without the panty part. Please and thank you.

"Planting" a New Wardrobe

As you move into the professional working world from high school or college, or move up in your profession, it is time to plant and build a wardrobe to complement your professional career. Retire your holey, as in wholly worn out, college T-shirts and jeans. Save them for the weekend or working in the garden. Here is a starter list for your new professional wardrobe:

1. A nice pair of khaki trousers: pleated or flat front is your preference.
2. A nice pair of dress jeans.
3. Two nice shirts or blouses whichever you prefer. Make them cotton and wash and wear.
4. A nice button sweater, which saves you in the summer from a too-cold office.

5. A nice belt.
6. Two pairs of dress shoes, preferably in black, navy blue or dark brown. Flat shoes or skimmers can look professional, can be worn with skirts or trousers and are better for your feet and legs. Low-heeled shoes are good, too. For you farmer folks, get a good quality pair of boots.
7. Trouser socks to wear with your khakis.
8. A nice suit consisting of a classic jacket and skirt. Navy blue or another neutral color.
9. A well-fitted bra.
10. Underwear that fits you well and does not show a panty line.
11. Hosiery if you prefer it.
12. A nice winter coat that will cover to the bottom of your skirt.
13. A scarf to accessorize and keep you warm.
14. A nice pair of small earrings. Other jewelry needs to be attractive, yet unobtrusive. Reminder: Jewelry should never be the musical guest at your office setting.
15. Your team's spirit clothes — T-shirts and jackets, etc. – need to be at the ready for game day or casual Fridays. Go team!

How to Be a Lady With Manners

- Courtesy, respect and thoughtfulness are with you always.
- Remember that doors are equal opportunity.
- Your smart mind and your good work ethic are more important than almost anything.
- Groom yourself in a way that shows you believe in yourself.
- Mental, emotional and physical strength in a lady is a very good thing.
- Self-deprecating humor is a classic trait.
- A lady always knows what she likes and what she doesn't like.
- Always tell the truth, especially when it is hard.
- Apologize when needed. Embrace the art of forgiveness.
- A well-mannered lady knows when to say "No."
- A well-mannered lady knows when to say "Yes."
- A great pair of earrings can be a lifesaver.
- It is okay to be vulnerable sometimes. It shows you are growing and learning.

- Assertiveness is different than aggressiveness.
- Admit your mistakes.
- In a couple's relationship, the strong woman will know each detail about the special man in her life:
    - His likes and dislikes
    - Cologne
    - Style of clothing
    - Shoe size
    - Favorite foods
- A well-mannered lady will know the type of flowers her guy prefers.

"I believe in strong women. I believe in women who are able to stand up for themselves. I believe in the woman who can stand on her own two feet and live a life that is successful and fulfilling. I believe in the woman who may have problems, but chooses to face those problems head on, in an honorable and respectful way, not blaming others, but facing down the arena. You face the world with good posture and a caring soul. I believe in the woman who chooses action over whining. I believe in a woman who chooses a man who can stand beside her, not behind her. I believe in the woman who carries the heartbeat of the universe within her and, indeed, the woman who moves the world."

- Dr. Patricia Tice

Chapter Nine

Specifics for Men in Agriculture

The average American farmer feeds about 155 people worldwide. In 1960 that number was 25.
Source: Iowa Farm Bureau Federation

Men have great clothes from which to choose. Their sportcoats and suits are generally classically cut, and designers don't mess around with men's clothes in terms of the cut, shoulder pads or wild colors. The wild colors are saved for ties and pocket squares, and this is a very good thing.

A recent piece in a national newspaper stated that men's fashions are creating a new look for gentleman, which means that even quiet, more traditional brands are working to gain the attention of young professionals. In some cases, the brands have been pushing the envelope of creativity with some men's clothes showing horizontal-striped suits, pants with oversized cuffs and formalwear in nontraditional colors such as crimson and lemon yellow.

Whether your take on clothes is more crimson, lemon yellow, denim or more along the traditional route of colors for men, the important thing is to fit your personality and the culture of your workplace.

Women love it when men get dressed up. For the man to take a bit of care with his shirt and his trousers – even if they are khakis or jeans – makes all of the difference. A man can display his personality through the way he dresses himself. A clever bowtie or braces (buttoned suspenders) can become the man's signature. A top executive wears beautiful sweater vests worn over his crisply starched shirt on casual days. He pairs it with pleated khaki dress trousers, and it looks fabulous. More importantly, its functionality and good looks works for him as he performs the duties of his high-stress job.

For those of us in agriculture, the key is to wear clothing that fits the work style you are performing. If you are working outdoors, be sure to protect your arms and legs by wearing sturdy jeans or heavy khaki pants with good socks and boots or shoes. Long-sleeved shirts will protect your arms from the harmful effects of the sun. A pair of leather work gloves come in handy.

Some farmers wear bib overalls with pockets to hold a screwdriver, a few nails, or a tape measure. For those folks in cold winters, insulated bib overalls are the key. Strong leather boots or shoes are a must and steel-toed are preferred.

Shoes Make The Man

Behold, the man walketh. Everyone from psychologists to archaeologists have studied shoes and their symbolic meaning and relevance. For most of us, the love of shoes is less cerebral and more institutional. Whether you are an athlete or a corporate lawyer or a farmer, here's what you need to make your shoe wardrobe work for you:

Black dress shoes – Your parents dressed you up with your first sportcoat and dress trousers along with incredibly uncomfortable "dress-up" shoes. Once you enter the working world, depending on the type of work you do, you cannot go wrong with a good pair of black shoes. Lace-ups or slip-ons are fine. Oxford-style or wingtip-style shoes are a little more dressy.

Boots – Protect your shoe investment with a pair of rubber outers that slip over your shoes to protect them from moisture during inclement weather. Four-buckle overshoes are optional.

Tennis/sports shoes – The vast array of high-tech sports shoes available today is mind-boggling. The bottom line: Choose a sports shoe that fits your sport and your budget.

Specialty shoes – Golf spikes and baseball cleats are specialty shoes that may be required if you play the sport. Have some fun with it. Choose a shoe with your team's color and logo on them.

What Not to Wear

White shoes – They never look very sophisticated unless you are going to a '70's party.

Sandals at work – They take you from spring into summer and are great with summer cargo shorts, but usually do not fit at work.

Socks with sandals – No, no and no again. The term schlocky comes to mind. Don't do it.

Sandals that look like car tires – They may be comfortable, but they only look good on the foot if you are less than 12 years old.

Shoes with toes that curl up – A Shakespearian play comes to mind.

White socks with a suit and dress shoes. Don't go there.

Nine Sartorial Tips For Your Professional Working Wardrobe

Fit: Once you enter the professional workforce, it is time to dress in a professional way. Put away your high school/college letter jacket. Lose the saggy, torn jeans. Making the leap into the workplace means your clothes need to look good from head to toe. Clothes should be more on the slim side. Your clothes should fit you well and flatter your body shape. Find a local tailor who can help you with your perfect fit, if needed.

Quality: Buy the best clothes you can afford. When clothes are better made, they last longer, wear better, clean better and usually fit you better. Invest in a couple of key pieces to begin with. You can't go wrong. If you need a suit for your work, get a nice quality suit and change it out with different shirts and ties. Crease-fee cotton can make your life easier by providing a wrinkle-free day through every wash, hang and wear.

Classic and timeless: Try to avoid anything that is trendy. Trends come and go. Colors come and go. Your closet needs to be classic and timeless with clothes that will look as good five years from now as they do now. Classic clothes tend to fit better and are more comfortable when you wear them. Basic stripes and solids are good in basic colors such as blue and white. Timeless style and classic good looks is what you are after. When your shirts begin to look worn around the collar or cuffs, then it is time to get a new shirt.

Jeans: Buy a pair of nice quality raw, selvedge jeans. "Selvedge" means the raw edges of the seams are turned under and professionally sewn. This is indicated by the distinctive seam along the edge of the jean's legs. "Raw" means the fabric in the jeans is unwashed. This means the jeans will break in and form to your body, looking and feeling great. Raw selvedge jeans will give you years of wear and look better than cheaper types of jeans.

Belts: Aaaah, the beauty of a belt. Belt loops on pants, jeans or trousers are sewn in for a reason: They beg for a belt unless one has sewn in buttons that beg for braces. Get yourself a nice leather belt. One that will fit your belt loops and keep those pants/jeans/trousers at the place they need to be, which is your waist. If one witnesses someone without a belt, they appear to be not finished with their dressing. Always wear a belt when you have belt loops. Otherwise, you may want to choose a pair of trousers without loops for a belt.

Shoes: Your first pairs of shoes for the new job should be two pairs of dress shoes: one pair of black shoes and one pair of brown shoes. Loafer style or wingtip style is okay, whichever you prefer. Try to avoid square toes, as they tend to date the shoe. Be sure to have dress socks to match both the black and brown shoes. White tube socks or any white socks with your dress shoes are a no-no. You may want to consider having rubber overshoes to protect your dress shoes during inclement weather. There are slimline rubber coverings that fit over the edges of the shoes. Not necessarily attractive, but they are certainly functional. You can always remove them once you have sloshed through the messy parking lot.

Coat: A nice dress overcoat is a great investment. Coats need to be practical, comfortable and go with almost anything. Many people tend to look like walking billboards during the colder months with all manner of advertising logos on parkas and outerwear. Having a nice dress overcoat will set you apart and make you look professional. Peacoats or a nice wool parka are also fine. Add a nice scarf when it is very cold and people will notice. On very cold days, a stocking hat may save you from the bitter wind, and a good pair of leather gloves will also serve you well.

Shirt: Invest in a few nice dress shirts. Make the shirts washable and permanent press, which makes them easier to care for and pack. Always tuck your shirt into your trousers, which makes for a neater look. You will also want to have a dressier shirt for special occasions.

Suits/sportcoats: Business is the time to suit up and look sharp. Colors to go for: navy blue or grey. Colors to avoid: brown. No black suits unless it is for a funeral. A small pinstripe is fine. A navy blue suit will serve you well on job interviews, special dates and weddings. Buy the best suit you can afford. Have it tailored, if needed. Pair the suit with a nice shirt, tie and shoes to create a look that suits your personality.

If your workplace is less formal, invest in a nice sportcoat. Never underestimate the power of a beautifully crafted sportcoat. It can be thrown on in a moment's notice and look good. Navy blue is a good color, as it will blend with chinos, khakis or jeans. A sportcoat can also be paired with a nice tie, open-collared shirt or even a nice T-shirt.

One designer for men has introduced what he calls the "broken suit" concept in which a jacket from one suit is paired with trousers from another suit in matching shades so it looks like a classic suit, but has a bit of a twist. This same designer also introduced an unconventional take on eveningwear: tuxedos without satin lapels paired with a polo shirt.

Among agricultural circles, the broken suit concept may or may not fly. It is up to you, of course.

"Planting" a New Wardrobe

As you graduate from high school or college, it is time to begin building your professional wardrobe. The first thing to do is to put away your letter jackets but get them dry cleaned first. It is time to step up to the adult world.

1. A nice pair of selvedge jeans.
2. Khaki trousers: pleated or not is your preference.
3. Two button-down collared shirts in cotton for easy washing.
4. A nice polo shirt either short or long sleeved.
5. A nice leather belt.
6. Navy blue sportcoat.
7. A tie and the knowledge of how to tie it.
8. Two pairs of dress shoes: one black and one brown.
9. Dress socks. Note: Select calf high socks. When you sit, your pant legs naturally pull up. When they do, others see more sock, no skin, giving a much more professional look.
10. Work boots if you are going to walk in the fields or operate farm machinery.
11. Boxers or briefs, your preference.
12. Nice undershirts.
13. A few nice T-shirts.
14. A washable blouson jacket.
15. A nice dress overcoat or a peacoat/wool parka.
16. Your team's spirit clothes – T-shirts and jackets, etc. – need to be at the ready for game day or casual Fridays. Go team!

Caring for Your Investment in Clothes

You work hard for your money, and you have worked hard to build the professional wardrobe you have always wanted. Now, how to care for those clothes? Make every effort to invest in clothing that is easy to care for. Wash and wear cotton blend shirts and trousers with timeless design are a given. If your clothes are made of fine fabrics – washable wool, polyester blends and cotton blends – it will make your life much easier. Finer fabrics also mean high performance and a style you can make all your own.

Wools: Most wool sweaters and coats will need to be dry cleaned. If you take good care of your sweaters and coats by folding them properly and airing after wearing, they will probably outlast your love of them.

Cotton blend casual and dress shirts and wash and wear trousers can be washed in the washing machine on permanent press. Damp dry the shirts in the clothes dryer. This means removing the shirt when it is still damp. Hang the shirt on a nice hanger in a place where air can circulate around the shirt. Button the top button. With your hands, smooth out the front button tab and collar while it is damp. You can also hold the top of the front tab with two fingers and put your other two fingers at the bottom of the tab. Then gently pull in opposite directions to straighten the button tab of the damp shirt. Ta-da! The shirt will dry overnight, and you are ready to go. No iron needed. Trousers work the same way. Damp dry, then hang on a hanger overnight.

How to iron your shirt without an iron:

- Use a hair straightener. Be sure it is clear of hair strands first.
- Use a hair dryer. Hang your shirt from the curtain rod and gently pull on it as you use the hair dryer over the wrinkles. If possible, mist a bit of water on the shirt first. This will help to release the wrinkles more easily.
- Spray and hang overnight. Use a mister bottle of water. Gently mist the garment but don't soak it, and then let it hang overnight.
- Take a shower first and then hang your garment on the shower rod once you have turned off the water. The steam will assist in releasing the wrinkles.
- There are new "wrinkle release" products available. Tuck a spray bottle into your suitcase.
- Best tips:
  - Buy shirts labeled "wrinkle free." They really are!
  - Have your dress shirts folded at the laundry. Then you can just pop them into your suitcase.

If you travel a lot, you may want to invest in a travel iron. Many hotels also furnish an ironing board and an iron in each room.

If you prefer a bit of starch in your shirt, then become friends with a nice dry cleaning store in your area. Starch comes in light, medium or heavy.

The heavy is very much like a hard board. You may prefer to have your shirts folded or hung on a hanger. Just let your dry cleaner know. There are few things better than a nicely starched shirt. Crisp and professional. They look good under a sweater or alone and are classic and timeless.

The Perfect Gentleman-How to Be a Man With Manners

- Thoughtfulness, respect and courtesy go a very long way both at work and at home.
- Open the door and let the lady go through first.
- For a revolving door, the man goes first. The idea is to make it easier for the lady.
- Let the lady enter the room first.
- Leave a note on the counter telling her how much she means to you.
- Offer a lady your arm, personal only.
- When walking along the street, walk on the outside of your lady.
- Be yourself.
- Show empathy for animals and other living things.
- Good grooming/pride is key.
- A gentleman knows how to present himself to the world. He knows what his likes and dislikes are.
- Always removes your hat when entering a building.
- Always tuck your shirt in.
- Admit your mistakes.
- Be honorable and always do the honorable thing.

- Don't take yourself too seriously. A sense of humor is key.
- Being vulnerable is sometimes very charming e.g., stopping to ask for directions.
- Kindness = strength. Kindness is contagious. Make sure to spread some around.
- In a couple's personal relationship, the well-mannered man will know every detail about his special lady:
  - Her likes and dislikes
  - Perfume
  - Style of clothing
  - Shoe size
  - Favorite food
  - Birthday
  - Wedding anniversary
- Value the art of forgiveness, apologizing and telling the truth.

"Anyone can be polite to a king. It takes a gentleman to be polite to a beggar."

—Unknown

Chapter Ten

Communicating With Style

The sun, with all those planets revolving around it and dependent on it, can still ripen a bunch of grapes as if it has nothing else in the universe to do.
– Galileo Galilei - Italian astronomer (1564-1642)

Communication

There is an old phrase that states, "Actions speak louder than words." Nonverbally, this may be true. Both social conditioning and imitation or modeling play a role in our acquisition of language, but neither can provide a complete explanation of how or why we learn to communicate. Human beings are biologically wired to communicate through language, regardless of the language. It could be Italian, German or French. Children tend to acquire most of the syntax of their native language by the age of 5.

When people listen to a familiar language, their perceptual system – the action of the mind by which it signals our eyes, ears, olfactory, feelings – permits them to hear the ebb and flow of the words and the spaces between the words. For us to understand language in general and conversations in particular, human beings use their knowledge of the given context and the world to make sense of what is being said. Additionally, understanding is directed by nonverbal cues.

In the communication pie, what are the pieces?

Nonverbal: This is the body language we present to people. This stimuli is presented to the listener and may contain a relational message. The stimuli are usually involuntary and are not actively sent in forms such as tone of voice, gestures, facial expressions, etc. This message can be an emotional clue indicating how the speaker is feeling about themselves, the situation at hand, or the content at hand. Do we have good posture? Are our arms crossed? Are we white-knuckling our pen? Our body language can speak volumes about what we are thinking or feeling. Body language is the physiological nonverbal cues that we give and we may not even realize it. Scientists have stated that up to 55 percent of our message comes through body language.

Tonality: By way of speech and language, tonality is a way of expressing meaning by tone. Is your voice high pitched or low pitched? Do you talk faster when you are nervous? The tonality of your voice will give clues to how you are feeling and what you are thinking. Tonality can be up to 38 percent of our communication message.

Verbal: The verbal part of our communication message are the actual words we say. Choose your words carefully, and finish all of your words. The verbal message is only about 7 percent of our message.

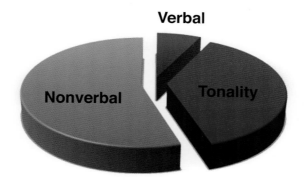

For effective communication, do a spot check on your nonverbal, tonality and verbal cues:

- Handshake: too strong or too weak?
- Posture.
- Are you smiling?
- Leg position.
- General fidgeting.
- Tapping your foot on floor.
- Head tilting.
- Crossing your arms over your chest.
- Clicking your pen.
- Chewing on your pen.
- Eye blinking.
- Breathing patterns.
- Talking fast?
- Talking too loud?
- Talking in buzzwords?
- Chewing your fingernails?
- Picking at your Styrofoam cup?
- Drawing on your plastic cup.

- Doodling when you need to be taking notes?
- Using too many hand gestures?
- Touching your hair or jewelry.
- Wiggling your leg.
- Twitching of eyes.

When it comes to business communication, it is important to remember to be open and flexible. If you are unsure about what behavior is expected, either ask or observe others. Different parts of the country will show big differences in the ways we communicate. Generally speaking, the eastern part of the United States is older and more established, and the western part is newer. These differences will show up in the ways we dress, leisure activities and business protocols, as well as cultural norms.

One way to navigate the differences from coast to coast is to understand some basics of how we communicate. One of the ways to understand is through neuro-linguistic programming (NLP).

Neuro Linguistic Programming

NLP is the science of modeling the patterns of human behavior. NLP explores the inner workings of the human mind: how we think, how we develop our desires, goals and fears, and how we motivate ourselves, make connections, and give meaning to our experiences. NLP grew out of the research activity of psychologists Bandler and Grindler in the 1970's.

Today, entire schools are dedicated to the teaching of NLP. For the purposes of this book, we will share the highlights. NLP is like the user's manual for the mind and allows us to use the language of the mind to consistently achieve our specific and desired outcomes. The name neuro-linguistic programming was invented as an attempt to describe in a comprehensive manner the scope of this extensive body of insights and skills:
- Neuro refers to how the mind and body interact,
- Linguistic refers to the insights into a person's thinking that can be obtained by careful attention to their use of language,
- Programming refers, not to the activity of programming, but to the study of the thinking and behavioral patterns or "programs" that people use in their daily lives.

NLP: "the study of success"

NLP has been variously described as the technology of the mind, the science of achievement and the study of success. It is based upon the search for and the study of the factors that account for either success or failure in human performance. For more than 40 years, NLP explorers have studied or modeled the behavior and thinking styles of particularly effective and successful people in business, education, sales, therapy, sports and personal development.

Basic NLP techniques:

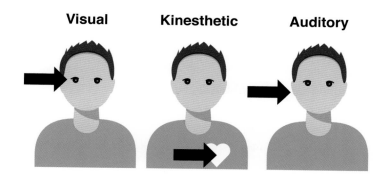

Visuals tend to speak quickly and often move their eyes upward toward the sky. They use verbs and phrases such as, "I see," "I picture this," "The sky is the limit," "Let me think about this" as their eyes move upward, etc.

Kinesthetics tend to speak very slowly, as they are trying to get a feeling of what is being said. They use phrases such as, "I'm not feeling good about this," "What are your feelings," "My gut is telling me not to move forward," etc. Their eyes often move downward when speaking.

Auditory folks also tend to speak slowly, as they are listening very carefully to what is being said. Auditories are exacting in their responses; the verbiage has to be perfect. Auditory folks tend to move their eyes horizontally and sometimes they have to work to not roll their eyes when they hear folks disgracing the English language by their usage. They use phrases such as, "I hear what you are saying," "This is music to my ears," "I've never heard anything so beautifully sounding," etc.

As you are interacting with people, whether meeting them on a sales call or a job interview, try to notice if the person is verbal, kinesthetic or auditory. The key is for you to become a chameleon and learn how to match and mirror your new acquaintance. This means to psychologically give back what they are doing in terms of behavior. This will allow you to create rapport with your new acquaintance. Rapport means that you have found common ground and meaning with this new person through your responsiveness to them.

NLP can be used in many areas of life:

- Management: NLP is a valuable tool for adapting to and utilizing the changes in the role of the manager or team leader today e.g., life coaching, mentoring, appraising.
- Relating with others: NLP enables folks to better understand what it's like to be the other person and how best to communicate with them. This makes it excellent for enriching and deepening relationships at home, socially and at work.
- Your inner self: It is very important to know how to manage one's thoughts and moods.
- Selling: A good salesperson knows that good relationships, repeat business and recommendations produce success over and over.
- Career: It used to suffice to be good at your job to move forward in your career. That has changed. Now you also need to (1) be a skilled communicator, (2) be able to network with and motivate colleagues and (3) be able to market and sell yourself.
- Sports: Mental attitude is critically important in sports. Whether you are an enthusiastic amateur or a professional sports person, NLP can be used to can give you an edge over your competitor.

Using NLP skills will enable you to improve how you:

1. Develop mutually beneficial relationships with customers.
2. Identify customer needs and motivations.
3. Manage your employees in a more effective way.
4. Match products and services with motivation.
5. Communicate more effectively with your co-workers.
6. Communicate more effectively with your family.

The Mechanics of Communication: Listening and Speaking

The Listening Process

Naturally, we tend to be bad listeners, even with those we love. We live in a world of sensory overload with lots of sounds demanding our attention. We have a tendency to swap stories, so we interrupt to tell our own story. We are sometimes uncomfortable with feelings and emotions, so we want to avoid anything unpleasant. We also want to have a quick fix if someone has a problem but, oftentimes, a quick fix is not possible because of its complexity.

It has been said that a picture is worth a thousand words, but some of us may have experienced communication with another person that can be akin to a landmine. Good listeners can overcome their natural inclination to fix the other person's problems and can keep the conversation brief.

The goal of active listening is to build and perceive correct images from the other person as they are speaking to you. As the speaker is talking, they are letting you know what their world looks like. By listening actively, you can enlarge the speaker's world and, hence, relate to each other more effectively.

To actively listen to a person, you need to master certain behaviors, some are verbal, some are nonverbal, that signal your interest. Researchers have called these "immediacy behaviors."

As listeners, we need to select whom we are going to listen to: our own inner voices or scripts, or the speaker. As a listener, if we do not separate our world from the world of the speaker, then we may have an image based on our own perceptions, rather than that of the speaker. As a result, the speaker will not feel heard, and the conversation will become one-way. Ask your question, then wait to listen for the response. Don't practice mental telepathy as to what the response will be, or it may stop you from hearing the truth of what the response is saying to you.

Phases of Listening Well

- The first step is to pick up on hints and nonverbal signals that the other person needs or wants to talk.
- Let the other person talk. Acknowledge and provide authenticity for their experience and feelings. You don't need to provide a solution. Feelings are just feelings. If you minimize or make light

of what the person is saying, the conversation will probably end.

- Encourage the other person to enlarge or explain more in depth with open-ended questions. Lean forward. Make eye contact. Use verbal cues to let the other person know you are listening.
- Show that you heard the other person by mirroring back and using a verbal check system. "I heard you say X. Is that right?"
- Continue to ask open-ended questions so you can work together on possible solutions.

When listeners display more active listening behaviors, the other person will perceive the listener as more emotionally present and feel better.

Roadblocks to Good Listening

Many of us suffer from inherent listening patterns that limit our understanding of what others are saying, often because the amount of stimuli coming from the speaker is distorted by our own thoughts.

Roadblock #1: *Ineffective listening.* If we are focused on sounds, tones and words, then we are probably not listening for purpose and meaning from the speaker. Meaning and purpose are the keys to understanding clearly what the speaker is trying to say.

Roadblock #2: *Feeling defensive.* If the speaker's message is critical of the listener, or if the message challenges the listener's world, then defensiveness may happen. It is a natural thing for the listener to want to defend by stating different facts, or questioning the integrity of what the speaker is saying. The listener may even counterattack the speaker. Instead of the listener hearing objectively what the speaker is saying, the listener spends all of the listening time trying to figure out how to defend themselves. Further, the listener then often feels negative about the interchange and may say, "I'm not dealing with that person anymore."

Roadblock #3: *Waiting for admittance to the conversation.* This roadblock resembles defensiveness, except the listener is not threatened by the speaker's words. The listener may even empathize with what the speaker is saying, but mentally turns off the speaker and becomes preoccupied with their own thoughts, feelings and needs. All the listener can think about is how they are going to respond. The listener may go so far as to interrupt the speaker with their own announcement. This causes the conversation to quickly turn into a one-way street. The listener is obviously not focusing on the speaker. Instead of being a listener, the person becomes a speaker, so we now have two speakers who are both listening to the stimuli from the other, but have no sense or feeling of what the other was really trying to say. In the end, this tends to minimize both people involved. If a person feels listened to and understood, this will allow them to experience a new depth and meaning in all of their relationships.

Roadblock #4: *Distracted listening.* At times, even the most skilled of listeners may not be able to actively listen. Maybe you are pressed for time. Maybe the emotional needs of the conversation are too complex to understand quickly, or we may feel frustrated or impatient with the speaker's own confusion or neediness. Sometimes the problem is simply the speaker cannot quite identify it. Another listening problem may be a preoccupation with other issues so demanding that we simply don't have the energy to focus on the speaker. If this happens, we need to admit it to the speaker instead of trying to pretend that we are listening. "Sally, I'm really sorry, but I have to confess that I am preoccupied. I received a call from my mother last night, and she was not feeling well. I am very concerned about her and am thinking of driving down to help her out. I've love to give you my full attention, but just not right now. Can I call you in the next few days? Thanks." Then, follow through. This will put your communication back on solid ground.

Roadblock #5: *Tired, low on energy or hungry.* If we are weary physically or mentally, or if our energy level is low, or if we are hungry, then it is going to be difficult for us to sort out the messages we are receiving. Listening is not a passive activity. It takes a lot of energy to process the stimuli and understand the message being sent to us. Hint: If you need to have a difficult conversation, do it when you are feeling more rested.

Roadblock #6: *Closed viewpoints.* One of the more serious roadblocks to listening is those folks who may have a closed perception. Because the listener is set on their own vantage point, the listening problem will not be changed by adjusting the circumstances. In this case, the listener may not be open to the speaker because the listener has a predetermined notion of what the speaker is going to say and purposely rebuffs the message. One of the saddest situations in active listening occurs when a speaker continues to send the same message over and over to someone who refuses to acknowledge it. This happens usually because the speaker is begging for someone to understand their viewpoint. It is important to remember that understanding does not equate to acceptance. A good active listener will always keep the options open on a speaker because a good listener is able to acknowledge the esteem of the speaker and the importance of the given message. [Do you know the average number of times an individual goes to see a psychiatrist or a psychologist? ONE.] We all want someone to listen to us. We all want to be heard and respected.

Roadblock #7: *Perpetuating stereotypes and clichés.* Language is a very powerful way to set up expectations about how people should act. Be cautious to not use clichés or perpetuate stereotypes. Some examples of clichés: "Like a girl," "Be a man," "Girls aren't good at math," and "Boys will be boys." These clichés do nothing to help good communication. In fact, they only provide a way to split us into gender scripts, which are not helpful. Clichés and stereotypes have no place in the workplace of today.

Roadblock #8: *Critical parent.* How many times have we been listening to someone and suddenly we feel as though we are being scolded like a child? This is because the speaker is emitting words and feelings that sound parental and mean-spirited. Nothing shuts down communication faster than a speaker sounding like a critical parent.

Roadblock #9: *A need to offer advice.* Feeling the need to offer a solution is a common communication roadblock. We all seem to want a solution to problems. We want to understand and help out. However, offering a solution short-circuits the listening process. Then we end up being a speaker, too, which is not helpful to the listener. Seldom is the speaker asking for solutions as much as they are asking for support and understanding. The speaker might be testing the listener's level of concern. Few of us can say to our boss, "I'm having a bad day. Can you hear me out?" Rather than offering advice, say, "Tell me more. What is going on?" Then actively listen for feelings and perceptions. This is a valuable chance to truly understand what the speaker is saying.

Five Critical Listening Skills to Master

These five listening skills can help to strengthen our relationships with others. They can also assist us in getting a new position, strengthen our teamwork at work and assist us in our personal relationships.

Accept the speaker: Try to accept the individual world of the speaker. A key to understanding is to ask "how" and "what" questions. A "how" question invites sharing and usually leads to an understanding of what the speaker is saying. Avoid "why" questions as they can easily become an allegation that requires a defensive response. Because of the complexity of life situations, the word "why" is often a difficult one to answer.

Check out your assumptions: Listen to the speaker from where they are at that moment in time. Do not try to fix the problem or change the person to feel better about something. We need to respect the right of people to suffer. We did not cause the suffering, and we are willing to respect the way they are feeling, even though it is a bit unpleasant or uncomfortable. Try to withhold judgment or blame. People feel the way they feel, and there is nothing wrong with feelings. Remorse and guilt are a healthy part of healing. An important part of communication is accepting others, regardless of whether or not their values are different or similar to ours. The goal is to separate the world of the speaker from the world of the listener.

Become comfortable with silence: An important part of active listening is becoming comfortable with silence in communication. This is true whether the communication is in person or by phone, e-mail or text. Sometimes a speaker needs silence to sort out thoughts and feelings. A listener needs to respect the silence.

Continue to be an active listener: This means to continue to be a listener. Do not interrupt and offer interpretations or your own experiences about what the speaker is saying. Offer a listener's response to show you are actively engaged in understanding what the speaker is saying. Being an active listener means also paying attention to nonverbal messages. A smile, a nod, shrugging shoulders, rolling eyes, leaning forward, gesturing: All of these nonverbal messages express valuable information about the speaker's message. Don't let the sound of your cellphone interrupt your good listening skills.

Offering authentic feedback: The speaker has sent you a message through conversation. The listener then needs to interpret the message authentically and in an unbiased way, and give back their understanding to the speaker. The speaker then acknowledges and confirms the listener did indeed practice active listening in a genuine, accurate and caring way.

These five critical listening skills not only help to strengthen our relationships with people, they also assist us in becoming a successful professional person. We all want to be understood. We all want to have some control over our professional and personal relationships, and good, active listening will help us to achieve that. [Communication hint: Never ask what you don't really care about.] Because listening is a learned skill, it is not always easy to learn. It may feel awkward at first as we try to eliminate a bad listening habit, but because it is a learned skill, practice will make us better, and the rewards are many.

People Skills

Superb people skills are one of the keys in having a successful career in agriculture and its related businesses. Regardless of your position or the type of customers you are working with, developing your skills in customer service will serve you well.

30 Skills for Excellence in Sales/What to Expect From A Professional

1. **Say "Hello".** Ask questions in order to understand more fully what your customer is saying. Summarize back to the customer what you heard them say. Show them you care by the tone of your voice. Show them you are interested in finding a solution to their problem or issue.

2. **Notice people.** When customers walk into a dealership with the motivation to purchase, make the time to notice them. Whether it is your job or not, whether you are busy or not, notice people by saying something like, "Hello! Great to see you. We'll be right with you." All people want is to be noticed that they are, in fact, present and welcome in the store.

3. **Learn to be a great listener.** Listen attentively, ask questions and summarize by speaking slowly and carefully. Being a great listener will show that you care, which will help you to gain the respect of your customers.

4. **Strong communication skills.** Practice knowing when to listen and knowing when to speak. Speak in a voice that is easy for people to understand. This means speaking clearly at a pace that can be understood by the listener. The communication process becomes much easier the more you practice. Strong communication skills will make the communication process much more effective with others.

5. **Practice patience and be calm.** Remember that some people were born crabby. That doesn't mean you have to be crabby too. Keep your emotions under control and stay in control. This will help you deal with unhappy customers. Expressing a calm attitude and showing patience will allow them to feel more respected and listened to while talking with you. After work, be sure to do a healthy de-stressor activity for yourself. Take good care of yourself nutritionally, emotionally and physically.

6. **Be well mannered.** Speak into the telephone with a smile on your face. Say "Hello," "Thank you" and "Good-bye" at the end of the conversation. Adding a cheerful phrase at the end also helps: "Take care now. Thank you."

7. **Make and keep your promises.** Keep your integrity intact by making good on all of the promises you make to customers. Your handshake should be your word. This is essential to you being taken seriously as a professional person in your company. Be familiar with company policies to assure that any promise you make can be fulfilled.

8. **Be as honest as the day is long.** Being honest and transparent with your clients will show them you truly care about their satisfaction and happiness with the products and services your company provides. Being honest is also very helpful when the message you have to share with customers is not a positive one. Show empathy for the customer by sharing their feelings when the news may be bad.

9. **Be friendly and caring** especially with those whom you may disagree. Having an outgoing and compassionate personality makes it easier to build long-lasting professional relationships while also improving your sales or problem-solving abilities. Difficult people make it harder to be friendly and caring but maybe those difficult people need a friend. Ask questions about your client's everyday life and why the services or products you represent could fit their lifestyle.

10. **Check in with your client.** Make it a habit to check in periodically with your client to make sure your product continues to work for them. Make a phone call and say, "I'm just checking in to see how our new corn hybrid is doing for you. Everything going okay?" This shows dedication to the product on your part and, perhaps more importantly, your client will know that you care.

11. **Become a pro.** Know your products and how they work with people. Know your clients and their expectations of your product. Communicate with your clients. See the section on Communication.

12. **Know your company.** The more knowledgeable you are of your company, the easier it is to have your customers trust your decisions and the products and services you represent. Be aware of your surroundings and fit into them. Get to know your co-workers and the hierarchy of your supervisory team. Being familiar with these groups and being friendly with them will allow you to not only earn the respect of your customers, but also open the option of solving complex problems together. All of this serves to enhance the esprit de corps of the team and makes you look like a hero.

13. **Good body language.** Open and inviting body language is important whether you are meeting a client in person or talking to them on the telephone. Square your shoulders, use good posture and speak with a smile in your voice. Having a conversational, friendly tone with your client will help to show the client you really do care about them and their happiness with your product or service.

14. **Good language skills.** As you are speaking with a client, your good language skills are a must. Finish your words. Speak in complete sentences. Slow down. Avoid insider language or buzzwords. Your client will appreciate you speaking to them in a way that honors them; that is, in plain and clear, proper English.

15. **Time management.** Managing your time properly as an ag professional means always being on time and making the best use of your time. Time is a limited commodity. Build in plenty of time to make a scheduled appointment on time. If you tell someone that you will meet them at 3 p.m., then it needs to be 3 p.m. or a few minutes before but no more than 10 minutes before. At times, circumstances are out of our control and you may be running late. If

this is the case, call or text the person that you are on your way and should be arriving in 10 minutes or whatever the amount of time is. In other words, if you're going to be late, communicate it. Let people know. It's a jungle out there and people need to know you are thinking about them.

16. **Persuasion and negotiation.** Your ability to convince others to use your product or service is fundamental to your success. Your ability to communicate effectively with others will not only increase your monetary bottom line, it will also increase your confidence and the trust and loyalty of your clients. Be eager to always learn more by taking a class, reading and practicing your skills.

17. **Confidence** in yourself and confidence in your product/service. By sounding confident over the telephone or in person, you will help your clients know that you believe in the products or services you represent. Confidence comes from the way you sound over the telephone, to the way you dress, to the way your conversational skills shine. Believe in yourself.

18. **Never give up,** never give up, never give up. As an ag professional, you have the training and skills to take your career to the highest levels. Be a goal-oriented person. Set your goals, then check them off as you reach them. Always push yourself higher. The more tenacious you are in the workplace, while being well mannered of course, the more likely you are to make more sales and earn the trust and loyalty of more customers and clients. Being goal oriented and determined will show your professionalism and dedication to yourself and your company.

19. **Handle surprises well.** Sometimes things will happen with your client or with your position that catch you off guard. Knowing how to handle confrontations, disappointments or disgruntled co-workers will improve your professionalism and ensure that an equitable and fair solution is found for all involved.

20. **Dealing with stress.** The ability to solve problems and work under pressure requires the skills of being prepared and thinking ahead in order to maintain your composure at all times. Temper tantrums have no place anywhere. If possible, do the most difficult tasks when you are rested and fresh. Be fully prepared for any meeting with all manner of pen, pencil, paper, computer, presentation, etc.

21. **Understand your customer.** As you talk with your client, begin to analyze the problems they are presenting. What if you were in their shoes? Put yourself in their place to try to understand what the client is saying to you by communicating clearly. Try to understand the customer's perspective. Present the customer with a win–win solution which benefits both the customer and your company.

22. **Learn the lessons.** With every person we meet and with every deal we do, there are lessons to be learned. It is just as important to learn <u>what not to do</u> as it is <u>what to do</u>. Mistakes are a part of life. Admit the mistakes to yourself. Learning from those mistakes helps you to become stronger, smarter and more focused on completing the tasks and objectives that lie ahead. Keep a journal for yourself and jot down the lessons you want to remember. Take time to reflect on issues you want to improve upon. The more you focus on the areas in which you are struggling, the easier it will be to make the life changes you need to make to improve your life skills.

23. **Understand the psychology** of human behavior. Become familiar with what makes people behave the way they do. Human psychology, body language and tone of voice all influence how we interact with others. Knowing how to pick up on tones, sounds and your client's body language will give you clues as to how to steer the conversation you are engaged in. When you can detect body language, you can then determine the best way to generate more interest in the products and services you represent. Getting into the client's world is a key goal as you interact with your new client or an existing client. Learning about human behavior will not only help you understand yourself better, it will also make it easier for you to influence others in a positive way and make genuine and lasting connections with others.

24. **Be system oriented** in your organization. Set up a system for your daily activities, then follow the system. Be disciplined in following the system you set up, and it will reward you exponentially. An example of a system is to keep a spiral notebook on your desk or in your truck. Within the notebook, write your to-do lists for each day, then check off when the tasks are completed. The notebook can also be used to take telephone notes and meeting notes. Keep all of the pages intact and you can refer

back to notes if needed.

25. **Use good language.** Any time you speak with a client, consider the language you are using and how effective it is. Do you use insider words or buzzwords? Positive language that is plain and simple goes a long way toward motivating and persuading your clients to make a purchase, accept a solution or get engaged with your company's services. Be cheerful and smile. Incorporate simple phrases such as "Please," "Thank you," and "It's so nice to see you again." Using Mr., Mrs. and Ms. also shows respect for the client. You can rarely err on the side of too much formality. If the client states, "Just call me Bob," then that is the permission given for you to call the client by his given name. Do not take it upon yourself to use the client's given name without their permission. This hints of arrogance, which is not always a complimentary trait, especially in agriculture.

26. **Good computer skills** and more. Knowing how to use a computer efficiently allows you to communicate with customers and others with whom you have a professional relationship. Learning how to type quickly can also save your time. However, be cognizant that work-related computers need to be used for work and not for personal use.

27. **Take the extra step.** Going the extra mile for a customer or co-worker results in loyal customers and a happy workplace. The goal is for you to offer to do more with the problems or issues clients or co-workers may be experiencing. As well, be the first to take the extra step to put away chairs after a meeting without being asked, tidying up the room after the meeting or doing that little extra thing, not because you have to, but because you want to. This shows your impeccable integrity and loyalty, not to mention a great work ethic.

28. **When communicating by e-mail** or text message or other mobile devices, use appropriate communication. Informality, roughness in wording, typographical errors and brusqueness are all pitfalls of responding to e-mails/texts on a handheld device. Don't say anything through electronic devices or sites that you would not say to someone's face. If you are unsure, then don't do it. After all, once the comment is posted, it is always there and can be forwarded to anybody at anytime.

29. **Be a leader.** A leader is not born. A leader is made. Demonstrate creative solutions to client issues, take the lead on a difficult project at work, be inclusive with your co-workers. Leading others in the workplace shows your natural capabilities of leadership and increases your professionalism. Be polite, well-mannered and tough as nails.

30. **Be enthusiastic.** Everyone loves to be around authentic, genuine, enthusiastic people.

> *"There is no shortcut to achievement. Start where you are,*
> *with what you have. Make something of it, and never be satisfied."*
> —*George Washington Carver*

Chapter Eleven

An Effective Image

The table is a meeting place, a gathering ground, the source of sustenance and nourishment, festivity, safety and satisfaction. A person cooking is a person giving. Even the simplest food is a gift.
Source: Laurie Colwin, American Author (1944-1992)

Dressing for the Workplace

"Respect yourself, and others will respect you."

—*Confucius*

How you dress yourself depends upon the nature of your work. For those folks working in an office setting, the key is to be consistent with the image of your organization. Often, the human resources department will have written guidelines about appropriate dress.

If your job is a plant scientist, you will probably wear a white lab coat, and if your job requires you to walk in soybean fields, then nice blue jeans and sturdy shoes or boots will be needed. The key is to be consistent with the company for which you are working.

Farm work often requires that work be done outdoors. Be properly protected with a hat and sunscreen. Seed caps do not protect the top of the ear or the back of the neck. Wear a hat with a wide enough brim to protect you from the harmful effects of the sun's rays. Your skin will thank you for it.

Sunglasses may also be needed to protect your eyes. Be sure to remove your sunglasses when you are talking with others. You need to make clear contact with your eyes so you can understand and read what they are communicating.

Clothes Manners

A friend of mine burst into laughter a few years ago upon learning that I possessed not one pair of blue jeans in my closet. Sans jeans. She was astounded. "Where would I wear them?" I responded simply. She rolled her eyes. At the time, I was working as a high-school guidance counselor and university professor, both of which required more formal clothing to meet with parents, alumni, scholarship donors and especially to be a role model for the students. Human beings observe each other in many different ways, not the least of which is clothes.

There are all styles of jeans today. Everyone from divas to rock stars to construction workers wears blue jeans, despite the sometimes high price of denim. The rock stars will spend hundreds of dollars to purchase blue jeans with carefully placed holes and tears in them. These are called "pre-stressed."

My generation called these "worn out." Throw them away. The only holes in the real jeans are the holes to place one's legs through.

Slumber Party Anyone? Yes, Jammies!

In America, we have many rules about clothing. Some polite. Some, well, not so much. Many cultures have very different rules about clothing.

This doesn't hold a candle to Shanghai, where men and women have exchanged their Mao suits for pajamas. People wearing pajamas are seen most everywhere: in the market, walking the streets and relaxing in the park. The Chinese adopted western pajamas not knowing the pajamas were intended to be worn only at home. They deemed the pajamas practical and very comfortable, and ta-da, a new tradition was born. This new practice also came about because the homes and living areas are so small, and the thought of changing clothes just to walk across the street to pick up dinner seemed silly. Plus, the wearing of pajamas in public deemed that money, style and a strong sense of cool was there for all to see. However, the government sees it differently and has recently been trying to convince Shanghai residents to change out of pajamas before going out in public.

Some years ago, an American entrepreneur designed a new kind of comfortable pajamas. This clever inventor and her associates marketed her wares by wearing pajamas in airports and other public places. It garnered a lot of attention. The trick must have worked. Her pajamas are now seen in major department stores across the nation. The entrepreneurial spirit is alive and well in America. We love our comfy PJs.

In England, the very proper British monarchs dress to the nines. Her Majesty the Queen always appears in public wearing a matching hat, coat, gloves and her ever-famous handbag, also matching. I once met the milliner in England charged with making Her Majesty's hats. There were samples of fabrics from floor to ceiling in the crowded and charming little shop, along with a detailed calendar of Her Majesty's appearances that signaled the milliner had to have completed the latest royal head covering, or risk offending the most well-known client of all.

Business Casual

The term business casual sometimes makes me nostalgic for buttoned braces, old-fashioned haberdashery and a well-dressed gentleman wearing a tape measure around his neck, saying gently, "Let's take in this much and mark here for the hem." Sigh. Of course, I am the one who dresses to travel on airplanes – yes, as in a dress or skirt – because it seems to get better service. People seem more humane when I present myself a bit better while traveling.

You may remember in 2010 when first lady Michelle Obama ascended from Air Force One wearing shorts. Yikes! Clothes police from coast to coast were all atwitter. Yet, the first lady was returning from a casual family getaway. Is the first family not to show any skin?

"When a woman is wearing shorts, her charm is enlarged without being enhanced."
–Beverley Nichols, English Journalist and Writer, 1898-1983

On any given street in America, on any given day in July or August, we will see a multitude of examples of American shorts, tank tops and halter tops. It makes one wonder if there is underwear under the wear. It's not that one is looking, you can just tell. Freedom of the clothes, I guess.

All of it reminds me to stick with capris, which are really pedal pushers with a new name, for my casual time. Or pressed capris if one goes out in public. Clothes call for the task at hand: garden pants with knee pads for digging in the soil, walking shorts for the daily workout and comfy T-shirts for weekly yoga class. Stretchy helps. We love stretchy.

Too many people seem to confuse dressing to work in the garden with dressing for the theatre. A formal theatre or concert series in a beautiful venue calls not for jeans and T-shirts. Quite the contrary. Dressing nicely shows respect for the actors, performers and musicians who have rehearsed so hard to provide a wonderful experience for you.

A nice skirt and top, usually in black or other dark colors, are the appropriate dress for a woman attending the theatre. Even dress trousers and a nice jacket or sweater will work. For the men, a sportcoat and nice dark trousers are appropriate. To take it up a notch, the gentleman can add a tie.

Of course, going to the theater is not the same if you don't have a small chocolate candy in tow. It makes the music in the theatre sound sweeter, does it not? No pun intended. Please do obtain the nice chocolates with the quiet wrappers. Nothing is more annoying than the lights going dim, then someone opening the crinkly paper on a piece of candy. Have you ever noticed how long it seems to take? Talk about spoiling the mood for all around. Please don't do it. Purchase candies that have quiet wrappers, then be sure to dispose of the wrapper in a proper way, which is in your pocket or purse and not the floor.

Attending the theater in England is a major event. People dress in sharp suits and fancy jewels and party dresses are the norm. Of course, built into the seating of the English theatre is a small holder to rest your wineglass, and ice, as in gelato, is being served at intermission. Ah, what a nice touch. One comes away from the English theater feeling like royalty. Why can't America do something similar? Just an idea, of course.

Dressing for church, synagogue or another house of worship calls for a similar type of dress as the theatre. Dress nicely, which will show your respect and honor for the place of worship. A house of worship is not the place to wear your play clothes.

We recently attended a worship service at which the music was lovely and the minister was very good. However, people were sitting in the audience enjoying their donuts and lattes. Children were sipping water out of portable water bottles.

Maybe this is modern, but it reminds me of a home movie night, complete with greasy popcorn and sugary sodas, with people checking text messages on their smartphones while they sit comfortably in their holey T-shirts and sweat pants. Maybe it fits for some folks.

Slovenly means sloppy, careless, disheveled, untidy, messy and unkempt. Examples of slovenly:

- Food or other stains on clothes.
- A shirt that appears to have been under a pillow for two weeks.
- A shirt that has not been laundered since the new millennium.
- Rips or tears especially those tears in, ahem, private areas.
- Shirttails hanging out.
- Wearing pants with belt loops and no belt.

- Undergarments that have not been changed.
- Clothes that reveal more information than we want.

While every venue is different, are there some basic guidelines we can all follow when it comes to business attire? It seems business attire has taken a confused turn. I know of one business that requires a coat and tie for the gentlemen and skirts or dresses for the ladies. Bravo for them. While your business may not be this formal, there are some general rules:

1. Do follow the dress attire of your business or office. Most training departments/human resource departments will have an employee handbook or document the person received when being hired.

2. Resist the urge to be slovenly in your dress. Enough examples of down dressing can be seen on most any street or college campus.

3. Remember the abnormal psychology rule: Viewer discomfort makes for an uneasy working day, especially during the warm summer months. Get outside of yourself enough to be aware of how your dress makes other people feel. Why? Because how they feel about you is going to effect how they interact with you. Saggy, torn jeans and bra straps hanging out may cross the line of good judgment for dress at the office. After all, you are a grownup who is in the workplace.

4. Casual and comfortable is not the same thing as slovenly.

5. Casual is friendly with starch and an iron.

While many businesses today do not require a suit and tie, upon entrance into any office, one can usually notice that people are dressed in nice khaki trousers with a nice polo shirt or other nice shirt and well-kept shoes. My rule of thumb: Dress one step up from your customer. For example, many farmers will wear denim. You, as a salesperson, should wear khakis and a buttoned shirt unless you have a heavy labor task that day.

Be cautious not to make the folks in your human resources department uncomfortable by wearing clothes that appear to be one step up from a bikini top or bottoms that reveal too much. The workplace is not the place to test the limits on clothing do's or don'ts.

If the business has a formal dress code, it needs to be followed to the letter. If dress code violations are in order, then members of the training department will seek to rectify the situation. It becomes even more uncomfortable when a male from the training department has to address a newly hired female whose manner of dress is too revealing.

It may be that a female may be the best one to address a female about a clothing mishap. However, the supervisor may give the job to the male trainer. This is sticky territory. Help yourself out by not going there to begin with. Purchase a few key pieces of workplace type clothing to begin your career.

A beginning wardrobe? A nice pair of khaki trousers, collared shirt, belt and nice shoes with matching socks for the guys. For the gals: A nice pair of khaki trousers, a nice skirt no shorter than the middle of the knee, a nice blouse, sweater and nice shoes that you can wear all day. This may or may not include stiletto heels (your choice). The type of wardrobe you have will depend upon the nature of the workplace.

One especially good trend has been that of businesses putting their logos on specially colored polo shirts. They are usually very sharp, help to promote the business and fit the business casual model nicely. Be sure to keep your polo shirt tucked into your trousers.

We tend to behave the way we dress. I once worked at a large high school that had dress-up day as part of the homecoming festivities each year. On that day, 1,400 students who usually wore saggy jeans, low-cut tops and micro short shorts with high heels came to school outfitted in dresses, skirts, pleated trousers dress shoes and French cuffed shirts.

Delightfully, none of them were recognizable. The students stood taller, had better posture and talked more comfortably and confidently. The trousers fit, the skirts were a better length. Students were being more cordial and affable to each other in the hallway. Their hair was combed and coiffed.

In short, they were different people for the better. It was an amazing transformation. Beautiful! We can only hope dress-up day will catch on in a way so as to become more regular.

"Clothes make the man. Naked people have little or no influence on society."
—Mark Twain

On Pockets and Carrying

In high school, our biology teachers taught us we stand apart from other mammals because of two main characteristics: We stand upright, and we have a working brain. However, the one thing we do not have is a built-in way to carry our stuff. Kangaroos with their built-in pockets are so lucky. We have pockets, backpacks, luggage, briefcases, purses and satchels, etc. Oh, and we have our after-work gym bag with the too smelly socks in it. We carry things that are near and dear to us.

We carry things we need – lip balm, money and so on – and we carry things we are required to carry, like military knapsacks. We see children carrying backpacks that are twice the size of the child. Look out ahead! We carry our wallet in the back pocket until the fabric wears out a line around it. We carry on our backs, on our arms and in front of us. We load ourselves up, front to back, top to bottom. It brings to mind pack animals.

Our pockets and all of the things we need are important to us. After all, we wouldn't want to climb Mt. Everest only to arrive at the summit and discover that our backpack contained a linen tablecloth and bone china teacups. Oops. Plan ahead. Packing the correct items you need for your event is part of being well mannered.

Manners hint: List the items you travel with on a 3x5 card. Keep the card in your suitcase as a reminder of what you need.

Some manners rules about pockets and carrying:
- Pockets in clothing are meant to be decorative or hold things such as a pack of chewing gum. Never let your pockets hold your hands for an extended period of time. This looks unprofessional and makes you appear to be insecure.
- Be aware of your backpack. If the backpack extends past your personal space because it is overstuffed, you could easily wipe out that nice person beside you by simply turning to the left or right. The bad part is that someone could be writhing on the floor after being smacked by your attack backpack and you wouldn't even know it. Be aware of the space around you. Someone's grandmother will thank you for it.
- When packing a suitcase for flying, pack only what you need. Follow airline regulations. Otherwise, they will be quick to remind you and

not always in the nicest of ways. Please don't be one of the folks who tries to stuff an overstuffed bag into the overhead bin of an airplane while everyone else watches and waits. Sigh. After all, we are all together in a very crammed space, trying our best to be comfortable.

• The bag we use says a lot about us an individual. Is it a designer original? Or a hand-me-down with a broken latch? Present yourself in the best way possible, even while traveling. Your luggage and objects you cannot live without do not need to be sparkly new, but they need to be well cared for and clean. The cleanliness says a lot about you as an individual. Of course, one wishes the bag handlers could respect our luggage a bit more.

"A child of five would understand this. Send someone to fetch a child of five."
−Groucho Marx.

Etiquette Objects

The cravat was a piece of linen, lace or muslin edged with lace worn around the neck and tied in a bow as a type of neckerchief. From this, the modern necktie was developed and has lasted for generations.

The cravat took much time to launder, iron, pleat and fold, and as the Industrial Revolution took hold, men, and the women who supported them, had little time to launder, iron, pleat and fold. A much simpler solution was a one-piece length of fabric worn loose and knotted. Ta-da: The necktie.

A man's suit can take on a distinctive flavor by the pattern of necktie that is chosen. Now, we have the four-in-hand knot, the half- knot, the full windsor knot and the bow tie. Within the bowtie, there are five different styles: butterfly jumbo, slim line, very slim line, slim line diamond point and very slim diamond point.

Your Tie, Your Way

Dresses vs. Cocktail Dresses vs. Pantsuits

While women wear trousers and khakis, polo shirts and button-down cotton shirts, some occasions call for a dress. Dresses and skirts are a staple for many women. A dress is a one-piece garment and is sometimes worn with a sweater or a jacket.

Skirts come in long or short, pleated or not, zippered or not. Skirts are an important part of the wardrobe because you can pair them with different tops, sweaters and jackets. It is good to have skirts in basic colors, allowing them to be mixed and paired with other pieces more easily, as separates allowing you get more outfits for less cost.

A cocktail dress is a more formal type of dress worn to a late afternoon or evening event. The dress tends to be fancier and may come in many different colors. It is often worn with heels. It is appropriate to carry a small clutch purse.

A more formal occasion calls for a long skirt (floor length). This might be a gala affair or a formal dance. If the invitation says "black tie" dress, then you can wear a floor length skirt or gown. A very nice cocktail dress would also work for the black tie requirement, as long as the cocktail dress is fancy enough to be considered formal.

Pantsuits came into their own during the 1990s. A pantsuit consists of a pair of trousers or pants with a matching suit jacket. A blouse or sweater can be worn underneath the jacket. Pantsuits are comfortable and women love the ease of them.

Trousers vs. Pants vs. Slacks

In the United Kingdom and Ireland, the words "trousers" or "slacks" were historically used for women's pants. Trousers are also known as breeks in Scotland, a word related to "breeches." The regular word "trousers" is also used, but is pronounced roughly represented by "tru:zirz," which may be a throwback to the Gaelic word truis, from which the English word is derived.

In the early 20th century, female pilots and other working women began to wear trousers. In the 1930's, actresses Marlene Dietrich and Katharine Hepburn wore trousers in their films, helping make trousers become more mainstream for women, for which this author is very grateful.

Luisa Capetillo was one of Puerto Rico's most famous labor organizers. She was also a writer and an anarchist who fought for workers and women's rights. Luisa challenged mainstream society in Puerto Rico by wearing trousers in public in 1919. She was arrested and sent to jail for this, as women were not to wear trousers in public. The judge later dropped the charges against her. Retrieved from Wikipedia June 2, 2015.

In the 1960's, fashion designer Andre Courreges introduced long trousers for women as a fashion statement. This lead to the era of the pantsuit and designer jeans, and the gradual wearing away of social prohibitions against girls and women wearing trousers in schools, workplace and restaurants.

In 1969 Rep. Charlotte Reid of Illinois became the first woman to wear trousers in the U.S. Congress. She was shunned for the wearing them. In 1989, Sen. Rebecca Morgan of California became the first woman to wear trousers in the U.S. Senate, but it was not an accepted trend. Hillary Clinton was the first woman to wear trousers in an official U.S. first lady portrait. She told David Letterman, "In my White House, we all know who wears the pantsuits."

Women were not allowed to wear trousers on the floor of the U.S. Senate in 1993. In defiance of the rule, Senators Barbara Mikulski and Carol Moseley Braun proudly wore trousers onto the floor of the Senate in 1993. Female support staff members began following suit and, later that year, the rule was amended by Senate Sergeant At Arms Martha Pope to permit women to wear trousers on the floor as long as a jacket was worn with the trousers.

What are trousers?

In North America, trousers or "slacks" refer to a more tailored garment with a waistband, belt loops and a fly front. Some dress trousers may be fitted with buttons rather than belt loops to support the use of braces or suspenders.

Parts of Trousers

Pleats are just below the waistband and are typical of both formal and casual trousers, including suit trousers and khakis. There may be one, two or three pleats, which can face either direction. If the pleat opens toward the pockets, they are called reverse pleats and are typical of most trousers today. When the pleat opens toward the fly, they are known as forward pleats.

Cuffs finish off the legs by preventing fraying. Cuffs may be referred to as "turn-ups." After hemming, the fabric is rolled outward and may be pressed or stitched into place. The reason for cuffs is to add a finished look to the trouser and to add weight to the bottom of the leg to help the drape of the garment.

A well-groomed gentleman or lady will be sure the cuff of the trouser is the proper length. A cuff sitting on top of the shoe, making another front crease in the ankle area, is not okay. The cuff should only brush the very top of your shoe line. Of course, this means that you need to choose your shoes carefully so to fit the length of your trousers.

Fly: The fly is the covering over an open joint in the trouser, which usual conceals a mechanism such as a zipper, Velcro® or buttons. The fly usually covers the groin area, making the trousers easier to take on and off. The opening also allows men to do one's business without lowering the trousers.

Trouser support: Most trousers are held up by the assistance of a belt, held in place by the belt loops spaced on the waistband of the trousers. Traditionally, this was a style only for casual trousers or work trousers. Suit trousers and formal trousers such as a bridegroom's trousers were supported by the use of braces (the British version) or suspenders (American).

Suspenders, Braces, Belts

There are few things more sartorially fresh and forward thinking as a pair of braces. Meant to be used to replace the belt, braces come in a variety of colors and designs. Braces are made from leather, silk, smooth cotton and other beautiful fabrics. One can build an ensemble with coordinating necktie – your choice of bowtie or regular tie – braces and pocket kerchief. With braces and a French cuff shirt, a man is transformed into a true gentleman. Often, a double breasted coat is nice with braces, but it is not required.

According to the Oxford Universal Dictionary, braces are the European version of straps for gentlemen, which originally were known as a "pair of arms" or "armour for the arms," first "a pair of brace"- 1611. Braces attach to the trousers by buttoning either on the inside or outside of the waistband.

Many men believe the use of braces is more effective and more comfortable because it requires no cinching or occasional adjustment. In addition, the braces do their job of keeping one's trousers in the proper location. Suspenders, while also a version of straps, are designed to be more casual.

Suspenders also come in a variety of colors and patterns, including suspenders that resemble yard sticks. There is a popular show on public television where the stars wear one green suspender and one red suspender. It adds to the cleverness of the show. Suspenders attach to the trousers or pants by means of a snap at the waistband, so buttons on the trousers are not needed.

How do you remember which is which?

Braces *button*.   Suspenders *snap*.

Used by permission.

What are pants?

Pants is a general category of garments. Pants tend to be more informal, elastic waist, knitted garments. Pants may or may not have pockets, though we all know pockets are the best. One of the craftiest types of pants is a pair in which the lower part of the pants can be zippered off, hence, making cooler, shorter pants. For folks working outdoors, this would be a very good thing.

Society

In our modern Western society, males routinely wear trousers rather than skirts or dresses. Some exceptions may occur, however, in the ceremonial Scottish kilt and Greek fustanella, as well as robe-like clothing like cassocks for the clergy and academic robes, both worn for special occasions. British kilts: okay. You really want to know, don't you? What is worn under those famous

British kilts? Comedian Spike Milligan said it best: "Is there anything worn under the kilt? No, it's all in perfect working order."

Suits vs. Sportcoat vs. Tuxedo

The suit, sportcoat and tuxedo are different forms of suiting for men. Whether one wears a suit or sportcoat is based on the event one is attending.

The suit consists of a suit coat with matching trousers. The suit coat and trousers are worn together. A formal suit is paired with a nice shirt and tie, dress socks and dress shoes. The suit is generally more formal than a sportcoat, but not as formal as a tuxedo. Suits are appropriate for church, funerals, weddings and other more formal events such as business or political meetings. Suits used to be the general uniform for the office, but times have changed, and many businesses are less formal now, though suits can be seen in most any city.

The much loved sportcoat is a definite "yes" for any gentleman's closet. Often in classic navy blue, the jacket can be paired with khakis and a starched shirt for a very polished look. The sportcoat can also go well with dress jeans. The sportcoat is beloved because it always looks good and is usually comfortable to wear. Also, the sportcoat adapts well to different shirts with a tie or without a tie.

The tuxedo is a very formal suit consisting of a jacket, matching trousers, shirt, vest and often a cummerbund. Tuxedos are often worn with matching shoes as well. The tuxedo jacket can be cut in different ways, such as a peak tailcoat often worn at weddings to the classic white dinner jacket worn with black trousers. The dinner jacket often has a shawl collar and solid classic looks. A classic bowtie is always a winner with a white dinner jacket, but a traditional tie is also a very good thing.

The matching tuxedo trousers can be pleated or not and often have a satin strip on the outside of each leg, adding to the ensemble's handsome beauty. The trousers often come unhemmed, as the pants would need to be hemmed at the appropriate length for the gentleman wearing them and the shoes that will be worn with them.

The tuxedo is something that people often rent, as not many events will call for such a formal garment to justify the cost. If you are going to use your tuxedo at least six times per year, you might want to consider investing in a nice tuxedo set. In any given city, a number of shops specialize in renting formal wear. If your invitation calls for black-tie dress, then a tuxedo would work. If the invitation calls for black-tie optional, then a nice suit would work. Though if you have your new tuxedo, it would also be appropriate.

Shirts vs. blouses

There are shirts, then there are shirts. The best shirts are those that are cut well, no matter if the shirt is casual or dressy.

The Shirt's Fit

Shirts come in three basic cuts. The classic fit is cut generously across the shoulders, chest, waist and hips. Classic fit shirts usually have long tails that will stay tucked in. The slim fit is usually the regular, standard fit and works for most shapes and sizes. It tends to be trimmer at the waist for a neat and tidy shape. The very slim fit is cut closer to the body. It usually has extra back darts for a more modern look.

The Collars and Cuffs

Several styles of collars can be found in today's shirts. The most popular collars are the classic collar and the spread collar.

Classic collar: The classic collar is a solid and fail-safe collar that flatters most larger faces and necks. The classic collar will sport an attractive tie or a bowtie. The classic collar will also stand on its own as an open collar. A bit of starch enhances its beauty as the starch helps the collar to stand at attention.

Spread collar: The spread collar or cutaway collar has slightly wider collar points and flatters narrower, longer faces and necks. The spread collar is at its tailored best when paired with a silk tie, but will also be sharp standing on its own. The spread collar was made popular by the Duke of Kent in the early 1920's. This popular collar brings to mind a genteel, contemporary, well dressed and classic gentleman.

Button-down collar: The button-down collar is a classic look, albeit a bit more casual. Button-down collars are happy with a tie, or open collar, starch or not. A button-down collared shirt comes in many different colors and serves as a great first-time shirt for young gentlemen. The button-down collared shirt also looks well when introduced to starch.

Spread collar.

Button-down collar.

Cuffs

Shirts can come with a button cuff or French cuffs, which require cufflinks. Cufflinks have a variety of themes from sports, to coins, to miniature roadster cars. Let your personality show through your cufflinks.

Button cuff.

French cuffs.

Blouses

Blouses can be formal to casual, simply cotton to exotic silk. Blouses can contain ruffles or exotic buttons or folds. Some blouses work better with a suit jacket than others. Women tend to wear blouses rather than shirts. However, there are those among us who prefer the men's cut shirt made for a woman. Blouses tend to be more feminine and can define a distinctive style for you when paired with attractive jewelry.

Accessories

What accessories do we wear in the workplace? For the ladies, a smallish pair of earrings (one pair) will usually work. Obviously, your wedding rings are fine. Large loopy earrings and big bracelets that sound like the brass section of a symphony are usually not appropriate in the workplace. Large bracelets also get in the way when one is trying to type on the computer.

If your job requires you to work around machinery, be very cautious that your jewelry does not get caught in the machinery. Big, fancy cocktail rings usually do not work when one needs to wear work gloves on a daily basis as the gloves won't fit over the ring.

A nice watch is always appropriate to keep you on time.

For ladies, the key is three. Wear no more than three pieces of jewelry at one time: 1. A pair of earrings; 2. Watch; 3. Ring(s).

If one is wearing cufflinks, then forego the watch and/or bracelet, which tend to rub against the folded French cuff.

For the guys, wedding jewelry and a watch is usually de rigueur for the workplace. Earrings are optional, depending upon your workplace protocol.

Small lapel pins representing your company or an organization you support are wonderful. Be sure to wear the pins on your left lapel near your heart and wear no more than two pins at one time. The preference is one pin.

All in all, accessories you wear in the workplace need to support and enhance your work, not detract from it.

Perfume and Cologne

Is there someone in your office who lingers long after they are physically gone because of the amount of perfume they are wearing? Sometimes the smell is so strong that it is nearly suffocating. The individual wearing the perfume does not notice it any longer because their brain has acclimated itself to the fragrance making them not notice the scent any more.

In an office setting, people are often fairly close together, divided by cubicle panels. In this type of setting, the best thing to do in terms of perfume and cologne is to not wear any while at work. Err of the side of caution and forego your cologne at work. We have enough olfactory challenges while at work such as break room smells, the gym bag sitting in the corner, etc., so one more challenge is not needed. Save your perfume or cologne for your days off and special occasions.

When you do use the perfume and cologne, remember this guideline:

Spray... Delay... Walk away.

Spray the cologne into the air in front of you. Pause for a few moments, then walk through what was sprayed. You will get enough of the fragrance to enhance your being. Caution: Do not spray cologne or perfume on clothing or jewelry. Because many fragrances contain alcohol, this can yellow your clothing or damage jewelry. When you spray, delay and walk away, do so sans clothes, then get dressed for your evening out.

Chapter Twelve

28 Manners Points You Should Know

98% of all farms are family owned.
Source: Iowa Farm Bureau Federation

There is a difference between etiquette and manners. Etiquette prescribes certain conduct for certain situations. Manners allows for interpretation and adaptation.

Here are the 28 most important manners points.

1. What are you building?

At the back of your mind each day, consider this question. Whether you are working on your career, your marriage, your relationships, your education whatever it is, be conscious of the bigger picture of what you are building. Make your efforts, energy and resources all move toward this ultimate goal.

2. Time.

Time is not a limitless commodity. In fact, time is precious. It is the only resource that does not suffer insouciance, and we all have the same amount of time in each day. Be planful and organized. Take the time to write down your to-do list. You will get more done. It is important for you to take responsibility for your time. Whatever gets scheduled will get done. Be intentional, be willing and be determined to make the most of your time every day. You have two options: to manage your time in efficient ways or to have time control you. Be aware and make the most of your use of time, yours and others'. If you are a person who tends to be chronically late, try setting your clocks ahead to help you be on time. Whatever you do, do not waste others people's time by being late.

"Punctuality is the politeness of kings."

3. Talent and education *may* be rated too highly.

Results are what counts. Getting along with people is also what counts. You could be the most talented and charming person in the world, but all of it is for naught if you cannot show solid results and get along with people. You might have a Ph.D., but if you cannot get along with people, then this may be an indication that you need to work with things rather than people. Education is very, very important, but if you do not use the life skills you learned while in college, you run the risk of not reaching your full potential.

To do hints:
- Keep a checklist of your to-do list. Check off each item as you complete it. Do the most difficult items first.
- Keep a notebook. This will help you stay as close to your work as possible. Use the notebook to keep research, quotes, post ideas, pricing formulas, and anything that will help you present your work.
- Minimize interruptions as much as possible.
- Stay focused on the task at hand.
- Reward yourself once each item is checked off your list.
- Set up a personal system for your to-do list. Get a special notebook or special apps/pencils/pens/computer spreadsheet to manage your daily tasks, then follow your system.
- Try to handle each task only once.

4. Morning productivity.

People tend to be most productive in the morning after a good night of rest. Do the hardest tasks when you are fresh and rested. Be sure to breakfast your body in the morning. Strategic planning and important meetings will happen during the day. Always be at the ready with pad of paper, pen or other writing instrument, notes, iPad, etc. Press "silent" on your electronic device so your co-workers will not be disrupted by the clicking sound of the keyboard. Try to not be the person who has to be reminded that a pen and paper or a particular folder are needed. Organize your files by project, and be sure to bring the project file folder that fits the meeting. Establish a filing system that works for you, then let the system work for you. It is very nice to do what you have been asked to do, but giving before you have been asked shows you are paying attention and that you understand the task at hand, and your boss might be impressed, too.

5. Conduct yourself properly on social media.

Be careful what you are posting on social media sites, as everything is public information. Companies that are hiring will often look at social media to determine if a candidate has posted information that may be embarrassing or even harmful to the reputation of their organization. Mind your social media activities so that they always present you in the best light.

Social media is a very interesting phenomenon in our world today. Consider this in today's world: Uber, the world's largest transportation network company, owns no cars. Facebook, a social networking service, requires an e-mail address for its users to subscribe. Alibaba, the world's most valuable retailer, has no inventory. Airbnb, the world's largest accommodation provider, owns no real estate. We live in interesting times. Good social media behavior is needed to do business with nearly any company.

6. Many forms of media technology have made communication easier.

Busy, but easier. Voice messaging, caller identification, text messages, social media, electronic messages: We get information from many sources. Use this media to manage your day. If you are in the middle of a project and the telephone rings, let it go into voicemail. Retrieve the voicemail later when you have finished your current project. Electronic mail can be both a blessing and a curse. It allows for instantaneous contact, but also expects a quick response. Each e-mail is going to take some time as you complete the tasks involved in it. Respond to e-mails in the order received unless it is an urgent matter.

7. Be the first to arrive in the office and the last to leave.

By arriving early, it will give you quiet, uninterrupted time before the busyness of the workday begins. Follow your to-do list. It feels good to check off an item, and it feels good to begin your day by getting some things done that need your attention. A bonus: The boss may notice.

8. Be on time or early.

Employees new to the workforce have a lot of ground to cover. One way to do this is to work harder and smarter than your peers. Be steady, do quality work, keep moving forward. Be true to yourself first, then your work. In other words, take care of yourself or you won't be any good at work. Early to work never hurts and usually helps.

9. Show drive and initiative, then take action.

Don't wait for someone to tell you what to do. Ask questions. Show interest. Doing too much can never hurt.

10. Take responsibility for your mistakes.

Everyone makes mistakes. Some mistakes are bigger than others. Embrace your mistakes early in your career. Don't make excuses or call Mommy or Daddy to fix them. Own them. Grow from them. Learn the lessons, then remember the lessons learned. This is called being a grown up. No matter your chronological age.

11. Temper tantrums, hissy fits and general meltdowns.

Save them for the sandbox. It is not nice to throw sand in the form of a meltdown or temper tantrum at your office mate, even if you disagree on something. The early stages of your career are when you are most impressionable, vulnerable and valuable. A tough boss that pushes you will help you to develop and set good lifelong work habits. It is just as important to learn what *not* to do as it is to learn *what to do*. Remember, results count.

12. Unexplainable gaps or blank spots in your work resume.

Unexplainable gaps or blank spots in your work resume or a new job every year is not a good thing. Short employment stints or lapses in your resume that cannot be explained by a reasonable explanation such as going to school, life-threatening illness, etc. are red flags to potential employers. Employers are looking for reliability and dependability. It takes a few years to master crucial work skills. Demonstrate your good work ethic on a daily basis. Stick to it, even if you don't like it, and give 110 percent in a mannerly and respectful way.

13. People are more important than benefits.

Choose people. "Bennies," as benefits are affectionately called, are extremely important. No question about that, but don't pick the company with the popular extras. Choose a company that will help you to grow in your career. Is there a leadership program within the company? Sign up for it. What does the managerial structure look like? Is there room for you to grow? Look for effective managers while keeping in mind your long-term career plan.

14. Put together your career plan.

Put together your career plan for one year, five years, 10 years, etc. Write it down and review it on a regular basis. Are your daily behaviors at work consistent with your short- and long-term career plan? People who write down their goals are more successful in achieving those goals. There will be bumps in the road. The bumps are a part of life. The key is to navigate the bumps. All of life is an adaptation. When a setback is experienced, how do you cope? Do you adapt and learn from the setback to move forward, or do you get yourself into a rut, refusing to let go of the anger and disappointment? The anger may show in your work or your relationships. Worse yet, do you dig a hole for yourself that is difficult to get out of? In that case, stop digging the hole deeper. Seek help. Don't get discouraged. In every situation in life, there is a lesson to be learned. Pay attention and learn the lesson.

Key to good manners in life: Always learn the lesson and grow from it.

15. Learn to strive through even solid strides moving forward.

If you are asked to do things you don't want to do (and you will be asked), take the tasks in stride by staying focused on the future. For every task to be done, there are a multitude of other responsibilities that lead up to the culmination of the assigned task. Think of the final event as the commencement. A lot of hard work and time go into making a successful career. It is the same way with any project. Don't be afraid to do the dirty work behind the scenes. Put in the effort and time while carrying a good attitude. It will show your workmates that you are a solid team player.

16. Speak up, not out (part 1):

Do not talk badly about your boss, job or co-workers to other employees or to anyone for that matter. Rather, have a constructive and healthy conversation. There is an old saying that goes, "what goes around, comes around" or "as you sow, so shall you reap," which is the basic understanding of how karma, the law of cause and effect, works.

Karma means "action or fate" and can be divided up into a few basic categories: good, bad, individual and collective. The fruits of the karma can be sweet or sour, depending on the nature of the actions involved. The fruits can be sweet in a collective manner if a group of people work together perform a certain task or activity. Sometimes, a couple who dated years ago reunite, through no formal planning of their own. There is no logical explanation for why this happens, except that karma can be wonderful. Sometimes one lands a perfect position. Was there hard work and a good education involved? Quite possibly, but the bigger thing is the timing of it. The time was right for you to land the perfect position. Karma is alive and well.

All of life is a vibration. If we put out goodness, honesty and truth, then we will receive back goodness, honesty and truth. All life forms are symbiotic. Each life is interrelated.

If we speak ill of people or are disrespectful and rude to people, that is what we will get in return. People are not going to confront you on your rudeness. That in itself would be rude.

Everything we say and do determines what is going to happen to us in the future. Whether we act honestly, dishonestly, are rude or kind to others, help or hurt others, it all goes on record in our internal psyche and manifests as a karmic reaction at some later time.

There is no scientific formula for how and when karmic reactions may appear in our lives, but one can be sure they will appear in some form or other. Very few things in life happen randomly.

One may be able to get away with a crime they committed, or avoid paying taxes, or may steal from a business, but according to karma, eventually, they will have to answer in some way. It is interesting that once karma comes back to visit an individual who has harmed someone or something, the individual is often filled with anger and vengeance, while being completely bewildered as to how this could be happening to them.

17. Speak Up, Not Out (part 2).

Having a good and successful career also means that you sometimes have to deal with difficult situations or difficult people. When and if you are faced with such a situation, there are three basic things to remember:

- Separate emotion from fact. When you hear shouting on the end of the telephone line, your heart may start racing, but stick to the facts. This is just your fight or flight response, which is your body's natural intrinsic survival mode trying to protect you. Let the person vent, take a deep breath, then respond factually, in a cool and calm way.

- Have a Teflon back. Let the emotion slide off. Let go of it. Your feelings may be hurt but focus on the fact that you handled it in the best way you possibly could. Then sleep on it. In the days following, reinforce to yourself that you were professional and factual and kind in your response. This is not an easy thing to do, but keep practicing having a slick back, so you can let it go. The key is for you to be able to say to yourself that you did the best you could.

- Stick up for yourself. If someone has personally attacked you or been disrespectful to you, you need to let them know. In your quietest, but using very direct language, remind them you will not be disrespected, and you hope they will remember that in the future. You want and need to work with them, but the work will be much easier for both if the respect is mutual. You are not a human punching bag, after all. You don't have to like someone to work with them, but you do need to respect them, and they need to respect you. It is okay to disagree with someone, with mutual respect, of course.

18. Know your technical stuff/insider words and jargon, but not so much that people glaze over.

Don't speak in buzzwords or acronyms for the purpose of impressing people. Don't use complicated words when simple words make more sense. Your resume will stand out if you are more savvy in the use of the English language, which means saying it so everyone will understand. Finish the ends of the words you speak and choose your words carefully. The world is listening. Simpler is always better.

19. Build and maintain a professional network.

The quality and quantity of your network matters. You may not be friends with your colleagues outside the workplace, but then again, maybe you will be. It is who you know more than what you know. People tend to do business with those folks they know, trust and like. Build your network early in your career– college friends are a great starting place – and maintain your network as you grow in your career. The social networking service LinkedIn is a great networking tool to use.

20. Find at least two professional mentors.

Develop a relationship with them. Be sure to listen to them. Be like a human sponge and soak in everything your mentors share with you. Their advice can often fast track your career or help you avoid possible pitfalls. Do not develop hubris, which can be poisonous to your career. Hubris is exaggerated pride in yourself. Your boss would just call it being too full of yourself and therefore you cannot focus on the task at hand. This is not an attractive thing, especially with professionals.

21. Pick a professional idol on which to model yourself.

Choose someone who is a professional in your field. Follow their career, both the risks and the rewards. Mirror them. Act as if you are in the position of your dreams, which will cause your brain to start to believe you can truly do it. Then do the actions that will get you to where you want to be professionally.

22. Read more books, magazines and reliable Internet sites in your field.

Be prepared to answer someone who asks what you are currently reading/ learning. Challenge yourself to read or learn something new each month. It jump-starts your creativity and grounds your soul. Be continually thirsty to learn more by reading business books. Reading is a good indication that you are interested in becoming the best person you can be for your work and for your family.

23. Manage your budget and your money.

Spend at least 25 percent less than what you make in net income. If your material needs meet or exceed your income, you may be incapacitating your ability to be financially successful. Don't go there. Practice delayed gratification. You don't have to have everything right now. Building up to it makes it sweeter when you are able to get whatever it is you want.

Spending less money now will pay off in a big way down the road. Be sparing with your use of credit cards. Pay credit cards in full at the end of each month. If you cannot pay the cards in full at the end of each month, you are setting yourself up for financial purgatory. Remember, credit cards are borrowed money that has to be paid back, often at a very high interest rate. Focus on *needs* rather than *wants*.

A recent report from the Federal Reserve Bank of New York shows that millennials shape lifetime earnings potential in the first 10 years in the labor market. This long-term, subject-heavy study looked at the career paths of about five million workers over 40 years. Written by economists Fatih Guvenen, Fatih Karahan, Serdar Ozkan and Jae Song, the study found jumps in pay could be largely driven by steep learning curves early in your career.

"At 25, I choose a job that allows me to learn valuable skills," Guvenen said. "I'm investing in my future, and my employer is allowing me to invest in my future. Soon, I'm producing more for my employer and they are paying me more."

The study went on to find that workers projected to earn the median lifetime amount will see pay increases of 38 percent from age 25-55, with the strongest upward movement in the first decade. Workers in the 95th percentile can expect a 230 percent increase over the same period. Those in the 99th percentile – executives, doctors, attorneys, engineers – will see earnings jump an incredible 1,450 percent.

The bottom fifth of workers, in which jobs are typically manual labor, tend to have jobs that are more physically demanding. The study showed the low-skilled jobs tend to experience an income decline from age 25-55. In part, this is because the human body gets tired over time. Your back begins to hurt. Your knees begin to ache. As a result, one becomes less and less productive. Save your money and work hard in your beginning years of work.

24. Start investing in a retirement plan.

Start investing in a retirement plan on the first day you are eligible. Take advantage of your employers' matching plan, if offered, and match it fully. Do not touch it. Leave the money alone and let it grow. You will be grateful for this once you reach retirement age.

25. Protect your reputation.

Your reputation is priceless and irreplaceable. Think of the analogy of toothpaste coming out of the tube. Once the toothpaste is out, it cannot be put back into the tube. If you give your reputation away by ruining it, it may never return. Even if you forget that your reputation is dirtied, other folks will most likely remember and never forget. It can take years to build back up, but can be gone in an instant.

Key to good manners in life: Honor thyself. Protect your reputation.

26. Show pride in your work.

Every piece of work that comes with your name on it needs to represent the epitome of professionalism. This means correct spelling and grammar throughout. Your syntax or the (constructional uses of a word or form or those characteristics of a particular author) need to match with the organization's values and the established use of the company's grammatical construction.

Focus on the end results. If you cannot get something from work out of your head in order to relax at night, try writing it down. Keep a pad of paper or journal nearby. By writing, this will allow you to get the thoughts out of your head and on paper, which helps your mind take a break from thinking about it. Writing will also help you to sort through the complex sets of emotions and experiences that face us each day.

Part of the reason why writing helps is because you are labeling the experience and your reaction through writing it down, which can make a difference in how you think about the experience.

You are able to put the experience into perspective and perhaps find meaning in what happened. Most importantly, if you put the emotional confusion into words on paper, it is easier to get past it. You are able to sleep better, pay attention in other areas of your life and even become a better friend.

27. Stacking some Zzzzzzz's.

Get a good night of sleep every night. The older you get, the more you will realize that your body and brain need good, sound sleep. Not only does it make you feel better, it also helps your brain.

What your brain does while you sleep:
- Makes decisions,
- Makes creative connections,
- Creates and consolidates memories,
- Clears out toxins,
- Remembers how to do a physical task.

Get a good night's sleep every night. Each time you are sleep deprived, you can never get back the hours you lost. Your brain is counting on it.

28. Be the genuine person you are.

It is important to be the person you are meant to be. Through all of the screaming, dreaming and scheming, at the end of the day, you want to be able to say to yourself, "I did the best I could today. I respected myself and others. I made a difference, and I can't wait to go back tomorrow and do it again. I'm the luckiest person ever."

If you can have this type of attitude at the end of the day, then you probably are a good fit for the position you are in. If you cannot feel weary yet settled at the end of the day, then look for another avenue of employment that may fit you better.

We need people who can solve complex problems in practical, genuine and respectful ways.

Chapter Thirteen

Business Etiquette and Manners

**Agriculture employs more than
24 million American workers (17%
of the total U.S. work force).**
Source: www.farmersfeedus.org

Work Manners

A 2014 Gallup poll found that less than one-third of workers were actively engaged in their work. This represents the highest ranking since Gallup began tracking worker engagement in 2000. Gallup defines engaged employees as those who are involved in, enthusiastic about and committed to their work and workplace. A majority of employees, 51 percent, are still "not engaged" and 17.5 percent were "actively disengaged" in 2014.

U.S. Employee Engagement

Percent of employees	2013	2014
Engaged	29.6 %	31.5 %
Not engaged	51.5 %	51.0 %
Actively disengaged	18.8 %	7.5 %

Through daily tracking interviews of 2.5 million employees, Gallup has found the responses to key workplace elements to be indicative of important organizational performance outcomes. Among all job categories, managers, executives and officers had the highest levels of engagement in 2014: 38.4 percent. Note that farming ranks No. 2 in both 2013 and 2014 for engagement. This speaks very highly of the profession of agriculture. On the other end of the spectrum, employees in manufacturing or production recorded the lowest levels of engagement with an average of 23 percent.

U.S. Employee Engagement, by Job Category

Percent of employees engaged	2013	2014
Manager, executive or officer	34.7 %	38.4 %
Farming, fishing or forestry	36 %	33.6 %
Professional	30 %	32.4 %
Construction or mining	31.5 %	32.2 %
Clerical or office	29.3 %	31.8 %
Installation or repair	28.5 %	31.3 %
Sales	29.2 %	30.6 %
Service	27.9 %	28.2 %
Transportation	24.1 %	25.5 %
Manufacturing or production	22 %	23 %

Among the generations, traditionalists are most engaged at 42.2 percent. Millennials are the least engaged group at 28.9 percent. Though the economy may be improving, workers in this generation may not be getting the jobs they had hoped to get. Gallup's engagement data reveal that millennials are less likely to say they "have the opportunity to do what they do best" at work. This finding may suggest that millennials may not be working in jobs that allow them to use their best talents and strengths, thus creating disengagement.

U.S. Employee Engagement, by Generation

Percent of employees engaged	2013	2014
Millennials	27.5 %	28.9 %
Generation X	29.6 %	32.2 %
Baby boomers	30.9 %	32.7 %
Traditionalists	38.3 %	42.2 %

How can we create a work environment that engages people? How can we, as leaders, help to encourage and motivate employee engagement? One way is to create a culture of gratitude.

- Respect the fact that each individual has strengths and weaknesses. Play to people's strengths. All of us have things we are better at. People will feel more appreciated and valued in the workplace if they can work at tasks more suited to them.

- Invite a co-worker out for a cup of coffee. Maybe it is a new hire, or maybe it is someone you don't care for very much. Put yourself out there. You may be pleasantly surprised.

- Make the time to show appreciation for a job well done. Yes, even when the regular job of the day is done and done well. Look an employee in the eye and tell them "Thank you" in a sincere way. Recent studies have shown that, given the choice of a pay raise or hearing their boss say "Thank you," employees overwhelmingly chose the thank you.

- Write a small note of appreciation to an employee. This could be a thank you note or a note of recognition. People love this type of tangible expression of gratitude, and it only takes a few minutes a day. Plus, you will feel better after writing it.

- Use affirming, uplifting non-verbal recognition to affirm co-workers: smiling at them, thumbs up, high-fives, etc. Enthusiasm can be contagious when everyone works together as a team.
- What you do is more important than what you say. Actions really do speak louder than words.
- Have small cards printed with the company logo. Use them to give written "stars" to those workers who solve a problem, come up with a new idea, finish out a project, etc. This is a great way to reinforce positive, engaging behaviors in the workplace. Use these cards with everyone in the work force, from the custodian on up.

Cleaning out the coffeepot and doing other things can protect you

A recent study published online by the journal "Human Resource Management" has validated the idea that having a good attitude and being a good corporate citizen can also help to protect you if layoffs loom. The study's co-author, Chris Zatzick, set out to measure some intangible factors, specifically something called "affective organizational commitment," an interesting phrase for describing the emotional attachment employees feel to the mission and goals of the organization where they work (Zatzick, Deery and Iverson, 2015). The study looked at about 6,000 of 20,000 total employees of a bank in Australia.

According to Zatzick and his colleagues, effective organizational commitment is closely linked to what researchers call "employee citizenship" behaviors, such as taking time to help a new co-worker learn the ropes, staying late, volunteering to work on weekends or even cleaning up the break room.

The study found that higher ratings of commitment decreased the likelihood of being laid off. While traditional measures of on-the-job performance – structural, demographic and human capital factors – were still the strongest determinant of who was pink-slipped, having a good attitude and a strong commitment to the workplace gave average performers a measurable edge.

"There's a choice we make about how to spend our time at work," Zatzick said. Although performance may matter most, having a good attitude and being a good "citizen" can protect you as well.

Making yourself indispensable can be a very good thing: schmooze with the boss, offer to help the new person and be the very nice person who cleans out the coffeemaker.

What are work manners?

A recent study conducted by Accountemps found that managers and employees disagree on most common workplace etiquette issues. The study, conducted in 2015, included responses from 2,100 chief financial officers from a stratified random sample of companies in more than 20 of the largest metropolitan areas in the U.S. The study also included responses of more than 320 employees age 18 and older who work in an office environment.

The rules we were taught in school – pay attention, don't be late, and if you can't say anything nice, don't say anything at all – hold true in the workplace.

The most common civility faux pas cited by chief financial officers is being distracted during meetings (27 percent). Workers, on the other hand, pointed out gossiping about colleagues (28 percent) as the most common breach of workplace etiquette.

Accountemps Study, May 2015

	CFOs	Workers
Being distracted during meetings (e.g., checking smartphone, writing e-mails)	27%	16%
Gossiping about others in the office	18%	28%
Not responding to calls or e-mails in a timely way	18%	21%
Running late to or missing meetings	12%	12%
Not crediting others when appropriate	6%	12%
Criticizing others publicly	5%	11%
Staff members do not commit etiquette breaches	11%	0%
Don't know	2%	0%
	99%*	100%

*Responses do not total 100 percent due to rounding

In response to the study, Accountemps offered four tips for displaying appropriate workplace etiquette:
1. Be present. No matter how many deadlines you're up against, give your full attention during group discussions. You'll be surprised how

much more effective you are in meetings and conversations when focusing only on the topic at hand.

2. Avoid the rumor mill. Don't participate in office gossip. It is just another distraction that can reflect poorly on your character and damage others' careers.

3. Be responsive. Don't let your inbox fill up with e-mails or voice-mails. Set aside time each day to respond to messages so you can attend to the rest of your workload uninterrupted.

4. Give credit where credit is due. No one likes a glory hog. Acknowledge those who help you along the way, and they'll likely do the same for you.

Bill Driscoll, a district president of Accountemps, added, "Most jobs today require teamwork and strong collaboration skills, and that means following the unwritten rules of office protocol. Poor workplace etiquette demonstrates a lack of consideration for co-workers."

The Telephone

A lot of us believe there may be companies around that really do not have human beings working within them. This phenomenon is known as "automated answering services (AAS)." These AAS move the caller from one automated choice to the next to the next to the next, only to end up back to where one started. It is, perhaps, the single most exasperating new technology to be presented to the working world since the invention of the telephone.

One advertisement currently running on television is a furnace repair business where the competent young lady declares, "When you call, I will answer the telephone every time." I want to call her, just to hear a human voice, but, alas and gratefully, my furnace is working just fine.

Then, there is the company that does business "By appointment only." I once knew a business like that. They soon were not in business. No one could find them. Where are the employees in the business? Would someone kindly respond and respond in a nice way?

Let's take a look at work manners. These manners, when practiced regularly, just make the workplace a more pleasant place to be. Since we spend so much of our time at work, it could be a very good thing.

Professional Etiquette in the Workplace

Following professional etiquette shows you are a polite, well-mannered and civilized co-worker who knows how to be nice and congenial to others. It also shows that you can represent the company in a constructive and confident way.

If you don't show good manners on a consistent basis, you run the risk of ruining your reputation. Once a reputation is ruined, it is very difficult or impossible to get back.

Basic professional manners rules in the office setting:
- Always arrive on time or early.
- Dress appropriately for your particular office environment.
- Never interrupt a conversation of other people.
- Don't overstep your boundaries at work.
- If you must eat at your desk and you work in a cubicle, avoid foods with strong odors.
- Remove your papers from the copier, fax machine and scanner after you are finished with the task at hand.
- Refill the copy machine with paper if it runs out on your watch.
- Shake hands in a professional way.
- Use good posture while sitting at your desk.
- Praise others for a job well done. Give credit where credit is due.
- Never take credit for other people's work.
- Emotion nearly always dominates logic. If you become upset, take a moment to get your emotions under control. You will then be able to respond in a logical way rather than reacting in an emotional way.
- Be friendly to clients, visitors and guests. Offer them a comfortable seat if they have to wait. Offer them water, coffee, etc.
- Use a professional voice and avoid shouting.
- Don't touch other people's personal or professional belongings.
- Observe proper etiquette with regard to personal space.
- Participate in office donations if you can afford it, but don't make an issue of how much or how little you give.
- Try to refrain from having a full-length mirror in your office. Use the washroom for your personal needs.

- Keep office correspondence brief and factual. Offer your opinion only when it is asked.
- Maintain a professional image when decorating your office or cubicle.
- Straighten your desk each day before leaving work.
- Make a to-do list for the following day before leaving work.
- When socializing with your colleagues, don't say or do anything you don't want mentioned at the office later.

Greetings

In daily life, purposely ignoring someone when they say "Hello" is considered an all-out act of full-scale nonverbal hostility. Even if you do not care for the person or they beat you out of a new project, or even if they are your mortal enemy, you still respond to them with a pleasant nod of the head or by saying hello. It is not about becoming friends with them; it is about being civilized and polite on your part.

The reverse also holds true. Say hello to people. Recognize their presence. It is not about being forward. It is not about groveling. It is about being respectful and noticing people.

Greet people the first time you see them during the day however late it is. Do this before you launch into the current business at hand.

Senior staff members suffer the most from lack of being greeted. Say hello to your boss.

Also say hello to the custodian and the secretary. These are the folks who will oftentimes give you information when others can't or won't. They are often the jewels of the office.

Door Manners

The endless number of doors have created a silent manners crisis in the workplace. Be aware of the space five feet behind you or in front of you. If folks are within five feet of you, hold the door for them. Do not let the door slam in their face. This is rude.

If you are preparing to enter a door at the same time someone is coming out of a door, step aside so the person can exit before you enter. It would be nice of you to hold the door for them as they complete their exit.

Doors are equal opportunity. If you notice someone directly behind you, or someone with arms loaded full of packages, hold the door for them. Hopefully, they will then respond with a thank you. If they do not respond in such way, you still did the right thing, and you can feel good about that. Door manners are important.

At the Start of the Work Day

Everyone, from Jill Schmo to Bill Gates, needs a few minutes to start the workday: putting your coat away, turning on the computer, grabbing a coffee, de-stressing from the commute to work, etc. Let them have five minutes at the beginning of the workday to get themselves going. If you are waiting for an appointment with the individual, take a deep breath. Hopefully, it will only be a few minutes.

Under no circumstances should you follow the individual to their office as they are arriving for work with a request of help. On the other hand, if the individual says, "Come with me." Then by all means, do so.

Say What is On Your Mind

Does the tone of an e-mail strike you the wrong way? Instead of responding to it via e-mail, which might create further confusion, speak to the sender and find out what is going on. Say what is on your mind. Your emotions, needs, wants and respect deserve it. Your authenticity to yourself and your co-worker will help you feel better. Remember, though, when you acknowledge feelings that are uncomfortable such as fear, anger, sadness, taking the risk to talk about it means to also have to be willing to hear a "no."

Make Yourself Vulnerable Sometimes

Vulnerability can be a new and surprising way to test your true capacity. Your ability to take on a difficult project that requires creativity and hard work is closely tied to your willingness to be real and vulnerable. The courage to take on a challenge that might have some missteps, which can be good, because you can learn from them, and you will be showing your bosses that you have drive and ambition.

If you happen to fall on your face, just have a good laugh about it. No one is perfect, so have a good sense of humor at your expense, not others' when things don't go as well as expected. Everyone loves it when they can see a boss who is vulnerable and can laugh at themselves. It shows they are human.

Be Aware of Misinformation

Don't believe rumors. Always have your facts in hand. Take a pad and pencil or tablet with you to each and every meeting. The smartest people in the world are the ones who say, "I don't know," then offer to find out. Admitting where there are gaps in knowledge or facts is the first step to filling them in.

There was once a supervisor who picked up on a personal rumor being bandied about by a needy person who wanted to feel important. The supervisor sent an e-mail to the party involved in the rumor, while the supervisor was out of state at a business conference. This supervisor was either very green in terms of supervisory skills, or felt the need to throw their weight around by commenting on the information.

This scenario has ugly written all over it. First, the supervisor did not confirm that the information was true with the individual involved. Secondly, the supervisor was spending time on personal information that, whether the information is happy or sad, really has no place in the workplace day.

Bosses: kindly mind your own personal business as well as letting others mind their own personal business, and if you are going to comment on a personal matter you've heard, check with the person involved first.

In the Elevator

It is in elevators that normal life as we know it goes on hold. People become non-people, looking at the ceiling or staring straight ahead. Even family members do not talk to each other; everybody stares at the walls. Although, once in a hospital elevator, a woman asked her husband how his hernia was feeling. That was way too much information.

Elevators in offices are different. Didn't Melanie Griffith get her big break in "Working Girl" during an elevator encounter? Once, during my whippersnapper days, I stepped onto an elevator and did not turn around. I faced the small crowd gathered there. It was very uncomfortable. I am sure they thought me insane.

- Do not corner senior management or anyone, for that matter in the elevator to try to make an impression. It's not fair to them or anyone else within six feet. There will be other chances to talk to them. This will be a different scenario, however, if senior management makes the invitation to talk.
- Senior management, when in an elevator, needs to always make a point of speaking. Even if the senior manager does not know everyone's name, a cheerful "Good morning all" can do wonders for morale. If the senior management ignores people, this behavior will spread like a wildfire through the office.
- Please remember that everyone else in the elevator can hear every word you are saying.
- Refrain from talking shop in the elevator. It is boring to everyone else.
- Kindly refrain from talking about anything involving personal grooming or lack thereof.
- Allow people to exit the elevator before you get on it.
- Don't block the entrance of the elevator as people are trying to exit.

Professional Grace

Observe Corporate Culture

I know of one business that requires a coat and tie for the gentlemen and skirts or dresses for the ladies. Bravo for them. While your business may not be this formal, you do need to follow the dress attire that is suited to the corporate culture of your business.

Resist the urge to be slovenly in your dress. Enough examples of "down-dressing" can be seen on most any street. Be polite by observing your office protocol. If you do not know your office protocol, ask. People will be happy to help you out.

Do introduce your dress shirt to a spot of starch, or, if you feel inept at such matters, kindly ask your favorite laundry to do so.

Co-Worker Manners

People are motivated to go to work for various reasons. Many people work to receive a paycheck. They do their work in an efficient way. They are good, solid workers. At closing time, they leave. They do not stay to work overtime. They receive their paycheck at the end of the week.

Other people see their position as a career. It may be a stepping stone to a higher position, but it is a full-fledged career. Those individuals have goals and aspirations for their working life. They do whatever it takes to be productive in their work and move ahead the business as well as their career. They do more, offer to take on more and are unafraid to work long hours.

Others work to get their social and emotional needs met. They may or may not need the paycheck, but it is apparent that they want everyone to know what is going on in their personal life. Not much work may get done, and others may not get their work done because of the person who is most interested in getting their personal needs met.

Are you going to work to get your personal needs met? I once knew of a secretary who kept food in her desk drawers. We are not talking M&Ms here; we are talking sardine sandwiches. The mere odor alone was nearly unbearable. The drawer would open and close each time someone approached her desk.

Work is not the place to get your personal needs met. Work is the place to work. A well-mannered and respectful person will attempt to understand the motivations of their co-workers and will make every effort to help them meet their goals. By understanding and respecting the needs of the people you work with, you can help them and you be successful in career.

Leave It As You Found It or Better

Our teachers used to say to us, "Is that how you would do it at home?" The hard truth is, it was the way some folks did it at home. We have all seen the microwave that has been splattered with cup-a-soup, leftover pasta and popcorn, and yet had no one had taken the time to clean out the microwave for over a month. Then, there is the coffeepot, left unattended with a small amount in the bottom, only to burn to a cakey, sticky mess.

There was a poster once that I greatly loved. It read: "If you open it, close it; If you un-do it, re-do it; If you dirty it, clean it, etc." You get the idea. Just because you are in the office doesn't mean that you have to become trampy in your habits.

• Tidy as you go.

- Clean up your own messes.
- If you put your coffee mug in the sink to soak, don't forget it.
- Check the office refrigerator every few days. If the food in the fridge belongs to you and it is beginning to look like a science experiment, then you are responsible for ending the science experiment.
- If you are emotionally attached to the food you refrigerate, put your name on it for protection.
- Leave it in better shape than you found it, whether in the break room, the conference room or your own office.

Negativity

There was a line spoken by Shirley MacLaine in the movie "Steel Magnolias" where she declared, "I'm not crazy. I've just been in a bad mood for 40 years."

Apparently, many people today have taken that notion to heart. If, for some reason, you have your underwear all twisted about something, then it is time to deal with it. Do not partake in office rumors or gossip. Avoid this as if it were a plague if you want to be liked and want to keep your integrity intact. Untruths or partial truths erode morale and tend to make people angry and upset, not to mention unproductive. Make your workplace a "no negativity zone."

Overdoing It In Various Ways

Who is the one most loathed in the office setting?

It is the one who suffers from severe braggadocio. The one without whose incredible talents the office couldn't function. It may come in the form of the monster of ambition, in the insatiable nosy one or the champion of them all, the self-important, full-time martyr.

Stories of unbelievable behavior abound. "We came in at 5 a.m. to get finished." "It took me the whole day to deal with it until 10:30 p.m." "I had 457 e-mails when I got in this morning." "I've had this cold for six weeks now."

It also shows up in nonverbal ways. Mary's secretary opens her mail, even though Mary has asked for the mail to be delivered to her unopened. It is not even opened with a letter opener or slider. No, it is simply ravaged open with uneven paper hanging everywhere. To add insult, the secretary then shuffles through everything contained within the envelope. Any amount of talking by

Mary to the secretary has produced negative behavioral change. It exhausts Mary to no end on a daily basis.

In England, children are taught that boasting is bad manners. Some American children are taught this as well. Part of this humble attitude comes from helping to prevent people from feeling badly when they haven't won the prize, and to keep possessions, grades, attractiveness, etc. in their place.

- If you are ambitious, try to keep quiet about it. Humility really is a virtue.
- Boasting of any kind provokes nothing but contempt and disrespect.
- Martyrs spoil the fun for everyone.
- Don't pull rank. Aren't we are all in this together?

Distractions/Interruptions

One of the pleasant things about working is that one can drop in to chat with legal, or pop by accounting for a moment or two. Dropping by creates, at times, a pleasant distraction from the people who are so busy climbing the corporate ladder that they do not say "Hello" in the morning. However, let it be said, that pleasant distractions can quickly become annoyances if one has to listen one more time to the color of towels being chosen for Karen's wedding or how well Joe's son is doing at the university. At the same time, we need to be respectful of co-workers.

- Ask permission to interrupt people. "Is now a good time?" Ask this even if the person has an open-door policy.
- Never walk into someone's office and assume they can see you at that moment.
- Always knock before entering someone's office, even if the door is open.
- If someone is on the telephone, do not interrupt them. The only thing that trumps this is if the situation at hand is truly an emergency, and the person on the telephone needs to know.
- Do not distract people if they are busy, even if their door is open.
- Do not follow people down the corridor, trying to maintain conversation with them if it is obvious they need to move on.
- Do not state the obvious: "I just stopped in to tell you I am going to send you an e-mail," or "Did you get the e-mail I sent?"

Is That Your Mug?

On a daily basis, the workplace yields its mysterious powers. Normally sane and morally upright people can turn into petty thieves. Matthew states, "I go through at least one mug every month." Fortunately, he is not one of those who gets emotionally attached to his mug. The thief is rarely caught in possession of the missing mug.

If it's not mugs, it's pens. "You've got a lot of pens," someone said to Mary the other day. Indeed, she had and most of them weren't hers.

The answer to these dilemmas is simple: If it is not yours, do not take it or use it without permission.

Lateness

Being late for anything is a no-no. By your being late, you are stealing time from everyone else. Don't do it. If needed, set all of your clocks ahead 15 minutes. This will force you to be on time.

Whining

It is important for you to behave in a fair and impartial manner on a daily basis. Do not respond to people according to how much you like or dislike them. Base your response on what is the objective, right thing to do.

How many working people do you know who whine? It makes one want to gently remind them to take their PDAs and day timers and go find another office sandbox to play in. You are working to move the organization forward.

Separate emotion from fact. Get over it and move on. Politely, of course.

Cubicle Manners

Open-plan offices and cubicles have made their way across countless offices at breakneck speed. They are efficient, cost effective, though somewhat homely in design, yet house thousands of employees during business hours.

Cubicles work. The architecture of office cubicles seems to suggest that workers are available all of the time, despite the mountain of paperwork sitting next to them inside of the cubicle. While useful for the business at hand, cubicles may not provide much personal space for the human beings who occupy them.

Most human beings like boundaries and personalization, even at work. This is part of the reason why we put family photos in our cubicle and pin drawings from our kids on the fabric wall of the cubicle. New moms and dads plaster the fabric walls with their precious newborn for all to see.

This is all good. These personal mementos bring a sense of comfort, warmth and familiarity to the starkness of the cubicle and the pressures of the workplace. These small artifacts personalize the space for the worker. Since all of us spend so much time at work, it may as well be claimed as our space.

However, the voluminous space above the temporary walls of the cubicle invites stretchers and lookers, as in, "Is Sally there? Can we see the top of her head? No, she's not there that I can see." Don't barge into a cubicle. Try not to stretch and groan to discover if someone is seated in their cubicle. It needs to be treated as if it were an office because it is an office. Announce yourself, either verbally by saying "Excuse me," or "Knock, knock. Are you available?"

Just because someone is physically sitting in their office chair within the cubicle does not presume they are available. They may be on a deadline to finish a project, or may be awaiting a conference call.

After knocking, always ask if the person is available. Say, "Is now a good time?" If the individual says no, then respect that and move on. Try again later to make a time with the individual. Even better is to consider calling or e-mailing in advance to ask if you can stop by at a pre-determined time.

Once a time is set, be on time or a few minutes early, but never be late. See the section on Time Manners.

Food in a cubicle

How many of us have winced at the smell of burnt popcorn in the office or the smell of Robert's sauerkraut baloney sandwich in the next cubicle? If you choose to have food with strong odors at work, that is fine. Be sensitive to your co-workers, and enjoy your wonderful food in the designated break room rather than your cubicle space.

Chapter Fourteen

Business Meeting Manners

Did you know corn has an incredibly long shelf life? Archaeologists have been able to pop 1,000 year old kernels.
Source: www.americasfarmers.com

Large Group Meetings

You can be with several hundred people at a meeting and, if you choose to commit a faux pas, it will register like a neon light to management. Everyone at the meeting will be on their best behavior because colleagues and/or clients may be present. Always put yourself in the shoes of the speaker. Even if you are completely bored, give it your fullest attention. Your rapt attention is needed with everyone, especially if a senior officer is the presenter.

If you are fatigued and feel as though you could fall asleep sitting up, wait for a pause or break in the presentation, then quietly and with as much politeness as you can, excuse yourself from the room. Go to the washroom to refresh yourself. Take care to not let the door of the room crash shut on your way out. Your main goal is first, not to interrupt the meeting, and second, to take care of your personal needs.

Later that evening, when at home, think of how you can better care for yourself so the fatigue factor will not impede your potential success.

General Guidelines for Meetings

Avoid at all costs hard candies with noisy wrappers. Even if you try to unwrap the candy slowly and deliberately, the noise it makes is still annoying.

Remember the person in the theater who unwrapped candy during the entire performance? You do not want to be that person.

If you must have candy, try to choose one with a quiet wrapper. However, if candy is provided for all guests at the meeting, that is again a different situation. In that scenario, do be sure that you dispose of the wrapper properly.

As a business professional, the emphasis is on the word professional. Have all manner of notepads, pens, pencils, sticky notes, at the ready for your use. You never want to delay the start of the meeting because you cannot find something you need, or you are shuffling papers. Also, be cautious of using a laptop computer. In no way do you want to distract the speaker or the business at hand by the clicking that emanates from a computer.

Meetings Manners

Be sure you have a reason to hold the meeting. Don't have a meeting simply for the sake of having a meeting. Outline a clear agenda for the meeting, including time and place details. Make the agenda available to all who attend the meeting.

I like to use a "parking lot" on the white board or large flip chart on which I outline all that will be covered in the meeting. Include everyone and value everyone's ideas, even if they may seem strange.

Stick to the agenda as much as possible. Adhere to your time schedule. For a treat, let your meeting out early every now and again. Serve light refreshments sometimes, even something as simple as a bowl of hard candies. People appreciate that.

Making a New Employee Feel Welcome

Be friendly. Remember the new employee is a person with feelings and a family. Say hello. Offer to show the new person the small stuff like where the coffee filters are, the candy jar, the pencils, etc. Put a handwritten note on the person's desk welcoming them to the organization. Include the new person in lunch plans, coffee breaks, etc. "Hover" gently for a day or two to help the new person feel welcome.

Socializing and Networking

People tend to buy emotionally, but tend to make decisions intellectually. Given the sometimes rough-and-tumble world of business these days, how do you make the most of your socializing and networking efforts?

First, you need to think of your product or service in terms of how your customer thinks of it. There is a hierarchy of effects everyone goes through when they are considering a new hire or a new product or service.

1. Awareness – Has the customer/client heard of you? What can you do to build awareness of your attributes or service?
2. Knowledge – Many people like to intellectualize the decisions they make. Make sure your client has the correct knowledge in order to make the decision.
3. Liking or disliking. Start to develop what you do as a selection set. People might be more interested in one category/selection or another. People like to have choices.
4. Preference – Another term for this is short list.

5. Conviction – It is not a yes until they sign on the dotted line.

6. R-E-S-P-E-C-T is as important as the agreement.

7. Purchase/hire – The transaction takes place. It is official.

This hierarchy of effects is cyclical in nature; it repeats itself over and over again. Always keep your assumptions in check and put your best foot forward.

Networking

Networking is a process by which you begin to build a systematic network of professional relationships that are win–win for all involved.

As you talk with people, keep the following ideas in mind for networking:

- Know your organization's history in bullet points. Have an elevator speech prepared that positions your firm and its mission.
- Talk about its services and products, less about people.
- Keep your phrases succinct and lead with strengths.
- Avoid talking about yourself or personal matters.
- Highlight your strengths and how it helped the business.
- Attend luncheons, business after-hours gatherings, etc.
- Arrive early, attend often.
- Sit with different people each time.
- Ask other people about themselves.
- Have plenty of business cards handy.

The key to networking is building relationships. Don't keep score, and don't burn bridges. Even if someone wrongs you, keep the bridge open. It's the mannerly thing to do.

If you are by nature a shy person, then build up your courage and go for it. It helps to have a script in mind that you can say. Make it your goal to give out a certain number of business cards or meet a certain number of people.

If you are a gregarious person, then keep it in check. Be conscious enough to conform your personality to the situation at hand. Be especially careful about alcoholic beverages, which tend to enhance those characteristics we may not consider our best ones.

How to Stand Out At Work

There is an old joke about farmers: They are "outstanding" in their fields, or is it "out, standing" in their fields? Seriously, sometimes doing a good job isn't good enough. You need to raise your own profile at work. Here's how:

1. Talk to your boss on a regular basis. This builds a nice routine of regular, relaxed communication that can boost your boss's opinion of you.
2. Always show up on time or even better, be early. Latecomers often get noticed, but not for the right reasons.
3. Dress properly. Whether your office is casual or formal, the way you dress has a big effect. You can never go wrong by dressing up rather than down.
4. Network, network, network. Share your expertise with everyone you can. You will gain a reputation as someone who is on top of their game.
5. Find a mentor. Ask for help from people who can mentor you. Their advice can be invaluable to push your career forward.
6. Be at your best every single day. Do not settle for less.

"Never grow a wishbone where your backbone ought to be."
—Clementine Paddleford

10 Simple Ways to Show Employees You Care

Perception is reality. For each of us, what the world presents to us each is our reality. Are you a leader who wants to show employees you care or do you want to be a strong-armed controller that people fear? Employees who feel valued and appreciated by their bosses are immeasurably more likely to go above and beyond in every aspect of their work. They hold themselves accountable for every project they are involved in, and they are happy in their work. One way to connect with employees is to show them you care.

1. Go out of your way to personally help.

Assist your employees with daily work issues, but take it a step beyond. Keep your radar out for personal issues that employees are having to deal. If the employee needs a little extra help with a personal issue, step in and help. This will solidify a powerful new bond for your employee, which is a loyalty that cannot be bought for any amount of money.

2. Make yourself one of them.

Don't act like you are above them in your attitude or behavior. Nothing will turn off workers more than a boss who is acting in an omnipotent way. Show your vulnerable side and include employees in the decision making process.

3. Show a genuine interest in their families.

Include families in some of your organization's events, like holiday parties. Why wouldn't you want to include your workers' greatest supporters? Including families will give you a big return from workers by knowing you care about their families, too.

4. Do things that set you apart.

One company I know gives a cash bonus to all employees based on the sales volume it achieves each year. In addition, some of the employees are eligible for a fully paid Hawaiian vacation for their entire family. Talk about setting yourself apart and building loyalty.

5. Be real and genuine.

Transparency is sometimes accompanied with a few uncomfortable conversations, but those conversations can show that you care enough to know the truth can only help in the long run.

6. Take time.

It is difficult for employees to realize they are appreciated when their leader is too busy to take time for a face-to-face chat. It is easy to get caught up in the busyness of the day-to-day activities, but employees will feel valued and respected if you make yourself accountable for regular, respectful conversations with them.

7. Little things make a big difference.

A quick e-mail containing a note of encouragement following a big project can go a long way to build morale and loyalty. Take the time to thank people for working so hard. Show your appreciation for the efforts they put forth. It doesn't have to be lengthy. Just a few brief sentences will do the trick.

8. Don't micro-manage.

Respect people enough to let them do their jobs. If needed, ask employees to explain how they conduct the project. Ask them if help is needed. Then move out of the way, and let them do the job.

9. Always be open to new experiences for your employees.

If someone has a passion for another position within the organization, keep your ear to the ground. If the position becomes open, and you can put in a good word for them, this will reap untold rewards in terms of gratitude.

10. Practice being a human being.

Many bosses like to remind people they are the boss, which is okay, unless you mind people thinking you are omnipotent and no one can touch you. Managing by fear is never a good way to conduct your daily activities, as it shows the insecurities you are feeling within yourself. Practice being a real person with feelings and vulnerabilities. Your employees will appreciate it.

Before employees will believe in and care about the long-term success of the organization, they need to feel that, as a boss, you respect and value each of them. Not just as people who will perform your to-do list or clean up your messes, but as people who are there to support you and the long-term success of the company.

This starts with you, as their leader, investing in them and showing them how much you value them as workers and as people.

Entertaining Clients

Entertaining clients can be one of the most joyful things you do in your work. After all, it is because of clients that you and/or your organization are so successful, so celebrate it.

Following are some parameters for honoring your clients:

- Maintain good communication. If changes are happening, make sure your clients are made aware of the changes.
- Consistent, clear, confidential: These three "C" words are very important in terms of your clients and their ongoing business with you.
- Do the unexpected: Surprise your clients with a thank you card, birthday card or other note to express your gratitude to them.
- Clients enjoy any sort of promotional items with the company logo on them: mugs, portfolios, caps, pens, etc.

If you have the opportunity to take clients to a nice dinner or luncheon, bravo! Here are guidelines for the meal:

- You don't have to choose the most expensive restaurant, but choose a nice restaurant where the clients will feel special.
- Brush up on your table manners before heading to the restaurant. See the section on Table Manners.
- To keep your budget in good shape, gently make a suggestion to your clients about the type of wine that might be good. This may sound something like, "We really have enjoyed the pinot noir from California." Make sure the wine you choose is a mid-range in terms of its price. Do the same thing with the meal itself. People will generally follow your lead.
- Conversational questions: Ask open-ended questions to help your guests feel appreciated and honored.
- Don't fuss over who gets the bill at the end of the meal. If two or more of you from the same company are attending the dinner, decide before going to the restaurant who will take the check. A smooth handling of the check and its subsequent payment will make your clients feel better as they will have witnessed a business group that is in control of the situation. This is a direct correlation

to how they feel about doing business with you.

- What to do if the client wants to pay for the meal? My rule is to thank them but say you are delighted to pay. If they insist a second time, be sure to let them. After all, they are the boss! Be sure to offer to pay the tip.
- Thank your guests for coming to the dinner and tell them how much you appreciate doing business with them.
- Wait until all of your guests are safely on their way before taking your leave. Once folks are in the cab or their own transportation and are heading down the road you can exhale and congratulate yourself on a job well done.

The Business Thank You

Saying "Thank you" when goods and/or services are exchanged for money is a cardinal rule in business etiquette. All other things being equal, people prefer to do business with those they know, like and trust. It is an added bonus when the business shows gratitude by saying "Thank you." Nothing can kill good will faster than a business that is slipshod in showing appreciation to customers.

Meister Eckhart, a German theologian from the 13th century, wrote, "If the only prayer you said your whole life was 'Thank you,' that would suffice." Offer a genuine "Thank you," followed by "Have a nice day" to each and every customer and mean it.

William, a young friend of mine who has just entered the world of work, says this, "Why should I thank someone? It's their job." Technically, William is right, but a little appreciation can go a very long way.

We hear many stories about how workplace morale is in the pits and that no one feels appreciated or valued. It is time to change this. The bottom line can only get better once employees are engaged and feel appreciated and valued.

- There can never be too much thanking in the workplace.
- It isn't only the boss who should do the thanking.

Chapter Fifteen

Manners with Ag Producers, Dealers and Corporate Managers

The top five states producing soybeans are Iowa, Illinois, Minnesota, Indiana and Missouri. The U.S. exported 1,790 million tons of soybeans, representing 43% of its crop in 2014

Source: www.soystats.com

Photo courtesy of AgriLife Studios, www.agrilifestudios.com

Manners with Ag Producers, Dealers and Corporate Managers

To interact successfully with those involved in the agricultural community and earn their respect, it is imperative to know as much as possible about the individual, their organizations and what makes them tick.

The Ag Producer

Much has been written and talked about over the years about what makes an ag producer. Because ag producers are people, they are as unique and complex as any other person. Though ag producers may be different as individuals, they are all cut from a similar cloth. They are hard working, dedicated, willing to help others and love feeding, fueling and clothing the world. Their passion for the land knows no bound, and they are very independent.

Progress comes when ag producers roll up their sleeves and engage in solutions. In most cases, they've been doing this for a very long while, as have their ancestors, passing the land on to family members for generations. They are entrepreneurs at heart, and they take huge risks to do right by the land. They face and must contend with market price risks, weather, insects, weeds and all the other curveballs Mother Nature throws at them.

Manners with the Ag Producer

For all of the important work ag producers do, few people really understand them. A new acquaintance was telling me recently that she was interviewing an ag producer for a story about what he was doing on his farm.

"He showed me around the farm and all of the activities that are going on. He talked and talked and talked. Then we got back to the barn for our sit-down interview. I asked him some questions about himself and he clammed up. Didn't want to talk anymore."

The ag producer didn't want to talk about himself because of a simple reason: The work they do is not about them. Many ag producers are humble people with strong integrity and willpower. Their work is about feeding, clothing and providing for other people. Ag producers are internally motivated. No one tells them they need to work in the field until midnight, but they do on a consistent basis.

When calling on an agricultural producer, do not chase them down in the middle of a field. Wait until they come to the edge of the field. Better yet, make an appointment first.

You often hear ag producers say, "I do not own this land, though I do, on paper. I am here to care for it and maintain its quality for future generations. I rely on the health and safety of our land to continue farming each year."

This is demonstrated in small-town cafes across America. As the noon meal approaches, ag producers take a break for lunch, wearing their seed caps. (And yes, I would prefer they remove their caps in a restaurant.)

If a stranger comes into the café, they will look up and nod. When they discover this stranger just purchased land in the area, everything changes. The stranger is now a friend and part of the inner circle. The stranger is invited to join them at the table. Another person to care for the land they love so much. The new person is now part of the inner circle.

The Farmer Wave

Driving on rural roads, I get the "farmer wave." They lift one or two fingers from the steering wheel to say hello. Of course, I can't resist waving back in the same way. What fun, but what does it mean? When you receive a farmer wave, they are telling you:

- Hello.
- Be friendly.
- Good to see you.
- Anything I can help you with?
- I see you and honor you.
- I recognize your existence.
- I mean you no harm.
- Hi, neighbor.
- It is almost saying: I trust you.

The farmer wave really brightens someone's day.

Anatomy of the farmer wave:
An index finger
Two fingers

[No three fingers]
Whole hand

Extension of the farmer wave:
Nod of the head up (watch the western hat go up)
Nod of the head down (witness the seed cap going down)

If you happen to pass an ag producer without seeing a wave, go ahead and wave at them, then look in your rear-view mirror. You will most likely see them, holding up his entire hand in a generous wave.

Terry Branstad, governor of Iowa, has noted that it was Iowa's reputation as a friendly, welcoming state that brought China's President Xi Jinping back to Iowa in 2012, nearly 30 years after he first toured the state.

Let's spread a little kindness and goodwill by doing a farmer wave, whether you live in the city or the country. A simple farmer wave can brighten anyone's day. The farmer wave is an international and intentional sign of good-neighborliness.

Manners with Dealers

Providing ag producers with the products and services they want and need is the local dealer (I prefer the term retailer).

There is the machinery dealer, the crop input retailer, the seedsmen, the insurance broker, the credit provider, the landlord. A larger ag producer will have as many as a couple of dozen organizations from which they purchase goods and another three dozen who are trying to get their business.

Dealers come in all shapes and sizes. Some are family owned with one location. Some are part of a co-op system. Some are part of a regional organization. Some are branches of huge organizations with hundreds of locations around the country.

Some dealers are aligned and represent just one manufacturer's product line. Most, however, offer multiple company's products and/or services. They are introduced and trained to many products throughout the year. Ag producers rely on their dealers to stay current on new products/services/ methods which they must do, while continuing to move inventory and provide service to existing customers.

Dealers (and all vendors) do have many things in common. The vast majority were raised in a farming/ranching environment but for some reason are not an ag producer themselves (perhaps there wasn't room for them in their parent's farming operation). Or, they prefer to participate in many farming operations in their areas rather than just the "home" place.

Dealers and their employees have a passion of giving assistance to the agricultural community and working with ag producers. They may have a farm/ranch "on the side." I personally know many ag bankers who do so. In addition, most are college graduates.

The new technology being introduced in the agricultural market is very exciting and dealers love being involved with it. For example, most of the new ag machinery has satellite guidance systems of the "Star Wars" nature.

They are a congenial people who are often collaborative, cooperative and have to be competitive. They want to be around interact with people. They are trusted members and leaders of their communities and many times their organizations are multigenerational.

And, they are driven by sales, service and their organization's profitability (need to have a profit to stay in business.). That profitability, however, is directly impacted by commodity market prices. If an ag producer is making money, they are more likely to invest in new equipment and better goods. If the markets are moving against them, they will cut their expenses. I'll bet it was a farmer who invented the phrase "Save it for a rainy day."

When calling on dealers, call ahead for an appointment. If possible, make an appointment with the decision-maker and then go in with a great attitude and smile. Shake hands in a professional way. Be enthusiastic about your product or service and how it can help the dealer. Have your business card ready. Start building rapport and establish common ground. How can your business help make the dealer's business be more profitable? Treat dealers with respect, dignity and courtesy. Hopefully, you will receive the same back from them.

Manners With Corporate Managers in Agribusiness

Corporate agribusinesses that develop, manufacture, market and provide technical support to ag producers and dealers are a crucial part of the ag community. Though many changes have come about in agribusiness due to mergers, acquisitions, etc., the fact remains agribusinesses are under constant growth patterns to launch the next product or service that will serve America's agricultural industry in a healthy and beneficial way.

A survey conducted by *Agri Marketing* magazine found agribusinesses launch an average of 7,000 new products/upgrades annually. This is a staggering amount of information to understand and absorb to be current and on top of the game.

What is a corporation?

In the most general sense, a corporation is a business entity that is given many of the same legal rights as an actual person. Corporations may be owned by a single person or a large group of people.

Corporations exist as virtual or fictitious persons with limited protection of the actual people involved in the business. This limitation of liability is one of the many advantages to incorporation and is a major draw for smaller businesses to incorporate. A corporation may issue stock, either private or public, or may be classified as a non-stock corporation. If stock is issued, the corporation will generally be governed by its stockholders either directly or indirectly. The most common model includes the organization's management staff who make all key decisions for the organization, reporting to a board of directors who are to serve the best interests of the individual shareholders.

Corporate Etiquette

Corporate etiquette is sometimes called business etiquette. It is a set of generally agreed upon rules for behaving well in the corporate business environment. Essentially, it focuses on manners for the corporation and for its individual players. This has to do with the way an individual interacts with its customers, clients and other businesses.

When etiquette is observed throughout the corporation, there is the opportunity to present a seamless, well-mannered image to the rest of the world, which can then increase the respect the world gives the corporation in return, which results in a potentially more profitable corporation.

What to Do When Calling on Corporate Managers

1. Discover the structure of the corporation e.g., where are the headquarters, divisional offices, etc. What is their history? What are their major product lines?

2. Learn as much as possible about the corporation before making an appointment. Study their website and discover as much as possible so you can be knowledgeable when talking with your contact at the corporation.

3. Visit trade shows, conventions and other venues where the corporation may be exhibiting. Attempt to meet and greet as many folks from the corporation as possible. Talk about your business services and how they could fit well into their corporation structure.

4. Exchange business cards with your new contact at the corporation.

5. Establish a clear future with them. "I will contact you in two weeks so we can set a time to meet."

6. Start the process of getting an appointment by sending an e-mail. Managers are extremely busy people, and they can respond to an e-mail when they have time to do so. If the manager fails to respond in two days, resend the e-mail and on the subject line include the word "Reminder." If they still fail to respond, call them on the telephone number they provided to you.

7. If you are making the appointment with an administrative assistant, be sure to let them know that you and "Greg" talked at the convention and you are now following up.

8. Follow the 12 effective ways to make a progressive and lasting first impression earlier in this chapter.

9. Always follow up your meeting with a thank you e-mail. Include the key points you discussed.

Corporate etiquette might include the polite way to interact with other people. It might involve specific behaviors and manners in the way people talk on the telephone or the way they speak in person, all of which will influence how you or the public perceives the corporation. Written communications including e-mail will be governed by certain protocol required by the corporation.

Show and practice respect and honor as you call on the corporate manager and, hopefully, the respect and honor will be returned to you in increased business and a new and healthy business partnership for many years.

Today, mid-sized and larger farming and ranching operations are multi-million dollar enterprises. They make many purchases annually (and in some cases daily) for items such as seed and traits, crop protection, plant nutrients, animal health, genetics, feed, livestock, land rents, insurance, labor and many other items required by their operation.

In addition, they spend a huge amount on capital equipment such as tractors (I just saw a brand new model whose list price is $650,000!), combines, planters, tillage, sprayers, haying, transportation, GPS guidance systems plus items for their farmstead including buildings, grain bins, handling, irrigation, tiling, fencing, livestock gear and other.

Then there are the pickup trucks, ATVs, trailers and automobiles. And don't forget the farm's mortgage. Nor the credit that is required.

These are important business decisions, all in the hope of having a good harvest and strong market prices.

Manners in the Ag Community

There is an old saying: "You never get a second chance to create a great first impression." It takes about seven seconds for you to decide if you are going to like the person you are meeting, and the other person is thinking the same of you. Your opinion may change once you get to know the person better, but the first impression will always stay with you.

Making a good first impression is imperative to winning clients and creating your own success. We all want to do business with people who are trustworthy, likeable and honorable. People who put us at ease and make us feel good about ourselves are an important part of giving meaning to our individual lives.

For this, we are grateful. Fortunately, you can project the qualities you want to show through your actions and nonverbal cues in those first crucial seven seconds.

Appointments: Always make an appointment when you want to meet with someone. Making an appointment shows respect. It also gives the person you are meeting with a chance to think about your discussion ahead of time.

A telephone call or an e-mail asking for an appointment is the way to go. If you have been given a direct number to call for the appointment, then call it.

Identify yourself, speak clearly and enunciate properly. Give the reason you are asking for the appointment. State the amount of time you need for the appointment, then stick to the allotted amount of time.

Once the appointment is secured, repeat the time, date, etc. of the appointment so it is clear for everyone. Add the date to your calendar. End your phone call or e-mail with a pleasant sentence, such as "I look forward to meeting you on (fill in the day). Meanwhile, have a great day!" Be sure to thank them for their time on the telephone or e-mail.

Send them an e-mail confirming the appointment's time, date and location.

Be on Time: Always be on time when arriving for the appointment. Arriving 5 to 10 minutes ahead of your scheduled appointment is best. Give yourself enough time to park, find the correct building, etc. If you have arrived more than 10 minutes early, wait in your car until about five minutes before the scheduled time.

Use this time to mentally prepare and get your best attitude on tap. Review notes if needed. Have your identification handy should you need it to enter the building. Double check yourself in the mirror to be sure you are groomed properly: tie is straight, collar is straightened, jacket is ready, no food in your teeth, hair is combed, etc. It is show time and you are the show.

Sometimes, things happen in life that may cause you to be late to your scheduled appointment: the car breaks down, your child becomes ill, etc. These things are called life, and all of us deal with life on a daily basis. Slight ups and downs happen in life. I call them "ripples and waves" or "ebb and flow." The ripples and waves from life are part of the overall journey.

If something happens that would cause you to be late, the best course of action is to immediately notify by telephone or text the contact person of your circumstance. Tell the truth: My car has broken down and I have called a tow truck, or school has called, and I have to go pick up my son.

The truth is best because we are all human beings and we understand that sometimes things will happen that are unpleasant or inconvenient.

Interestingly enough, whenever something inconvenient happens, it will rarely be at a convenient time. Think about it. Take a deep breath. It is an unavoidable circumstance. Try to make the situation better in the most productive and positive way possible.

In the same phone call, immediately reschedule the appointment. You don't want to start the whole process from the beginning by saying, "Let me get back to you for a reschedule. I'll call you next week." This sounds lame and gives the impression that you are not really interested in rescheduling the appointment, which, in turn, makes you look not so good. Make every effort to reschedule the appointment then and there. Be sure to thank the person for their understanding and time.

Your Arrival: Wash your car before driving to your appointment. You do not need to have a brand new fancy car to boost your image, especially if you cannot afford one. Why wash the car? Because it demonstrates earned respect in the things you own, and it shows you take pride in your things.

Showing care and respect for the things you own indicates a caring and respect for the life you are living. This involves your car, your shoes or clothing, your apartment or home, etc. This caring and respect will carry over in your professional work.

My grandpa, a large man and a retired farmer, used to have a saying: "A person can tell a lot about a man by looking at three things: his car, his shoes and his elbows."
Elbows?
"Yes, elbows. The car or tractor doesn't need to be new, but it needs to be respected and cared for—serviced and cleaned. Same way with shoes. And elbows, because they give us so much service, need to be scrubbed clean."
Got it, Grandpa.

When parking in the lot, use the visitor parking spaces. If there are no visitor spaces, or if they are filled, then park on the edge of the parking lot. You don't want to be the person who happens to take the spot of a regular employee, who loves to tell everyone about the "jerk who took my parking space." Don't risk it. Just park at the edge of the parking lot.

If you have to use metered parking, be sure to put in enough coins to cover the time needed for your appointment. You don't want to be distracted by thinking that you need to plug the meter or risk getting a parking ticket.

Be sure to lock your car and put the keys in your pocket or purse in a place where they won't turn into a musical instrument.

13 Effective Ways to Make a Suitable and Lasting First Impression

1. Check and adjust your attitude.

People are going to notice your attitude immediately. Before you greet someone, enter an office setting for a business meeting, or step up to make a presentation, think about the situation and make a conscious choice about the attitude you want to personify.

Attitudes that appeal to people include friendly, happy, enthusiastic, receptive, patient, approachable, welcoming, helpful, curious and respectful. Attitudes that are deal-killers include angry, impatient, rude, bored, arrogant, afraid, disheartened, boring, mistrustful, loud and skeptical.

2. Stand tall with good posture.

Center your shoulders over your hips. Imagine a helium balloon is attached to your sternum, pulling you forward. Look straight ahead so your head is held up. This is the posture of success, confidence and healthy self-esteem. Practice good posture whether you are standing or sitting.

3. Smile.

A smile is an open invitation, the human body's welcome sign. It says, "I'm friendly, trustworthy and approachable." Make your smile convey genuine caring and warmth.

4. Silence your mobile phone.

Silence your mobile phone prior to the meeting, and do not check the phone while in the meeting unless it is information for which both parties are waiting.

5. Make good eye contact.

Looking into someone's eyes conveys energy and indicates honesty, openness and interest.

6. Raise your eyebrows.

Open your eyes slightly more than normal to simulate the eyebrow flash that is a general signal of recognition and acknowledgement.

7. Shake hands.

This is the universal way to establish rapport and affiliation. It is also the most effective way. Make sure you have a firm handshake, where the web of your hand meets the web of the other person's hand. Grip firmly for two to three seconds. Do not pump the hand or squeeze very hard. At the same time, do not do a wimpy handshake. Rather, grip the person's hand firmly for a few seconds while maintaining eye contact.

8. Lean in slightly.

Leaning forward shows that you are interested and engaged, but be respectful of the other person's space. Never go behind a person's desk. Maintain appropriate space levels, which means, in most business situations, about two feet away.

Never enter a person's office without their permission. If you are to meet someone and the individual is on the telephone, wait until the person if off the telephone before you enter their office. Do not stand outside of the office. Rather, have a seat in the waiting/reception area.

9. Dress appropriately for your interview/meeting.

If you are unsure of what to wear, it is always better to overdress in a coat and tie or skirt and stockings than to underdress.

10. Always have your business card ready.

Make sure the business card is accurate and professional looking. Have your writing utensil and notepad at the ready so you can begin taking notes immediately. Electronic tablets are fine too, but have it charged and ready to go. The thing to not do is fumble around in your briefcase or bag, searching for something. This indicates disorganization on your part. It wastes time and can be very annoying to you and the person with whom you have an appointment.

Present your card at the beginning of the meeting. Ask for their card. When presented it, take a moment to study it. Then place it in your shirt pocket or briefcase. This shows respect. Do not fumble or play with it during the meeting. (I've actually seen this happen many times.) That is disrespectful.

11. Use their most formal name.

As you greet your new acquaintance, call them by their most formal name until they give you permission to call you something else. "Hello, Dr. Smith. I am happy to meet you." "Oh, you can call me Dale." "Great, Dale it is, then."

12. Start building rapport.

From the first moment you shake hands with your new acquaintance, start building rapport. This means to talk a little bit, but not a lot. After all, you are there to listen to your new potential customer/client. Recognize and learn your customer's communication style by reading body language and listening. Always think about the other person. You are building a new relationship and relationships are the key to getting ahead.

Match your customer's personality. If the person you are meeting with is somewhat quiet and laid back, then you need to match that. By matching the customer's personality, this will encourage the customer to be comfortable with you and trust that you are looking out for their best interests. Meeting the customer's needs is why you are there, after all.

13. Establish a clear future.

Be sure to establish a clear future once you complete your meeting. By having the next steps laid out for you and your new acquaintance, both of you will be on your way to building a successful future together.

Every encounter you have, from meetings to conventions to business lunches presents an opportunity for you to meet people, network and expand your professional associations by making a positive first impression. You've only got about seven seconds, but seven seconds is all it takes to make a great first impression.

"Doing unto others as you would have them do unto you only works when you both have the same preferences. The golden rule is good, but the platinum rule is better. Find out how they want to be treated, then do it."

—Unknown

Professional Dining Etiquette When it Involves Work

A lunch or dinner is more often the setting these days when organizations are interviewing a job candidate. How the candidate conducts themselves during the meal is an indication of how the candidate may respond to clients and/or co-workers.

As a candidate, do your table manners enhance your overall self-confidence level? Are you secure in how to order and how to navigate the table setting? What about alcoholic beverages?

Consider the following tips when having a meal with a potential customer, client or prospective new boss:

- When a job interview involves a meal, it is safest to follow the lead of the senior people. One of the quickest ways to build rapport and understanding is to mirror the other person. People tend to trust people who are similar to themselves. By acting like they do, it will put them at ease, which will make the conversation go more smoothly.
- Whatever the senior people order, order the same or similar. What if your host has a four-course meal and dessert at lunchtime with coffee after? Follow their lead. You want to be eating or appear to be eating at the same time they are eating. It is somewhat uncomfortable to watch someone else eat when you are not eating.
- If your host orders a rather light lunch, a salad and soup, for example, then you also order a salad and soup, even if you are famished.
- Do not unfold and place your napkin on your lap until your host does so. Review the section on Table Manners.
- Try to time your meal so that both of you finish at a similar time. This means you need to slow down or speed up how you are eating. Try to match your acquaintance in this way. It is very awkward to have your companion finish their meal and ask you a question only for you to have food in your mouth, making it difficult to answer.

- If a question is asked while you have food in your mouth, it is okay to hold up your index finger, which is a nonverbal sign saying, "I'll be able to answer in a moment." Don't forget to use your napkin.
- Whatever you do, do not order the most expensive item on the menu. It is safe to go midrange, price-wise. Better yet, ask your companion what they like at this restaurant. Whatever they order, then you can order something similar.
- If you have special dietary needs – vegetarian, semi-vegetarian, gluten-free, etc., – don't feel as though you need to order a steak if your companion orders steak. What you can do is order something a bit more substantial so it is comparable.
- Interviews held at a restaurant may seem casual and fun. Make no mistake about it though. If you are meeting someone for a job interview or having lunch with your boss or co-workers, it is still considered work.
- Conduct yourself properly. Don't get caught with your guard down. If you are famished before heading to the restaurant, your body is trying to tell you something. Eat a little bit before you go. The last thing you want is for your G.I. tract to announce to the world that you are ravenously hungry by growling for all the world to hear.
- Eat slowly, take small bites, use your napkin and don't talk with your mouth full. Say please and thank you.
- Alcoholic drinks can be a very slippery slope. If your host orders an alcoholic drink, that is fine. However, this is the time for you to not follow suit. Despite the fact that you may think one drink might not hurt, think again. Even one alcoholic drink can impair the brain in ways you may not realize. Don't chance it. You can always say, "No, thank you. I need to drive home and want to be safe." This shows a responsible and caring attitude.
- If you are at a happy hour interview, stick to one drink and consume only half of it or less. You want to remain in complete control of all of your faculties. Your future may depend upon it.

Chapter Sixteen

The Right Way to Apologize

Hamburger from a single steer will make about 720 quarter-pound hamburgers.
Source: Iowa Farm Bureau Federation

Photo courtesy of AgriLife Studios. www.agrilifestudios.com

Mistakes are a part of life. A very important part of life. It has been said that if you do not make mistakes, then you are not taking risks.

Several things come into play when thinking of mistakes: the habits we have, how we apologize and accept responsibility for our social blunders and how we encourage and show support for ourselves and the people around us.

At times your organization may under deliver, overpromise, not follow through or in some way be less than professional in dealing with customers. We have all heard the phrase, "I am just the messenger," but, the fact is, customers expect and deserve an explanation.

Sometimes, there are situations that are out of your control, such as a late delivery of parts, a snafu in the manufacturing process or shortage of a popular product. There is always potential for human error. And in the agricultural sector, weather can create unwanted surprises.

Don't make it harder on yourself than you need to. We are all just human, after all.

How do you respond once a mistake is made?

Correcting a Mistake

- The first rule is to address the cause head on immediately.
- Communicate posthaste with the client by issuing a genuine "I'm/we're sorry."
- Ask the right questions to learn their concerns.
- Offer an honest explanation of how the situation happened as much as you can.
- Ask what you can do to fix the problem.
- Ask the customer what they believe would be fair to them.
- Fix the problem in as timely a way as possible and sooner rather than later.
- Explain the measures that are being taken so the problem does not happen again.
- Thank the client for their business and again offer a sincere apology. Go an extra step by saying, "We are here to support you through this. Here is a number to call if you have further concerns or issues."

When a mistake has been made, people often want to be heard. They want someone to really listen. They want to feel understood. Customers have high expectations around service levels and responses in a difficult situation. Once the customer feels understood, they are usually very supportive with comments like, "We've been through the same thing."

There are plenty of stories about how brand loyalty was built or shattered by a company's response during a breakdown in the regular processes or performance. Before Twitter and Facebook, unhappy customers told as many as 15 others about their bad product or service. Now, who knows how many people hear about it?

Machines will break down sometimes. The wrong fields can get sprayed. The preferred seed size isn't available. An incorrect diagnoses and remedy can get made. A computer program may have a bug in it. The list, unfortunately, is endless. Competent people can make mistakes sometimes.

Communicate to the client in a clear and effective way and in a way that helps the customer feel better about continuing to trust your products/ services going forward. This is one way to build brand loyalty for your business.

Say "I'm Sorry"

The high majority of mistakes are unintentional. If this is the case, then a genuine "I'm sorry" goes a very long way. The "I'm sorry" can come in the form of (preferred) a personal visit, telephone call or a letter. E-mail also works, but is somewhat less personal.

If you send a letter, take the time to personalize the letter. Don't do a "Dear Customer" letter. If at all possible, take the time to personalize the letter with the individual's name. Size the response to the breadth and scope of the presenting problem. Listen to what your instincts are telling you. Put yourself in the other person's shoes. If it is an isolated issue, then a telephone call from the manager or other leader can go a long way.

If the problem is more widespread, then the business needs to be ready to respond in a more comprehensive way. Whatever action is taken on the part of the company, be sure that it is personalized communication. It needs to be a letter that expresses a real person who genuinely cares about the unfortunate inconvenience they have caused for another real person. The letter needs to be personally signed by the leader of the business.

Don't wait too long or ignore the problem. When people think they have been mistreated, they tend to remember it and you may not ever know it. They will tell everyone else about the problem they had with your company. Social media may take the issue far and wide. Be mindful that an apology will only go so far. Follow up the apology with action to correct the problem, and set up a system of action to avoid the problem going forward.

Offer Encouragement

All of us have 24 hours in each day. How we live our 24 hours will depend in large part on our internal fortitude, our attitude and whether or not we have taken good care of our bodies through good nutrition and rest.

People who live in rural areas or who work in agriculture have a remarkable perspective on humanity. We are moving toward a healthy and productive life and navigating the bumps of life with grace, understanding and a good sense of humor. Taking the responsibility for being less than perfect is part of this path we call life.

To offer encouragement to people along the way is to do angelic work. From the farm field to tables across the world, people are always looking for a bit of encouragement. To help them feel better. Consider the following 7 Ups:

1. **Wake up.** Decide to make it a good day.
2. **Dress Up.** The best way to dress up it to put on a smile. A smile is an inexpensive way to improve your looks.
3. **Hush up.** Say nice things and learn to listen. Respect people. We were given two ears and one mouth. Listen to the sounds of the earth.
4. **Stand Up.** Stand up for what you believe in. Stand up for someone else who cannot stand on their own. Stand for something or you will fall for anything.
5. **Look Up.** Take time to be silent and be thankful for all you have.
6. **Reach Up.** For something higher than yourself.
7. **Lift Up.** Your thoughts. Don't worry about anything. Do your honest, humanitarian work. You will be rewarded for it.

Show Respect and Support at Work

If you are a full-time working American, you spend at least 40 hours at work each week. With so much time spent at work around the same people, it is important to make sure you are showing respect to them and you.

- Take care of your working environment. Your colleagues walk past your cubicle or work space daily. They can see what it looks like. Are your common areas clean and tidy? If so, everyone will be calmer when they are around you.
- Focus on your goals daily. Write down what you want to accomplish then focus on checking them off your list. Don't look for excuses to not work. Go to work to work. Your career will benefit.
- Mind your manners. "Please" and "thank you" are the gold standard, of course, but also be aware that work time is not when you bring up your personal problems from home. Don't try to force your political or religious beliefs on co-workers. There is enough stress in the workplace. Don't add to it by bringing up topics that will stress people out unduly.
- Never make excuses. If you make a mistake, admit it and be respectful about it. Successful people, when faced with an obstacle, see an opportunity, not an insurmountable hurdle.
- Always be on time or early. You do not have any more time in the day than your co-workers. Don't steal time from them by being late.
- Let the buck stop with you. This means to take responsibility for your failures and for your successes. Do not claim other people's work as your own, and do not push your failures onto someone else. Work as a team and give credit where credit is due.
- Respectful, successful people are willing to fail. "No risk, no reward" is a theme with these folks. They are not interested in failing, of course, but they push themselves in a way that failure is often impossible.
- Come up with polite ways to respond when you feel you are not being respected. This could sound something like, "I am interested in hearing more detail about this, but I would appreciate it if you could make it less personal," or "I appreciate your thoughts. Could we talk more about this in private?"
- Take care of your spot in the break room. Your old lunch in the refrigerator that is beginning to look like a science experiment gone

bad, your soaking coffee cup in the sink; if it is yours, clean it up and put it away.

- Practice good daily habits. Examples include: straightening your desk before leaving at the end of the day, writing down a to-do list for the following day, etc.
- Successful people often do not think of their job as work. They love what they are doing and that positive attitude gives them a fresh perspective on the daily grind. They entertain new and novel ideas, try new approaches and include other people in their projects because great ideas come from everywhere. These folks go to work to prosper, not just to work.
- Respectful and honorable people would be willing to work at their jobs even if they didn't get paid for it. They have a depth of passion for their work and the people involved in that work. They have a drive, an inner self-focus that pushes them to get something tangible done, and they often succeed in doing it.
- Use good sense when doing your daily tasks. My dad used to call it "horse sense." Be practical and think of others when making decisions. Teamwork can be a very good thing. No one can be successful alone. It takes a whole village.
- Embrace change. We often grow the most when we are pushed out of our comfort zones. Embracing change is key to moving ahead successfully.
- Surround yourself with positive people. If you happen to have people around you who are negative and sour, still be courteous to them. Don't lower yourself to their level.
- Express your incredible drive to succeed, but do it in respectful ways. This means to not brag about your accomplishments, rather be humble and firm in your beliefs and keep pushing forward. Respectful, successful people keep doing the hard things even after everyone else has given up.

"I never worked a day in my life. I enjoyed every minute of it."
—Dr. Denny Pilant, Emeritus Professor, 1966-2002.

Chapter Seventeen

Essential Manners

Cotton is a unique crop in that it is both food and fiber. Cottonseed is used as a supplement for dairy feed and is also processed into oil. Uses for cotton fibers range from heavy industrial to fine fabrics.
Source: www.americas farmers.com

Cocktail Party Manners

Creating a Good Professional Impression While Still Having Fun

There was a time when the cocktail party was meant for only top executives. However, with the passage of time, the office cocktail party may now be open to rank-and-file folks within the company.

How do you handle yourself while at the cocktail party? Here are some tips:

1. RSVP. In the context of social invitations, RSVP is a request for a response from the invited person or people. It is an acronym derived from the French phrase Répondez s'il vous plait, literally "Reply if you please" or "Reply please." For further information, see the section in this chapter on RSVP.

2. Attire for the Cocktail Party: What you wear to a cocktail party will depend whether the party is a cocktail buffet, cocktail party or a cocktail reception. For a cocktail buffet, semi-formal or casual attire will do just fine. A cocktail party would require you to dress up semi-formally. Finally, the cocktail reception would require a very formal dress. If the cocktail party is prior to a formal dinner, then follow the guidelines on the dinner invitation for your attire.

3. A cocktail party is the perfect place for you to mingle with new people, strengthen your connections or strike a deal. When introducing people, make the introduction simple, but give enough information for the new folks to strike up a conversation. "Mary, please meet my friend, Tom. Tom has been working out of the Albany office and has expertise in logistics." This simple sentence will give Mary and Tom a common ground on which to start a conversation.

   Whatever your do, mix and mingle at the cocktail party. A cocktail party is not the time for you to sit in a corner alone nursing your drink and thinking of ways to feel sorry for yourself.

4. Easy on the palate: At a cocktail party, you need to follow proper etiquette rules. This means to always have a napkin with you whenever you eat something. If appetizers are carried around on plates by server staff, pick up one piece of food at a time and place it whole in your mouth. If the appetizers on the plate are

on sticks, pick it up by the stick. If the appetizers are not skewered but rather carried in a natural vessel, such as stuffed mushrooms, then it is okay to pick up the mushroom with two fingers. Place it directly in your mouth if you do not have a plate. If a plate is offered, place the food on your plate before eating. If food is served in a buffet line, do not make more than two rounds of the buffet line. After all, the cocktail hour is a pre-dinner event.

5. Plate, cocktail, fork (part 1): Often, when plates are offered during cocktail parties, then silverware utensils are also offered, as are high tables at which you can set your food so you can enjoy meeting new people while eating. This is very manageable and creates a nice focus for you to have conversation with those at your table. You will often be standing at such a table. High cocktail tables are designed for people to move around from table to table.

6. A separate, lower service table may be provided along a wall or edge of the room. This table is used to place your depleted/used cocktail plates or glasses when you are finished. Waitstaff may also be working the room by picking up used cocktail plates and glasses. If the party gets too busy, it may be the waitstaff cannot keep up with everything that needs to be cleared. If this is the case at your cocktail party event, do your part by placing your expended plate and glasses on the service table.

7. Plate, cocktail, fork (part 2): Someone wants to shake but my hands are full! Don't panic. Find a table on which to set your small plate of food. Once your right hand is free, you are ready to greet your new acquaintance. Always carry your cocktail in your left hand, leaving your right hand free. Wear your name tag on your right, as this is where people's eyes will automatically go.

8. Straws, stir sticks, etc. Straws are very fun. They come in bright colors, some twist and turn, and some do perfect curly-cue shapes, but straws are for children. Didn't you blow bubbles in your chocolate milk when you were a kid? I did. Great fun.

If a straw or a stir stick is served in your drink whether the drink is iced tea, lemonade or a cocktail, it is meant to be used to stir the drink, not to sip through. Once you have stirred the drink, remove the straw or stir stick and place on the cocktail napkin beside your glass.

Do not try to sip the drink while the straw is still in the glass. Haven't you seen people wedging their straw off to one side with their finger while trying to take a drink out of the glass? Does this even need to be mentioned? Under no circumstances should you slurp or blow bubbles while using the straw.

9. Navigating conversational groups: If you see someone you would like to talk to and they are engaged in conversation with another group, approach the group. Wait for a pause in the conversation, then say hello to your acquaintance and the rest of the group. If you do not know anyone in the group, make eye contact with someone in the group and ease into the conversation when the opportunity presents itself. There is always time to introduce yourself after you have started interacting with the group. After all, they came to the party to meet people as well.

10. Drinking. Whatever you are drinking at the cocktail party, be sure to put it in a glass beforehand. Drinking from a bottle or a can just looks tacky. It is really a no-no. Save it for your garage or garden time at home.

If you are enjoying wine, remember that the red wine glass is held by its bowl. For white wine, the glass is held by the stem. Be careful to never place your glasses on surfaces that may stain. Ask for a coaster if needed.

Never drink alcohol to excess. After all, a cocktail party for work is still work, no matter how late it lasts.

11. Conversation. There are several topics that one can approach at a cocktail party. You could talk about the marvelous host or hostess, or talk about a unique piece of jewelry someone is wearing, or a great bowtie. These conversations could lead to talking about the latest family vacation, or the upcoming holiday weekend. A great starter question is this: "Tell me about you. What is your position? What do you like best about the

position? What are the challenges?" Use your best listening skills when talking with someone. You can also talk about an interesting news report you just learned of, which means you need to keep up on your reading.

12. What to avoid: Avoid conversing about anything that is off limits or emotionally charged: health, money, sex, religion, politics, racist remarks, sexist remarks. All are a no-no. If you are having any doubts about talking about something, then it probably means you shouldn't talk about it.

13. Basic manners 101: Certain basic manners need to be followed at a cocktail party. For example, do not imbibe too much alcohol and end up getting inebriated. Continue to maintain eye contact with people. Be polite when you request something from the party staff. Make it a habit to say "Please" and "Thank you."

14. Exiting: Always take the time to say thank you to your host or hostess before you take your leave from the cocktail party. Bid farewell to other guests as well, though it is not necessary to say goodbye to everyone, especially if it is a large party. In that case, just say goodbye to the most recent group of folks you had talked with.

Cocktail parties are like any other social event. The more you are out and about, the easier it will be for you to enjoy yourself. Cheers!

Country Road Etiquette

During the time of year when farmers are driving large pieces of equipment on the road, it is imperative to practice patience and good manners. In my home state of Iowa, this means more than 30 million acres of land (an acre is the size of a football field) are planted, cultivated and harvested annually. To get all this work completed, farmers transport large pieces of farm equipment down the road, across bridges and on the highways moving from field to field.

Farmers need to move as efficiently and safely as possible when traveling on the roads. They need to pull over as much as possible to the side of the road while proceeding to their destination. Drivers need to defer to the farm machinery when they are behind it. Doing otherwise could be very unpleasant or, even worse, deadly. Do not crowd, tailgate, honk your horn or otherwise try to hurry a tractor, combine, sprayer or other type of machinery driver.

Farmers would appreciate your help in understanding their need to be on the road and to take precautions. Most of all, be patient, safe and respectful. These are the folks growing and harvesting your food. Practice good country road etiquette, and, be sure to give them the official farmer wave.

Conversation

Don't underestimate the power of small talk. Small talk is an essential part of the social contract. It allows us to engage with someone and identify common ground within safe topic areas. When you meet someone for the first time, it takes about seven seconds for the person to size you up. This means that you need to master the basics:

1. Start with a firm handshake, lasting three to four seconds.
2. Make eye contact with your new acquaintance.
3. Try to use the new person's name at least two to three times in the first two minutes of meeting them.

Your conversation tells who you are more clearly than anything else. If your conversation is dull and uninteresting, you either do not know interesting things to talk about, or you have never learned the art of expressing yourself. If you use slang, and cut your words short, or slur them until there is no beauty left in the sound of them, you mark yourself clearly as a careless person. If you use profanity, you mark yourself as one who is insensitive to others. If you talk loudly, you are not considered refined. If you talk about yourself most of the time, you will be branded as someone who has an uncontrollable ego.

On the other hand, if your topics are well chosen and your words are beautifully spoken, your powers of conversation will win you a place in any group of people. Remember, asking questions is one of the ways of showing people that you are truly interested in what they are saying.

Things To Avoid

Try to avoid these things in your conversations:

1. Hearsay or gossip. Avoid this if you want to keep your integrity.
2. When you are listening, do not become a speaker. When you are a speaker, listen.
3. Thinking aloud. Who wants to sit idly by while you try to recall some obscure fact, or date or figure? "Let me see if I can remember." Do your thinking, then speak.
4. Discussion of your personal issues such as family problems, illnesses and so on. Some issues are private. Keep them private.
5. If you are nervous about having a conversation with someone, bring your biggest fear to the front. "I am very glad, but very nervous to meet you, Mr. President." Often, by dealing honestly with your fears first, it allows the situation to diffuse and ends up being more enjoyable for all.

One of the most important issues of good conversation is simply to be yourself. If you feel confident in yourself and know you will be able to put your best foot forward, you cannot help but succeed.

Overused Phrases and Words

There are some words and phrases in the English language that have been used so much they have become annoying buzzwords that cause many to immediately roll their eyes as in "Oh, no, not again." Let's take a look at some of these words and phrases.

1. **"No problem."** Let's say a co-worker helps you with a project. You would not have been able to complete the project without his help. You are very grateful to your co-worker, so you say, "Thank you. I'm not sure I could have done it without you." To which, the co-worker says, "No problem. Glad to help."

   Let's dissect what just happened. If you had not completed the project by the deadline, it would have been a problem for you and all of your team members. Your co-worker very deftly minimized your angst over the project by stating, "No problem. Glad to help." This is insensitive on their part. Your feelings about the project were very real. For the co-worker to dismiss your investment of time and energy on the project was a disrespectful thing to do.

People have a tendency to say, "No problem" because it wasn't a problem for them, which misses the point. It was you who had the challenge of getting the project completed on time, which is why you reached out for help. A better response from the co-worker would have been, "I'm happy to have been of help to you" or "Glad to help" or "You're welcome." Can we please stop saying, "No problem" in response to help asked for and help given?

2. **Using "Hey" in place of "Hello."** When did this happen? Have we become so casual in our speech that we have adopted the language of the street? "Hello" is much more civilized and opens the way for a friendly conversation.

3. **"Whatever."** This word is often used when we are feeling exasperated about a situation. It is really not a helpful word as it signifies "I don't care." A better phrase to use when feeling frustrated or exasperated is, "Oh my, now what?" or "Oh, dear."

4. **"Tell me about it."** This phrase often comes from the individual who has experience with the current situation. It is often accompanied by a roll of the eyes, or perhaps a sigh. A better phrase to say is, "Tell me more." Say it with sincerity and don't roll your eyes. Be genuinely interested.

5. **"OK, whatever."** This phrase implies that the person saying it is not feeling valued or listened to and probably is ready to quit sharing ideas. This is not a good place to be for any manager or worker because it indicates they are giving up by not contributing. If this type of thing happens once, it probably happens more than once, which means the team is not working together as efficiently as possible. This probably means they really don't want input from others.

6. **"I don't care."** The phrase "I don't care" can mean one of two things. In the first case, Worker A may truly feel they don't care about the outcome. In this case, Worker A will be okay with

whatever the team decides. In the second scenario, "I don't care" may be the cynical attempt of Worker C trying to help because they never feel as though their ideas are taken seriously anyway. Nothing makes morale erode faster than when a manager invites ideas, then takes none of the ideas seriously. The unfortunate thing is that Worker C and those around them will always remember how their ideas were rejected. This type of scenario also contributes to disengagement in the workplace.

7. **"Like."** The word "like" was like, very good a few years ago, and like, wow, it has now, like, taken over, man. Can we please say a phrase or sentence without using the word "like" four times? Also, let's use the word "like" in a good sentence such as "I really like the fresh lettuce from my garden."

Conversation Starter Questions

Instead of the common questions people ask such as:

- Hey, man. What's happening?
- Hey.
- What's up?
- Where are you from?
- Where did you go to school?
- What is your position?

Ask open-ended questions that invite people to tell stories, rather than give bland answers.

The open-ended question will not only encourage the person to talk, it will also open up a deeper and more engaging conversation for you.

Open-ended questions that pack a punch include:

- How <u>are</u> you? Best when spoken earnestly.
- Tell me about (fill in the person's name).
- Where were you raised?
- Tell me about your career.
- What is the best thing about your work?
- Tell me about your responsibilities for (organization).
- What brings you to this event?

- What is the most interesting thing about your hometown?
- What is it about (fill in the city) that I need to know?

As you meet new people, consider yourself in the role of "chief schmoozer" and then listen. No more talk.

Ask your question, then wait and listen for the real answer. Don't play mental telepathy with the answer you desire, or it may stop you from hearing the truth of what the speaker has to say. One of the keys in meeting someone for the first time is to remember their name and engage them in a meaningful conversation. Make an attempt to say the new acquaintance's name three times in the first two minutes you are talking with them.

Example:
- "Hello, Jim. How are you doing?"
- Shake hands with Jim for three to four seconds. Make eye contact.
- "Tell me about your career, Jim. You've had a few changes, I understand."
- Jim tells you about his new responsibilities. Listen for cues in what Jim is saying, so you can ask more in depth questions of Jim.
- "It sounds so interesting, Jim. Where do you see it going?"

Keep listening and cueing in to what Jim is sharing with you.

As good as an engaging conversation can be, there comes a time when the conversation needs to come to an end. Speak with confidence and sincerity and tell the person that it was wonderful to meet them and say you need to meet other people in the room as well and that you hope to see them again soon.

Phrases to Avoid While at Work
1. "I don't have time for …" or "I don't have enough time for …"

Often, when workers state these phrases or some semblance of these phrases, it indicates the worker is feeling overwhelmed and overstressed by the job demands, or the worker does not know how to prioritize their work projects.

Solution: Supervisor needs to sit down with the individual and assist in establishing a list of priorities and a clear to-do list. The worker can then proceed through the list one task at a time. Once the worker has a sense of accomplishment, they will then be motivated to finish the other tasks.

2. "We've never done it this way before." Or "That's not how we did it at my last company."

Every organization is different and though you may have mastered how to do the task at your previous company, it may be a different ballgame at your new firm. Adaptability and willingness to learn new things is key to your growth. This phrase sends the message that you are not a team player, and you may not be aligned with the organization's goals and objectives.

3. "It won't work."

This phrase paints you as someone who is not a team player, is negative, or simply not willing to give new ideas or tactics a try. Even if what is being asked of you did not work in the past, it is better to say something like, "Great idea. We tried this before, and it didn't work as well as we had hoped, but we realized some things that would make it work better once the project was completed. Let's give it a try."

4. "To Deal With (the idea brought up yesterday or the situation that occurred)…"

For many organizations, the focus is on their people. As Fortune 500 executive Jim Autry states, "… Business exists only among people and for people." The phrase "to deal with" suggests a negative connotation, a burden, or a general negative attitude toward work, co-workers or previous managers. This choice of words can come across as if the activity or the person was more of a chore than the aspect of the job itself.

5. "It's been brought to my attention …"

Never use this phrase when dealing with internal issues. This phrase makes the person feel as though others are talking about them behind their back, which leads to mistrust, apathy and low morale. Instead, say, "I've noticed that …" Your relationship will be helped by your honesty.

6. "Because I'm the boss" or "I'm in charge"

This is the business version of a parent saying to a naughty child, "Because I told you so" with finger pointing. Supervisors who use phrases such as these are supervisors who tend to be more interested in power and control than in getting the job done. These phrases automatically put a wall between the supervisor and the worker by making the worker comply, but in a mistrustful and morale-crushing way. Treating people with respect and dignity will go a long way toward building good rapport and trustworthiness, which is good for business. Trust people to do their jobs, then let people do their jobs.

Finally, remember this:

Businesses are made up of people. All people are human beings, and sometimes human beings make mistakes. If you make an error at work, it is good to apologize, but be sure to back up the apology with action. The best way to get back into good graces is to follow your apology with a solid solution. If you come in with ideas of how to avoid this problem in the future, you are destined to move ahead. Honesty and integrity still count.

Dining Out Manners

Dining out can be a beautiful event with delicious food delivered to your table by a well- trained and well-mannered server. Then, at the table next to you, a shriek emits from a toddler who is strapped into a highchair pulled close to the table. The parent, sitting next to the infant, is mortified, but the damage is done. Suddenly, your beautiful meal is, well, not quite so much fun.

What is the protocol for dining out?

1. **Make a reservation.** Not all restaurants take reservations, but for the ones that do, making a reservation helps the restaurant to plan for food and table space. Another great option for making reservations is the "Open Table" app. When making your reservation, give your name and the time you will arrive.

2. **Be on time.** We all know that traffic is bad, and your wife has a tendency to take a bit longer to get ready, but you need to be on time. When we are running late, everything seems to take a bit longer. Being late not only affects how much money the restaurant makes, but also

the timing of the party booked after yours is seated. Your being late also means the restaurant may be losing business because they haven't filled the table because they are waiting on you. Be aware the restaurant may move to the next reservation to fill the table, which means you will lose your spot. Be respectful and be on time or call and change your reservation.

3. **Think positively.** Head into a restaurant thinking and believing you are going to have a good time and you probably will. Everyone has off days. Don't use your waiter as a human punching bag or the busboy as the complaint recipient. It is poor form, and it is not fair to them. In fact, consider giving out a compliment to the hostess or waitress. Ask for the manager on your way out or coming in and share positive feedback about a server or the food. It makes a big difference. "We wanted to come here again because we had such a great time last time." They will probably go out of their way to make sure you repeat your good time. There are few other industries that take as much grief from their customers as the hospitality trade. Think positively and be nice. Leave the crabby at home.

4. **Don't sit at a dirty table.** If tables are at a premium and you see people get up from their table, don't rush to the table and sit among the ruins of the previous meal. Ewww. Let the wait staff know you would like to have the table once it is cleaned up and ready to go. There is a system to the way the wait staff works. Don't mess with the system. Wait until someone has a chance to clean and reset the table before capturing it.

5. **Let the server know of any food allergies.** If there is a food allergy with any member of your family, let the wait staff know before you order. Be honest and truthful about the situation. They will bend over backwards to accommodate you. Afterall, they want you back as a customer and not a lawsuit. Do not say you have a food allergy just because you don't like it. Be sure to thank the staff for their understanding.

6. **Be proactive.** Never assume a restaurant can handle your special dietary request. Always call ahead and spell out what you need to avoid, then

repeat the same to your server. You might be pleasantly surprised by what some chefs can do for you given a little notice.

7. **Use your inside voice.** We would all like to think our particular table has a bubble around it, securing our privacy so we can say anything we want. Guess what: We are still in a public place for the duration of our meal. Avoid strong language of any sort. Keep in mind that your competitor's wife may be sitting in the booth behind you. Be aware and conscious of what you are saying and do so in a voice that only your tablemates can hear.

8. **Large tables of people** tend to be louder than tables of two or four. If you are a member of a large table of six or more people, be aware that having a conversation with Joe at the other end of the table will require a louder volume than if Joe were sitting next to you. Then other folks crank up their volume so they can be heard above the din. All of this is taking place next to the couple in a booth trying to have a quiet conversation. If you are a big table of people, enjoy it, but be aware there are other folks around you.

9. **Children in restaurants.** I enjoy seeing kids in restaurants, provided they're well behaved while in their booster seat, but it takes some parental coaching at home to teach them not to play with the saltshaker, not to scream or cry and not to throw carrots as missiles. Who knew babies could have so much lung power? Modeling and role-playing in the comfort of home is the best preparation for a child's introduction to dining out. Generally speaking, children below the age of 5 neither understand nor care about the intricacies of dining out. Is the little one getting fidgety? Take her for a stroll outside. Did Jamie throw his mac and cheese on the floor? Clean up as best you can, apologize and be sure to leave a generous tip. Then go home and continue to model good dining behavior at the table.

10. **If you are unhappy, file a complaint nicely.** The best time to let a restaurant know you're unhappy with something – your seat, a dish,

the server – is the moment the problem is developing. Most businesses will do their best to accommodate you. Just remember to be civil and fair in your delivery. The worst time to air a complaint is after you've eaten, which doesn't allow the restaurant a chance to make amends on the spot. If you do not want to speak up in front of your date or other guests, excuse yourself from the table and talk to a manager privately and out of view.

11. **"I didn't care for it."** Then why is it half gone? Don't do this, then expect to have money taken off your bill. Talk about uncivilized behavior.

12. **"But it's Aunt Sophie's birthday and we have to have her special cake."** If you want to bring in your own dessert for a special occasion, be sure to call first and ask for permission. Some restaurants are happy to oblige for a caking fee of several dollars per person. After all, you will still be using the restaurant's plates, utensils, napkins and the dishwasher, and the waiter to clean up after you.

13. **Ask to move to another table.** When you are escorted to your table and, for some reason, the table does not suit you, ask to be moved to another table before you sit down.

14. **Camping is for the great outdoors, not for restaurants.** When you're finished with your meal, especially in a bustling and busy eating establishment, ask for the check and pay it promptly. Want to continue talking? Head into the bar. They serve coffee and tea there, too.

Grooming Manners

Today's television programs could almost convince us that etiquette and proper behavior is out of style. However, good manners and etiquette are more important than ever. Following the basic rules of good manners shows respect and positive regard for other people. It also sends the message that you have earned the same respect in return.

Proper etiquette and positive regard for manners applies to all people, including men, women and children no matter what their station in life. However, there may be certain manners and customs that started long before you were born and they may not make sense to you. Be that as it may, some of the rules that may not seem to apply now actually do apply. By following these tried-and-true rules, you'll certainly impress everyone around you.

For the Gentlemen

Before leaving home, practice good grooming. The use of a good soap is never overrated. Take a shower, brush your teeth, don't forget to floss and comb your hair. Make sure your fingernails are clean and trimmed. A man who doesn't care enough to be clean repulses others. Take a glance in the mirror and trim anything you see that you don't want, and this includes nose hairs and ear hairs. If you wear facial hair, make sure it is trimmed and neat. Make sure you wear deodorant each day. On a daily basis, wear clean underwear, socks and shirt.

After you have visited the men's room, don't leave without washing your hands. Do a double check on your overall appearance in the mirror. Don't spread germs to the people you are with. If you are in someone's home (or anywhere), always put down the toilet seat when you have finished your business.

For the Ladies

Every day, be sure your hair is clean and brushed. Shower as often as your body type and hair will allow i.e., every day or every other day. Use a nice cleansing soap or gel that is good for your skin. Brush your teeth three times per day, be sure to floss, and apply make-up if you choose. I have always called make-up "special effects." The main purpose of these special effects is to (a.) help me feel better, and (b.) not frighten people so much when I go out into the world. Make sure your nails are well groomed, whether they are painted or not. Clean fingernails tell a lot about grooming skills. Don't forget some simple jewelry if you choose.

Check to be sure your professional clothes are enhancing to your rising position in the working world. Do not derail your career by having bra straps hanging out or short skirts taking too much attention away from the work at hand. After all, it is your mind and good heart that counts.

Change your underwear and stockings on a daily basis. Wear comfortable and well-kept shoes. High heels are fine. Just keep a pair of comfortable shoes nearby.

When leaving the washroom, but sure to wash your hands thoroughly. Check your clothing to be sure everything is tucked in, smoothed out and looking good. Be sure to check your backside, too, to be sure your slip did not get caught in your pantyhose.

Pack your work bag the night before with all of the essentials you need. This will allow you to dash out the door on time for your morning commute.

Habits Manners
And How Not to Drive Everyone Else Crazy Over Them

Human behavior is a very interesting thing to watch. Just observing people in their daily habits, whether it is the commute to work, or shopping at the supermarket, tells volumes about how they live their lives. Sometimes, we have to say, "You couldn't make that up." Changing behavior is hard for a very simple, yet incredibly complex reason: We are creatures of habit.

We like for things to stay the same, which makes the rhythm of our lives more predictable, and we like predictable. We sit in the same seat every week in church, not because it has our name on it, but because that's what we've always done. We like our coffee a certain way, in a certain cup, and if the cup gets stained and cracked, we still think it is the best cup ever. We park in the same spot in the parking lot just because it feels comfortable. We are creatures of habit. Plain and simple.

To make a change in our behavior, it means we need to take baby steps. This means to understand what we are adding, what we are subtracting and why we are adding or subtracting. If I want to run a marathon, I am not going to go out the first day and run 10 miles after I've been sitting on my sofa for five years. Rather, I'm going to break it down into baby steps: start out with a few steps, then a mile, then two miles, work up to five miles, then seven miles, etc.

It is best to regiment yourself to each day. Try not to think about it, just do it, even when you don't want to. Especially when you don't want to.

Realize there will be at least a million things that you can think of to do, to encourage you to not take one step toward your goal. Set a small goal for yourself. Do one day or one week at a time. If you're going to run, that is what you will do. Be specific in your goals.

Many people will make a long list of to-do's often at the beginning of a new year. That is a recipe for disaster, as you will take one look at the list and immediately feel overwhelmed. Then, because we are creatures of habit, we say to ourselves, "Forget it. I'm not doing any of it." Block it off in realistic, baby steps. Do one goal at a time.

Setting Goals

Most people do not complete their new year's resolutions for a simple reason: It is too overwhelming to think of that many things to accomplish. Specific goals are the goals that will work. Follow this simple formula to set a goal and achieve it:

S – Specific Make your goal one that is very precise and doable.

M – Measurable How are you going to measure your progress? Even a simple checklist is good. Writing it down helps you to be accountable to yourself.

A – Attainable Having a goal to be President of the United States or a millionaire is a worthy goal, but both are huge tasks. Making your first attainable goal to be elected to local public office is a more realistic first step.

R – Reward What is your Reward for achieving your goal? Okay, folks, it is time to practice delayed gratification. Think about a realistic reward for yourself once you attain your goal. The reward can be a great motivator. Another great motivator: Think about the people who want you to fail, but don't spend too much time on it. It can be a great motivator to think for a moment about those folks who were the naysayers.

T – Trackable – How are you going to track your progress? Don't think you will just remember. Find a tangible way to track it. This also allows you to look back on the progress you have made. Take the time to write down your progress.

Stay committed to your tangible goals. Taking small daily steps is one of the most effective ways to change human behavior. After you do this long enough, the steps will become automatic. Your brain will adjust to the new regimen, and ta-da: You'll be on your way. Consistency is key.

Don't be afraid to ask for help. Becoming part of a community is a great thing. The community will help to motivate you when you cannot motivate yourself. Take small steps that you can accomplish. Each time you reach another milestone, this will boost your self-efficacy, which means you are much more likely to accomplish your goals and change your behavior.

The habits you are trying to change are often personal, even though the changes you want to make are in your professional life. There will be few people who will understand or empathize with the hard work you are doing.

While you may have a co-worker you can share every milestone with, which is a good thing, try to refrain from announcing to everyone each little change or goal you accomplish. While it is huge what you are doing and you may want to shout it from the mountaintop, don't do it, as your co-workers may or may not relate to your accomplishments. The last thing you need is to see someone minimize your hard work by rolling their eyes or acting disinterested.

The Healthy Habits Behind Creative and Successful People

Some habits are harder to form than others. Here are some hints for helping you to establish good, healthy habits for yourself.

- Once the workday is over, put your electronic device in an inconvenient place. As frenzied workers, we have a bad habit of letting work creep into our leisure time. People want the feeling of being off duty. It is somewhat emancipating to start a daily walk without the cellphone in your pocket. Make the walk your alone time to regenerate your batteries.
- Carve out a specific time and place to do your work. Do the work and nothing else. Do not check your e-mail or Twitter. Do what you are supposed to do for the allotted amount of time.
- Figure out what works best for you. Each of us is wired differently. Some of us drink lots of coffee. Some of us work long hours every day. Some people go to bed early. Find out what works best for you to change your habit, then follow it.
- Just because you like to do a behavior does not mean it is going to be

easier. If you love bike riding and want to ride in a road race, then you need to practice daily. However, it is not going to make the practice any easier given the fact that you like bicycling. Some habits are going to feel a little less comfortable to put into place. Prioritize and do the habits that are most important to you.

- Establishing good habits means doing something on auto-play. This means the heavy lifting of decision-making is over and you have moved into automatic. Decision-making is hard work. Make the decisions you need to, then move ahead.
- Pay attention to how you use your time, especially late at night.
- The more consistent and persistent you are with a habit, the faster it will lock in for you.
- If you fall off the wagon, be compassionate and gentle with yourself, and get yourself up and moving again.
- Practice good self-control. Eat and drink properly, get plenty of good, restful sleep and move; even a little bit of exercise will help to clear out the cobwebs. Unclutter your life: Cleaning out stuff from your life helps you to feel more in control of your life in general.
- Put your goals down on paper. It helps to see the goal put into a framework, and it is a good reminder for us.

Holiday Food Days/Celebrations And Being Well-Mannered

When the holidays roll around, your office may have a holiday party. People can take a moment to enjoy the company of their co-workers, holiday goodies and a cup of cheer.

Some office settings celebrate the holiday season by doing a community service campaign such as collecting canned food for the food bank, or gathering coats and mittens for children in need. This is a marvelous way for the business to demonstrate a convivial spirit of the holiday season and assist the community in which the business is located.

If your office has an in-house celebration, there are some basic rules.

If there is a sign-up sheet for bringing different types of food, be sure to sign up. Holiday time is not the time to hold a grudge, or somehow withhold holiday goodies because you are upset with someone at work. Rather, be cheerful and partake. If your office does not do a sign-up sheet, then talk to others and find out what type of food is needed/wanted.

Fundamentals of office parties

- With holiday parties, especially those held within the office setting, set up and tear down play a big part. A person or persons needs to be designated to set up and tear down the infrastructure of the party. Tables, chairs, serving tables, tablecloths are all considerations. Place the tables near a wall electrical outlet for hot dishes requiring a cord.
- Make sure the fundamentals of the party are in place such as napkins, plates, silverware, etc. Attractive disposable plates, cups and silverware are easily found to accommodate this.
- Be sure to have a large trash can available. Place it away from the serving table, yet convenient enough for people to use.
- Keep a supply of cleaning materials handy, such as towels. This will be handy in the event of a spill or other accident with the food.
- Please pick up/clean up after yourself. If a saucy, smoky sausage slides to the floor under your watch, be sure to pick it up immediately. Place used spoons back in their holders and pour the punch carefully. If you accidentally spill, drop or splash, take the time to clean it up immediately.
- Whatever dish you bring, be sure to have it ready for folks to place the item on their plate. Cut it, prep it and have it on a platter ready for pick up. Be sure to have a tool ready with which to pick up the food Picture this: A beautiful cake on a beautiful platter that no one takes because it has not been cut into portions.
- Try to avoid bringing foods that do not travel well e.g., a cheese soufflé or are difficult to eat like baby-back ribs.
- Be sensitive to ethnic/religious foods.
- Do bring your favorite family dish.
- Proper hygiene and handling of food is always paramount.
- If someone is feeling ill, they need to consider refraining from the activities. Appropriate personal habits while in the company of others are always appreciated i.e., covering your cough with your elbow, etc.

How the rules differ for workplace celebrations with gatherings of friends and family

- The holiday office party has matured so plan on a relaxed, convivial atmosphere.
- Try as much as possible to socialize. The holiday party is not the time to talk serious business issues, though it is okay to talk about funny things that have happened in the office/workplace. Do not tell funny stories at the expense of others.
- The office party is the perfect opportunity for the CEO, president, owner, etc. to express gratitude to the workers for a job well done. A simple "Thank you" works wonders. Research shows that most people, when given a choice of a raise or a compliment, would choose a compliment. IDEA: Send a personally written thank you note from the boss. One for each worker, yes, each and every worker, presented to them in a dignified way. It demonstrates caring and respect.

If the company is too large to write individual thank you notes, an appearance of the CEO/manager with the message of "Thank you for the work you do all year. We couldn't do it without you" would do marvelous things for the morale of the workers.

- The No. 1 way to show gratitude is to notice people. By noticing people – saying "hello", "thank you", etc. – this is the beginning of demonstrating civility, which is one of the cornerstones of manners and etiquette.
- A small gift for each of the workers helps to build loyalty and allegiance to the company. Wrap it in an attractive way. Some examples: coffee mug with the company logo on it, paperweight or pen with the company logo, etc. This type of gift builds company loyalty while demonstrating appreciation to workers.

Organization Culture

Each organization setting has its own culture and structure. In very large organizations, different divisions may hold their holiday gathering, but together with the CEO, they might celebrate with a company-wide party. For smaller businesses, people often are treated like family. The bottom line is the personalization of the party. Make the party special for all, no matter if you work in a large or a small organization.

Dos and Don'ts for the Business Holiday Party
DO'S
- Remember to RSVP in a timely manner.
- It is the business holiday party, which means that even though you are in a party atmosphere, your bosses and co-workers are still present.
- Refrain from airing the company's dirty laundry.
- Arrive on time.
- Mingle. Try to meet new people.
- Try to not talk shop though humorous stories are okay.
- Say "please" and "thank you" every chance you get in a sincere way.
- Sip. Don't gulp.
- If the organization presents you with a gift in the form of a bonus, etc., make the time to show your gratitude. Write a personal thank you note.
- Be cordial when you greet people. Holiday time is not the time to be angry with people.
- Refrain from asking: How much do you think this is costing us?
- Be sensitive to those who may be of a different faith, i.e., saying "Merry Christmas" to folks that may not be Christian.
- Observe corporate culture.
- Be yourself and enjoy.
- Bring goodies if goodies are needed or requested.
- Write a thank you note to the organizers of the party.

DONT'S
- Do not imbibe before the party.
- Do not bring your significant other if they are not invited.
- Do not stay away from the party if you feel you have been wronged in some way. This is the time to be cordial and civilized, despite the fact that someone else got the promotion.
- Do not have your cellphone on unless you are having a baby or someone is terminally ill.

- Do not be late.
- Do not avoid people that you do not enjoy working with.
- Do not be the company Grinch.

How to Weather Rudeness or Criticism

Following are some effective responses to almost any confrontation, criticism or rudeness. These phrases work because they tend to disarm the individual attempting to do the harm:

- "Hmmmm."
- "Oh."
- "Glad to know that."
- "Really?"
- "Never knew that."
- "Very interesting."
- "That may be true."
- "That could be."
- "I'll think more about that. Thanks for sharing."
- "Tell me more."
- "Wow."
- "Okay."

For an especially hostile comment:

- "Would you mind repeating that?"
- "Okay. Hmmm."
- "Say that again, please?"

Practice silence. Do not give a response. Just look at the person. Walk away if you need to.

Your body language needs to match your tone of voice. If a topic is upsetting to you, it is especially important to control your voice tone and body language to separate fact and emotion.

If a situation at work is upsetting to you and your feelings are hurt, brace yourself and think of the facts of the situation. Keep a written timeline of events on your personal calendar so you can document the events leading up to this point. The more detailed your notes, day, time, etc., the better.

Sometimes, it is important to remind yourself that this may be a difficult situation, but you have done the best you can. If you have not done the best you can, revisit and relearn what you can do to be better the next time.

Managing Conflict in a Mannerly Way

First, understand that conflict just to have a conflict is counterproductive. Do not become a human hammer in search of a human nail to pound upon. If there is a conflict or some other workplace issue, then the conflict can become a breeding ground of ill will and low morale. On the other hand, the conflict can become a shared place for co-workers to find common ground, and grow and build based on shared interests, good communication and shared respect.

The most productive way to grow and build on common ground is to respect and honor workers enough to hear them out. If a manager wants everything their way, or shuts down all ideas except their own, then the business ultimately will not grow. This often gets down to whether the conflict is a matter of principle or a matter of territory. More often than not, a conflict is a matter of turf or a matter of a supervisor with an out-of-control ego.

Any child can become impatient and throw a temper tantrum. Mature, well-mannered people keep their cool. The payoff for doing so will be huge.

It is the same way with hurtful words. Make every effort to not say poisonous words that harm. There is no taking the words back and, chances are, they did harm to someone. People have memories like elephants: they never forget. They may forgive, but they will not forget. The end result is low morale and disengaged workers.

There are problem people in the world. I have worked with some of them, and I have worked for some of them. When the problem person inevitably shows up next to you in the workplace, there is only one thing to do. Be honest and direct with them and try to solve the problem with the person directly. If the person has a tendency to be unreasonable, then distance yourself. Be respectful, but distance yourself.

Key to good manners: Remember that one cannot reason with an unreasonable person.

Sometimes, if the problem person or situation persists, then the most mannerly thing to do is to focus on your own work. Be cordial and say hello to the problem person, but avoid asking the person to work on projects with you.

Whatever you do, do not lower yourself to the offender's lower standards. Take the high road. Sad, but true. Agree to disagree and move on.

Any challenging situation you face will have a different outcome if you come from the perspective of kindness vs. the perspective of loyalty or ambition. Prioritize your values and decide what is most important as you focus on the most fitting solution.

We also need to recognize that some people are difficult to work with and some people are not kind. Sadly, it is what it is…what it is…what it is.

A Little Bit About Toxic People

Weathering rudeness or criticism can sometimes often involve people whom I consider to be toxic in their approach to others. Bosses showing favoritism among workers, people who are quiet in demeanor, yet lethal in their approach to people. These are examples of toxic people in the workplace. Other examples are people who overstep or blur professional boundaries.

There was once a woman who worked in an office setting. I'll call her Jean (not her real name). She was well-educated and had earned an advanced degree. Jean was petite in size and often wore very tight clothes to work. She paired her outfit with knee-high, heeled boots. When she walked down the hallway, one could hear her heavy boots hitting the floor with each step. It brought to mind a big bass drum.

She kept a full-length mirror in her office. In the ladies room, she placed a large wicker basket of personal toiletries, including deodorant, toothpaste and toothbrush, mouthwash, hair brush and comb, and a curling iron. She said any of the workers could use the items in the basket, but, really, does one want to share brushes, etc.? Probably not.

She was the only person I ever knew that could reach a large auditorium with her voice without a microphone. It was kind of amazing to watch. In her new position of supervising about 100 workers, Jean wanted everyone to know who was the boss. It didn't matter that people were working hard and doing good work, Jean's goal was to pick someone out and hammer them because she was their boss. She wanted to demonstrate her authority.

She would pick out an individual, then work to find things wrong in the individual's work. The worker was conscientious and thorough. It would be difficult to find something wrong with their work.

This did not deter Jean. She would pick apart and micromanage other people's projects, though she knew nothing about the projects. She would pound on her chosen individual through written evaluations that were critical and demeaning of the individual. Endless face-to-face meetings would follow the written evaluations in an effort to "correct" the worker. Jean would not let up on the person until the worker was nearly in tears, as the hammering went on for weeks.

People would hear those heavy boots stomping down the hall, and fear would strike their hearts. Jean thought she knew everything about the work (even when she didn't), was not open to suggestions from anyone and when suggestions were given, Jean claimed them as her own.

Morale plummeted and workers became fearful they would be on the receiving end of the next trouncing by Jean. Formal complaints were filed against Jean. After what seemed a very long time, Jean left to go to another firm.

The employees at Jean's previous firm joked they should send the new firm a sympathy card, for they were unfortunately well aware of Jean's battering behavior.

Humor can become a lifeline to help you cope with a difficult situation.

People in the workplace or in your personal life can sometimes exhibit what is called a toxic personality. Individuals who present a toxic personality are often external people. This type of personality places any type of blame outside of themselves. It is never their fault, even if they were involved in the project. Whatever happens, it is always someone else's fault.

The offenders may act omnipotent or above the fray, knowing that someone else will be the fall guy or gal. They may even become hostile about denying their involvement. Hostility can be silent as well as in-your-face. Nonverbal cues almost shout louder than if the person would raise their voice and can be just as harmful.

What are the traits of someone with a toxic personality?
- Very self-absorbed.

- Takes up a lot of space in the relationship. This means the relationship is focused mostly on them.
- Are often critical about anything and everything. The sky is not blue even when it is blue.
- Uses sarcasm and humor to hide or defend their toxicity.
- May be new to the job, but know everything about everything and are not interested in hearing what experienced, talented workers have to say.
- Instills a sense of heaviness or dread before you spend time with them, while you are with them and after they leave.
- Not supportive of your achievements or, if something wonderful happens to you, they may respond with jealousy or a contemptuous tone or they may ignore you.
- Toxic people may also overstep their boundaries, blurring the line between personal and professional correspondence.
- Often, they will be dismissive of your feelings.
- Toxic people will be hot/cold. They may be nice to you off and on, but will do nasty things just when you think you can trust them.
- Not interested in knowing you as a worthwhile and special person.

The more of these traits you recognize in the individual, then chances are you are dealing with a toxic personality.

How to recognize and end a toxic work relationship

Our working relationships can be some of the most rewarding relationships in our lives. After all, we spend much of our time at work, and it is important that the relationships we have are healthy for us and for our co-workers, but, of course, you have no control over them. You only have control over yourself.

There are times when a good working relationship we have built with another person slowly begins to deteriorate. The changes may come slowly or quickly, depending on the circumstances. You may begin to dread seeing this person, or even begin dreading going to work. Over time, you may feel as though spending time with this person does more harm than good. Your ideas may be rejected, or you may feel as though, suddenly, the skills and talents you have brought to your position are suddenly dismissed or not valued.

If you care about and love your position and the value you bring to it, then it is time to take stock of the working relationships that may be interfering. The question to ask yourself: *Am I being honored in this relationship, and am I honoring the other person?*

Dissonance and conflict are bound to happen when a person is not feeling honored in a relationship. This is a good question to ask yourself whether the relationship is professional, platonic, romantic or familial.

In a harmful relationship, you may feel the other person is critical, selfish, petty or insulting.

A toxic person does things such as taking information you have created, then pull the information out of context in order to zing or upstage you. They reframe your information to make it their own, factual or fictional. A toxic person will take ownership even when the ownership is not justified.

A toxic person is sometimes like a human hammer, looking for nails (reasons) to pound on you over anything and everything. You may begin looking over your shoulder, and yes, the toxic person can sometimes be your boss or your client. You begin to feel anxious and fearful and suddenly, your once solid self-confidence begins to erode, leading to low self esteem.

If the work situation continues to make you feel horrible for any reason and if the situation has become perpetual and chronic, it may be time for you re-evaluate if you want to stay there. When the relationship begins to have this type of an effect on you, it is time to ask yourself these questions:

1. Can I trust you?
2. Are you committed to honoring me?
3. Do you care about and respect me?
4. Do we bring out the best in each other?

If you do not feel valued or honored, you may need to look elsewhere for a position where you can feel valued for the contributions you can make.

Sometimes it is in your best interest to cut communication with people who exhibit toxic characteristics. If the toxic person happens to be a family member, it is still okay to consider cutting them out of your life. Difficult, but fine. It is also fine to say to them, "If you talk about X or complain about Y, then I'm hanging up immediately or I'm leaving."

It is okay to walk out on anyone, even if it is a sibling or parent who is toxic. Having a biological relationship does not give carte blanche permission for a family member to be poisonous to you. Eliminate toxic people from your life, even if they are family. Life is hard enough. Surround yourself with loving and supportive people, personally and professionally.

So, ask yourself again:

Key to good manners: Am I being honored by this person and am I honoring them?

Something to think about: Carrots, Eggs and Coffee

When placed in boiling water, carrots, eggs and coffee differ. Each of these objects face the same adversity: boiling water. Each reacts differently. The carrot goes in strong, hard and unrelenting. However, after being subjected to the boiling water, it will soften and become weak. The egg is fragile. Its thin outer shell protects its liquid interior, but after sitting through boiling water, its inside will become hardened. The ground coffee beans are unique, however. After they are in boiling water, they can change the water.

"When adversity knocks on your door, how do you respond?
Are you a carrot, an egg or a coffee bean?"

Medicine Manners

Despite our daily workouts, healthy diets and avoidance of almost all things fattening, there comes a time in many of our lives when the doctor uses the dreaded phrase "Well, you are getting older now." Is that phrase not one of the most exasperating ever? Sigh.

Be that as it may, sometimes the doctor prescribes medicine that we need to take to help our bodies continue to be healthy. Can there really be manners associated with taking medicine? Actually, yes.

I knew a man, Don, once who belonged to his church choir. The church was a prominent and popular church in the city and known for its glorious choirs, whose numbers ranged in the hundreds. The chancel choir held their rehearsal every Wednesday night in the church sanctuary.

Don recounted the scenario with dismay, "We were in final rehearsals for our sold-out holiday performances. People were attending rehearsal who had not been there for weeks. Every seat was filled. Suddenly, a few people were distracted at the front of the group.

"Sally (not her real name) had retrieved an insulin syringe from her purse and proceeded to give herself an insulin shot to treat her diabetes. The entire choir waited for her in rapt, uncomfortable stares, while she completed the injection."

Sally certainly was doing the right thing by taking care of the treatment of her diabetes but her timing and placement were inappropriate. In what could be considered a major viewer discomfort, Sally chose to do something very personal and private in public.

What this behavior screams to everyone around Sally is that she is starving for attention and is gaining attention by doing this. Unfortunately, Sally didn't realize this or chose not to realize this. After all, haven't we heard of the phrase, "Negative attention is better than no attention at all"?

Unfortunately, the human mind remembers things it doesn't want to remember. Chances are that some members of the choir, while in the midst of performing the glorious "Messiah," will remember the faux pas by Sally on the fateful night during rehearsal. We hope this isn't the case, but the human mind is the human mind after all.

If you need to take insulin shots, oral medicine, or use a topical salve on wounds, etc., this is a good thing. Choose a private place, such as a lavatory in which to conduct your personal tasks and needs.

If you are in the middle of a meeting or important conference and realize you need to take medicine, then politely excuse yourself to the washroom to take care of yourself. It is not necessary to announce to the people around you what you are doing. Simply say, "Please excuse me for a few moments." and then exit yourself. When you return to the meeting, be sure to return as unobtrusively as possible.

Recently, our beloved geriatric kitty cat needed some animal penicillin to treat an infection. Our wonderful veterinarian got us all fixed up with the medicine needed. After arriving home, I studied the literature the veterinarian had sent home with us. Clearly stated was the following phrase:

Note: Federal law prohibits the transfer of this drug to any other patient or person. If you have any questions concerning how to give your pet medication or on any reactions your pet may be having, please call us promptly.

Have we really stooped to the low point that there are those among us who would give pet medicine to human beings, or vice versa? Unfortunately, this is more common than we think. Oh my. If you believe you may have a problem with substance misuse or abuse, please get help for it immediately. Nothing will derail a career faster.

On traveling with your medicines: Obtain one of those handy dandy medicine travel kits where you can put your medicines in by the day. They are a great help and with all of the things you are thinking about on your business trip, your medicines will be taken care of. One less thing to think about.

Names Manners

Proper Names

The use of a person's given name is a sensitive area. If you are introduced to a person as "Mr. Ronald Brown," you must refer to him as "Mr. Brown." Under no circumstances are you to call him Ronald, unless you get to know him on a more personal basis and he gives his permission to be called Ronald.

At the same time, do not take it upon yourself to shorten a person's name to a nickname or otherwise shorten the name. For example, do not assume that Robert can be called Bob or Rob, or that Elizabeth can be called Liz. This is the pinnacle of insensitivity. If you are unsure of how to address a person, simply ask, "Do you go by Elizabeth?" Elizabeth will appreciate your genteel and mannerly approach.

A friend of mine from long ago used to love saying her full name. I loved hearing it: Christina Lynn Treski Topschephski. She rolled her tongue while saying it, making the whole thing sound like a wonderful, exotic dessert. My best friend is Betty Lou Fretty Blue. Doesn't it rhyme wonderfully? Names are delightful in their lyrical quality.

For all of the trouble we have remembering someone's name, it could be worse. We could have to remember someone's title, as the British do. Lord Justice Elizabeth Butler Sloss is actually addressed as Dame Elizabeth. Aren't we glad we don't have to do that?

Names, names, names. How do we handle them all?

- There is an American tradition of repeating names when first introduced. This is supposed to help you remember the name. It usually works, but try not to blubber the name out with so much emphasis that it's horribly obvious what you are up to.

- Never say, "I'm sorry, I don't remember your name." Nobody likes not being remembered. Does minimalized come to mind? It is a kindness to conceal your ignorance, even where it is obvious.
- Rather, gently say, "Please help me out with your name. My mind is getting older, you know." Self-deprecating humor usually works.
- If you have no recollection whatsoever of the person, just grin and bear it. All being well, the stranger will help you out in some small way through conversation.
- Resort to invention. Be prepared. If you know who is going to be at a particular event with people whom you've met before and you only remember them as "the olive oil salesman," or "keen on soccer" or "was in my night school class," plot to find out their names in advance. This can be an amusing game in and of itself.
- If caught by surprise and we usually are, try to corner the host or another unlikely guest for a covert briefing.
- A nightmarish situation is where your mind goes blank just as you are about to introduce someone whose name you know perfectly well. Mercifully, people are more and more coming to the rescue to help you out. Bless them. Rest assured, this happens to all of us at one time or another.
- Practice self-introductions. Be prepared.
- With the wonderful mix of ethnicities we have in our world today, we often come upon names that are difficult to pronounce. If you meet a wonderful person whose name is Aziz or Keshaun, for example, it is okay to practice their name out loud for their pronunciation approval e.g., "Hah-zeez. Am I saying it correctly?" People will appreciate the care you are taking to correctly pronounce their name.
- Be gently insistent that your name is pronounced correctly.
- At the same time, insisting on the exact nuances of pronunciation can be cruel as well as pointless. If you have a completely

Impossible name – some Polish names or the Chinese surname Ng – you might need to accept that people are doing the best they can.

- If you are the forgotten one, don't say, "You don't remember me, do you?" It will sound like a criticism, which will cause the entire interchange to slide downhill. Rather, say, "Let me help you out," then give your name, or "Hello, I'm Patricia. It's great to see you again."
- Being embarrassed about not remembering a name will not help the situation. It happens to all of us.
- Avoid inside nicknames when talking with people who aren't inside.

Call me what you'd like. I don't mind.

In America, our names seem to be directly connected to our self-esteem, as evidenced by the endless gadgets one can personalize with names: keychains that say Gary or Post-it notes that proclaim "From Shelly's Desk." I didn't know that Shelly's actual desk did correspondence, but in our world of constant new gadgets, it may well be so.

Our names are among our most precious possessions. Treat them as such.

Posture Manners And Good Posture Matters

Many of us recall our parents reminding us to "Stand up straight." or "Sit up straight." After which, we would roll our eyes, because we couldn't understand the importance of standing up straight.

The truth is posture really does matter to our overall health and the way we present ourselves to the world. We have witnessed the hunched over forms of older adults who have carried bad habits for a lifetime. Many of these fine people are turning into human question marks as the passage of time displays their bad posture habits.

Why posture matters

The benefits of practicing good posture are many. According to the American Chiropractic Association, keeping your spine aligned properly:

- Makes certain that bones and joints are correctly aligned. This helps muscles to be used properly, which then lessens the irregular wear that eventually leads to joint pain and degenerative diseases.

- Puts less stress on the ligaments which join the spinal links together. It is this precious spinal column that allows us as Homo sapiens to stand upright.
- The body uses less energy and gets less fatigued by creating efficiency within the muscle groups.
- Reduces the overall chances of back and muscular pain later in life.

Electronic devices and posture

We love our electronic devices. Do we ever, but despite all of the convenience and fun our electronic devices bring to us, they can also do damage to our body and general health in some surprising ways.

Research suggests that spinal pressure actually doubles each time you bend your head down to look at your smartphone. Some smartphone users spend an average of two to four hours a day hunched over. As a result, neck and back pain have increased among users of electronic gadgets, and the effects may linger for years.

Misalignment of your spine can affect your overall health and well-being. Anatomically, the spine protects your nervous system, which controls and coordinates all of the different functions of your body.

Designer posture

Notice how young women, mostly in the acting profession, are standing tall in their beautiful gowns with their legs crossed at the ankle. What is this all about?

This posture tends to direct one's attention to the more flattering parts of the body. By standing with one foot crossed over another, it makes the person appear taller and highlights any details of the dress. Since actresses like to say who they are wearing, as in who is the designer of their gown, standing with ankles crossed is one more way to bring more attention to individuals when attention is needed or wanted.

The Model-T Stance

The Model-T stance is a way of standing and sitting that will elongate your body, position your shoulders for proper alignment over your spine and overall make you look stronger and more powerful. The Model-T stance is used by fashion models all over the world to help them look strong and appealing on the runway or in front of a camera.

Here's how it is done: Stand with your left foot at the 12 noon position. Position your right foot two to three inches from the left foot at the 2 o'clock position. Let your shoulders settle in over your spine and take a couple of deep breaths. Ta-da! You now have perfect posture.

Another way to think of it: Imagine a helium balloon attached to your sternum. As the helium balloon rises, your spine aligns nicely over your well-positioned feet. If it is more comfortable for you, you can reverse your feet with your right foot at 12 noon and your left foot at the 10 o'clock position. Whether you are left or right-handed may determine which foot is leading at 12 noon.

To double check your posture in this position, stand very close to an unobstructed wall with the heels of your shoes/feet an inch or so away from the baseboard. Stand in the Model-T position. If you are standing correctly, your shoulder blades should touch the wall with a curve at the base of your back. As you pose for presentations or get your photograph snapped at the company awards banquet, always use the Model-T stance.

When you need to sit at your desk all day, be conscious to always keep your spine in good alignment. Have a good office chair that supports you ergonomically, and get a small foot riser to place under your desk.

If you are sitting for a business photograph, use your best sitting posture. Sit a bit forward in the chair so your back is not touching the back of the chair. This allows for better posture. Put both feet together, which will pull your knees together. For the ladies, cross your feet at the ankles, which will automatically pull your knees together. The knees may sway to the left or right, depending upon which ankle you cross over.

With your hands, rest them in your lap, with one crossed over another or gently rest your hands at the top of each leg. Do not clench your fists or stuff your hands into your pockets.

Maintaining Good Posture

No one is suggesting that you dump your smartphone. We don't want grumpy people here, but you need to be mindful of your posture while using your cellphone. Keep your posture in check by utilizing these tips:

- Avoid angling your head down for long periods of time while using your smartphone or electronic device. Raise the device closer to your eye level, or use a phone stand to prop up the screen.
- If you develop back or neck pain, which may signal a posture problem, do not hesitate to treat it. Regular chiropractic adjustments can assist in keeping your body balanced and functioning properly. Be sure to follow your doctor's suggestions.
- When sitting, try to avoid crossing your legs at the knees. Keep your knees at or below hip level. Use a lumbar pillow to support your lower back or maybe your ergonomic chair has a built-in lumbar support. Relax your shoulders throughout the day by taking three to four deep breaths. Our shoulders automatically tend to rise up throughout the day when we are dealing with the everyday stresses of work.
- Avoid sitting in the same position for a long period of time.
- Get up periodically and take a brisk walk. Take deep breaths. Adjust your shoulders. It feels good.
- While standing, keep your feet shoulder-width apart with your knees slightly bent. Assume the Model-T stance, then square your shoulders over your torso. Your shoulders will automatically pull back to their natural position.

Always practice good posture, whether you are standing, sitting or using your electronic device. Your spinal column and your overall health will thank you for it. Good posture matters.

Punctuation and Pronunciation Manners

Correct Salutations, Complimentary Closes and General Good Grammar to write a powerful letter or correspondence

The world is awash with pronunciation purgatory and electronic mail that sometimes does not even resemble the beautiful English language we know and love. While electronic media has its own language, which seems to work at least most of the time, you still need to be careful how you represent yourself, both online and in print. After all, most everything online is public information. Organizations, when looking to make a new hire, are making it a point to check social media sites to discover how the potential candidate represents themselves online.

When using written correspondence, it is important to represent yourself in the most professional way possible, which means using the appropriate salutation for the type of letter you are sending. What is appropriate depends upon how well you know the recipient and whether or not you are writing a posted letter as in snail mail or an e-mail.

Types of Letter Salutations

The salutation of the letter is the first thing the recipient will see. It is crucial that you display an appropriate level of respect and friendliness.

Dear – is often appropriate, whether you know the person well or not. If they are a potential employer, a supervisor or other business acquaintance, "Dear" works just fine. If you happen to know the person well, use their first name only. For a potential employer, use Mr., Ms., Mrs. or Miss when you know specifically that the individual is married or single.

Do not use a first name, unless the individual has given you permission to use their first name. It seems too friendly.

If you are on a first-name basis with a business associate or colleague, using a first name will depend upon how well you know the person. If you are not sure, use Mr./Ms. Last Name, or Mr./Ms. First Name, Last Name. If your contact name is gender neutral e.g., Taylor White, and you are unsure, then use "Dear Taylor White."

Dear Madam or Sir – Use an appropriate gender title if you know, or use both gender titles if you are unsure. This type of salutation should only be used when you don't have a personal name to use, as you want to address your letters as precisely as possible. Please note that "Dear Madam or Sir" can also be perceived as being a bit outdated.

To Whom It May Concern – This phrase is used in business correspondence when you do not have the specific name of the person to whom you are writing. It will always serve you well if you can't discover the name of a person to whom you can write.

Hello – Use "Hello" only in casual circumstances with people you know well. It is often used in e-mail correspondence, as in "Hello, Joe."

Hi – "Hi" is a very casual salutation and should only be used in friendly e-mail correspondence with people you know well.

Hey – "Hey" is a somewhat popular term used both verbally and in print. The word "hey" is really considered slang. Despite its popularity, it has no place in business communication, verbally or written. It is much too casual a word for business.

Familiar Salutations in order of decreasing formality

For Men	For Ladies
Sir:	Ladies:
My dear Sir:	Dear Ladies:
Dear Sir:	Madam:
My dear Mr. Jones:	Dear Madam:
Dear Mr. Jones:	My dear Ms. Jones:
My dear Jones:	Dear Ms. Jones:
Dear Jones:	My dear Miss Carter:
My dear Jack:	Dear Miss Carter:
Dear Jack:	Dear Sarah:

Examples of Salutations

Be smarter, better and wiser in all of your correspondence by minding the following examples of business salutations. Note the use of colons following the salutation.

One Woman, Title Preference Unknown

Dear Ms. Severson:
Dear Mary Severson:

Gender Not Known

Always be on the side of caution. Do not guess as to the gender of the individual to whom you are writing. If a name is not gender specific, or if the name is of an ethnicity that you are unsure of the gender rules, do not guess. Many people go by the name "Taylor," for example, and would be very annoyed at being called the wrong gender. When you are unsure, play it safe and use the full name instead of a courtesy title.

Business Letter Salutation

In a formal business letter, the greeting or salutation is always followed by a colon. Hence, "Dear Ms. Jones:" would be the correct version. However, you may find some businesses drifting away from this professional version and beginning to use a comma after the salutation, but the colon following the salutation is the epitome of professional.

Name and Gender Not Known

Dear Sir or Madam:
Dear Madam or Sir:
To Whom It May Concern: Note all of the words are capitalized.

Multiple Persons or Individuals

Dear Mr. Jones, Mrs. Eftink, Ms. Comet, Mr. Delway and Miss Eugenie:
Dear Friends or Colleagues, Members, Council, or some other appropriate collective term:

Writing to Underage Folks, Otherwise Known as Teenagers

Girls: Address them as "Miss" or "Ms." and respect the individual's preference if you happen to know it. For girls younger than 13, "Miss" or "Ms." may be omitted.
Boys: Address them as "Mr." For boys younger than 13, omit the title. Using "Mr." often helps young lads feel more grown up.

Name Known, Gender Unknown

Dear R.W. Jones:
Dear Adrian Parker:

Two or More Women

Dear Mrs. Jones, Ms. Pearcy and Miss Olant:
Dear Mrs. Schmidt and Ms. Elantro:
Dear Mesdames Schmidt and Elantro: more formal
Dear Ms. White and Ms. Ericson:
Dear Mses. or Mss. White and Ericson: more formal
Dear Miss Taylor and Miss Ross:
Dear Misses Taylor and Ross: more formal

Married Couple, Wife Uses Birth Name

I have long been puzzled by the use of the word "maiden" when asking for a surname of a female on any number of forms, governmental and otherwise. The term maiden is defined as "of, or pertaining to a maiden, or to maidenhood, befitting, or having the qualities of a maiden, 1591."

The literal use of maiden means "unmarried." This becomes matron when the female marries. It seems somewhat stodgy, like an old card game I once knew. Is there a similar term used for the unmarried status of men or has the phrase "maiden name" outlived its usefulness?

It seems that we need to hold women to the equal esteem of men by referring to the female surname as a woman's "given" name or "birth name."

Dear Mr. Reed (husband's surname) and Ms. (wife's birth surname):
Dear Dr. R. Jones (wife) and Mr. Robert Smith (husband):

Married Couple, Wife has Special Title

Dear Senator and Mr. (husband's surname):

Organization for Men and Women

Dear Ladies and Gentlemen:
Ladies and Gentlemen:
Dear Gentleman and Ladies:
Gentlemen and Ladies:

Organization of Men

Gentlemen:

Dear Gentlemen:

Organization of Women

Ladies:

Dear Ladies:

Mesdames: more formal

Hyphenated Names

If you are writing to a person with a hyphenated name, the complete name needs to be listed in the salutation.

Example: The letter is to Stanley Shafar and Brigid Jones-Shafar:

Dear Mr. Shafar and Ms. Jones-Shafar:

If the name is not hyphenated, treat it as a middle name.

Example: A letter to Stanley Shafar and Brigid Jones Shafar:

Dear Mr. and Mrs. Shafar:

In other words, pay attention to the hyphen.

Two or More Men

Dear Mr. Longet and Mr. Waterman:

Dear Mssrs. Longet and Waterman: more formal

Gentlemen: more formal

Dear Sirs: more formal

Sirs: more formal

Name Unknown, Gender Known

Dear Madam:

Dear Sir:

Name and Gender Known

Use the courtesy title preference if known:

Dear Mr. Longet:

Dear Mrs. Blue:

Dear Ms. Sampson:
Dear Miss Torpy:

Married Couple/Husband has a Special Title

Dear Dr. and Mrs. (husband's surname unless wife uses her own birth name or hyphenated name):
Dear Amb. Brown and Mrs. (husband's surname):

Married Couple, Both Have Special Titles

Dear Drs. (husband's surname):
Or Dear Major and Professor (husband's surname):
Use whatever the couple's personal titles are.

Woman and a Man

Dear Ms. Cuto and Mr. Wainright:
Dear Mr. Foro and Miss Landers:
Dear Mrs. Keystone and Mr. Jones:
Dear Mr. and Mrs. Blue:

Once you have completed your proper salutation and the body of your letter, it is time to close out the letter in a professional and respectful way. Be sure to check the letter for grammatical accuracy. Use spell check. Finally, read the letter backwards. This will help you spot any homonyms: one of two or more words spelled and pronounced alike but different in meaning. Also, have a fresh pair of eyes – a friend, partner, etc. – review your letter.

Now you are ready for your complimentary close.

Complimentary Closes

In order of decreasing formality.

Respectfully yours,

Yours respectfully,

Respectfully submitted,

Respectfully, I am,

Very truly yours,

Yours very truly,

Very sincerely yours,

Sincerely yours,

Yours sincerely,

Sincerely,

Cordially yours,

Yours cordially,

Cordially,

Kindly yours,

With kind regards,

With best regards,

Best regards,

Faithfully yours,

Yours faithfully,

Faithfully,

Finally, Sign Your Name

Be sure to sign your name in your best handwriting. If your signature is illegible, then type your full name below your signature.

There may also be an opportunity to use your electronic signature, or the signature on e-mails or other forms of electronic communications. These are usually set up ahead of time and can be very useful in terms of efficiency.

Other Important Punctuation

The placement of commas, periods and other punctuation marks will determine not only how the sentence is stated, but also how the sentence is written. Consider two examples:

1a. Woman, without her man, is nothing.

1b. Woman. Without her, man is nothing.

Each of the following phrases contains the same words. Note how the pronunciation of the words explains the meaning of the sentence. You think the English language is easy?

1. The bandage was wound around the wound.

2. The farm was used to produce produce.

3. The dump was so full that it had to refuse more refuse.

4. He could lead if he could get the lead out.

5. Since there was no time like the present, he thought it was time to present the present.

6. A bass was painted on the head of the bass drum.

7. I did not object to the object.

8. There was a row among the oarsmen about how to row.

9. They were too close to the door to close it.

10. The buck does funny things when the does are present.

11. To help with planting, the farmer taught his sow to sow.

12. The wind was too strong to wind the rope.

13. Upon seeing the tear in the painting, I shed a tear.

14. How can I intimate this to my most intimate friend?

English can be a tricky language. There is no egg in eggplant. No ham in hamburger. Neither apple nor pine in pineapple. English muffins are not a product of England, nor were French fries invented in France (they were developed in Belgium). Sweetmeats are candies and sweetbreads are meat. Quicksand works very slowly. Boxing rings are square and a guinea pig is neither from Guinea nor is it a pig.

The paradoxical nature of the English language is also part of its extreme beauty. Respect the English language and have fun with its quirkiness.

Pronunciation Manners

Our world of today consists of a beautiful mix of ethnicities and cultures that serve to make our world fascinating and interesting. Along with these ethnicities come beautiful languages and names that may be very different from our own. How does a well-mannered person navigate these sometimes difficult-to-pronounce names?

First, be mindful and respectful of the person, for their culture and country of origin are as important to them as your country is to you. In America, you can shake hands with your new friend to greet them. If you are in another country, then follow the protocol of that particular country.

For more information on proper introductions, see the section on Names Manners and Effective Introductions.

I was once charged with reading the names of 525 graduating seniors who represented more than 42 countries and languages. On an occasion as important as a commencement, it was imperative that every name be pronounced properly with respect and dignity. It took a bit of time, but the 525 names were listed in alphabetical order.

Beside each hard-to-pronounce name was written the phonetic version of the name representing the vocal sounds that express the pronunciation of words. The list looked something like this:

1. Abdo Ablar [Ab-doo ab-lar]
2. Cesar Guzman [Say-zar Gooz-man]
3. Edgar Little
4. Brenda Suares [Suh-wah-rez]
5. Christina Topchevski [Top-chef-ski]

Be sure to check with the individual if you are unsure of the phonetic version of their name. Consider having a phonetic listing of names to help your presentation go easier.

Names are very important to people. Be sure to show your respect to someone by making every effort to pronounce their name correctly.

R.S.V.P. Manners

In the context of social invitations, R.S.V.P. is a request for a response from the invited person or people. It is an acronym derived from the French phrase Répondez s'il vous plait, literally "Reply if you please" or "Reply please."

Anyone receiving an invitation with an R.S.V.P. on it is obliged to reply. To not reply by breaching this standard is unnecessarily rude and crude behavior. Everyone is busy. Please do not make "busy" your reason. It does not sound good and is almost lame. Anyone receiving an invitation containing an R.S.V.P. needs to respond within 48 hours of receiving the invitation.

"If it pleases you" is the pre-eminent phrase used in French for making polite requests and does not convey the formality or irony that "if you please" can carry in English.

R.S.V.P.s ask for significant information: the guests' names that are attending and any dietary requirements for catering purposes. R.S.V.P.s may be a printed card with an envelope or a postcard. The postcard style was designed as a less expensive option. Often, the envelope or postcard will include a postage stamp for mailing. This stamp is a gentle nudge to the recipient to follow through by mailing the R.S.V.P. within 48 hours.

Responding as notice of attending

While an R.S.V.P. request expects responses from both those attending and not attending, there is discussion suggesting many people misunderstand the concept and do not respond if they are not attending. In Las Vegas, where the R.S.V.P. is the lifeblood of social gatherings, there is some debate as to the modern use. Coined the "Cautela" version, one only needs to respond if accepting the invite.

R.S.V.P., regrets only

The phrase "R.S.V.P., regrets only," or simply "Regrets only," is a popular modern variation on the traditional R.S.V.P. The intention is to say "You need reply only if you are going to decline," with the effect "If you do not reply, that will be taken as an acceptance."

More specifically, if most invitations can be assumed to be accepted, a regrets only R.S.V.P. will reduce the communication required by both host and guests. The phrase "Regrets only" refers to the assumption that a decline will be worded with some variation of "We regret we cannot attend," and it follows that if the guest intends to attend the event, any regrets will be missing from the reply.

Save the date cards

Prior to receiving the R.S.V.P. invitation, the host may mail or e-mail out a "save the date" card to advise the date and location of the party. This may be used when the event will be held in a distant location to allow for travel plans, such as a wedding, christening or any other important event.

If, for some reason, you discover you cannot attend after submitting your R.S.V.P., then send your host a text or call to let them know. If you're bowing out, it will help your cause to give a valid reason for bowing out.

Electronic Invitation

Invitations sent electronically function in much the same way as an invitation sent by the postal service. They are often cleverly designed and delightful to receive. R.S.V.P.'s for the electronic invitation need to be sent by the due date. This is often done by a few clicks of your computer mouse.

One bonus to electronic invites is you can often view a listing of the other nice people who plan to attend the party.

Social Media Manners

We live in an age of frenzied social media. The good, the bad, and the sometimes ugly. ☹ A recent study by Edison Research reported that 67 percent of Americans have a profile on one or more social networks (Edison Research via MediaBistro, 2014).

As reported by *Agri Marketing* magazine in September 2014, Clara Jacob from Paulsen, a marketing communications agency located in Sioux Falls, SD, wrote: "The news about social media is overwhelmingly positive … social media allows you to have conversations with your customers and respond to their concerns immediately."

Jacob goes on to say, "Every social media post is like a press release. It's critical that your social media strategist have judgment as astute as your company spokesperson's … your social media shouldn't be just a fire hose of information. Make sure your strategy is guided by objectives, key targets and effective messaging."

We are in danger of becoming a nation of hyperconnected hermits, thumbs furiously working our smartphones and tablets. Along with our fatigued thumbs, invisible walls have been built by electronic tablets and phones that fit in our pocket.

The evening news recently reported that a city is building special lanes on the sidewalk for people to use while they are looking down at their smartphones and not paying attention to where they are going. No word was given as to how people crashes might be avoided within the electronic lane.

Along with the invisible walls, we seem to have forgotten the transformative power of human contact. As with the young ag leaders I worked with a few years ago, going without electronic devices for a few hours can be fun.

Restoring human contact becomes a simple management problem. We seem to be so distracted by digital information that we are forgetting the importance skill of conversing, listening and spending time with one another.

Our own self-importance seems to contribute to this phenomenon. Our own arrogance becomes one of the reasons we cannot put our devices down. The devices make us feel to important and needed.

People first, then technology.

Social Media Etiquette

Imagine if Twitter had been around hundreds of years ago.

TXT MSGNGS LK SPKN N CDE. (Text messaging is like speaking in code.)

Are you ok?	UOK?	Oh	:0
Be back later	BBL	Oh, I see	OIC
Before	B4	Oops!	:-★
Be right back	BRB	Please	PLS
Big liar	:----------)	Please call me	PCM
By the way	BTW	Really mixed up	:~/
Excellent	XLNT	Sad	:-(
For your information	FYI	Screaming	:-@
Great	GR8	Sticking tongue out	:P
Happy	:)	Surprised	:-O
Hear-broken	(:-...	Talk to you later	TTUL
Hmm	:-|	Thanks	THX
Later	L8R	Today	2DAY
Laughing	:-D	To keep a secret	:-X
Laughing out loud	LOL	Tomorrow	2MORO
Love	LUV	Want to	Wan2
Mad	>:-<	Winking	;)
My lips are sealed	:-X~	Wow!	:-0
No one	NO1	You	U
Not funny	:/)	Your	UR

Is Twitter advancing us or it is making us, ahem, stupid by breaking everything into emoticons? Isn't there value in speaking correct English with its full, deep meanings?

To Tweet or Not To Tweet? That is the Question!

Here are a few famous phrases in the form of tweets:

The Declaration of Independence: "We gots life, liberty, happiness now! Peace, King George!"

Shakespeare's Macbeth: "Macbeth killed the king. ☹ But he got his. Ambition will consume U!!"

Martin Luther King's "I Have a Dream" speech: "U R equal. I am equal. We R all equal. My dream is we have no more h8."

Gone With the Wind: "Frankly, my dear, I don't give a d@m ☹."

Jane Austen's Pride and Prejudice: "During dinner, Bennett's :-X~"

Twitter Etiquette: How to Tweet Politely

Christopher Null, a writer and journalist in the technology field, has provided a few simple etiquette rules for Twitter. Keep in mind that Twitter is just a messaging platform and is much less complex than Facebook. Some favorite etiquette rules:

- Reconsider the running commentary. Live tweeting a business speech may seem like a public service, but consider who is listening. If you normally use Twitter to post a once-a-week status, suddenly sending 30 tweets in one day may annoy folks who usually follow you. Consider composing a blog instead or offer one comprehensive observation each hour.

- Understand @ replies. Twitter's biggest downfall is its inability to organize conversations. Therefore, overuse of @ replies can be confusing to your followers. The proper time to do an @ reply is when you are adding to the conversation publicly, preferably with a tweet that can stand on its own.

- Go easy on abbreviations. Twitter was designed for smartphones. Go easy on the abbreviations unless you are crunched for space. Fitting tweets into a single message is a polite and admirable practice. Spelling still counts on Twitter.
- Think about the venue. Funerals, weddings, court and other solemn and serious proceedings are off limits for tweeting. Think about it.
- Up-to-the-minute spoilers. Twitter's beauty is that it operates in the here and now. It is a bit unreasonable for you to expect folks to suppress or censor their remarks for fear of spoiling a surprise. Avoid tweeting if you don't want to know the outcome of the game or the end of the movie.
- Following the followers. In the early days of Twitter, it was commonplace for all users to follow anyone who followed them, but Twitter has now grown to be very large. It has disabled the account option that let tweeters automatically reciprocate when someone chose to follow them. Today, reciprocating a twitter follower is strictly voluntary and there is no discourtesy in choosing not to follow someone. Be sure to look at the follower's profile before you do follow.
- Mind the plugs. If all you tweet about is yourself and your work, most of your followers will unsubscribe. There are exceptions for news feed services.
- Twitter is public. Unlike a Facebook update, a Twitter post can be read by anyone. Keep this in mind when you tweet.
- Send photos when you can. One photo is still worth 1,000 words.

Text Messaging Etiquette

Text messaging can be fraught with pitfalls that can turn normally reasonable people away, and it can turn relatively well-mannered folks into rude and thoughtless jerks. Follow these simple tips to not embarrass yourself or annoy others.

- Too many texts? Think of a text conversation as a telephone call. Think to yourself if you are imposing upon the other person. A good rule of thumb is to consider how many times you would be comfortable calling someone in a day.
- Personal relationship issues. With texting, the medium is the message.

It is not appropriate to break up with someone via text or to propose marriage to someone via text. Major life events or critical work issues require a more thoughtful, meaningful conversation, as in person to person, face to face.

- The personal space issue. It is not necessarily rude to text while in the presence of other people. However, do not let the texting prevent you from being fully engaged in what's going on. Again, think of texting as a telephone call. This should be your clue in how to behave.
- Keep it simple. As business professionals, the common abbreviations involved in texting are fine: LOL, FYI, etc., but leave the cumbersome long abbreviations to the teenagers.
- A reply is not needed now. Don't feel the need to respond immediately with a reply. People are busy, and sometimes it just takes some time.
- It is considered civilized to return the message, call, etc. in the same medium it was received (i.e.: reply to a voice mail with a phone call, e-mail to an e-mail, etc.) unless the sender requests otherwise. In other words, if someone calls you on the telephone and leaves a message, and requests you reply via a text, do so.
- Never be the one who texts during a public performance movie, theatre, etc. The light from your smartphone is a rude distraction to those around you. Whether in a public or private setting, please excuse yourself and slip away to a private location before engaging in text messaging.

What Social Networking Behavior ranks worst?

Some crimes are just unforgiveable. You're en route to the grocery store to buy milk and eggs and you decide to text while driving? Now, now. Find some self-restraint. The top four Facebook felonies:

4. Do you respect the English language? Emoticons are a popular tool and shortened words are plentiful on electronic media. Be careful to still spell words properly as much as you can.
3. Willful, unauthorized distribution. Do not distribute if the content is dishonorable or potentially shameful to someone else. Last year, a university professor sent what she thought was an assignment to her undergraduate class. What the "assignment" contained was actually a

photograph of the professor and her lover engaging in a sexual activity. Immediately, students began resending the information to everyone on their electronic contact list. Not a good thing for anyone involved.

2. Contributing to delinquency of friends' lists. Beware of embarrassing photographs. Respect your friend enough to not use photographs that may harm or humiliate them.

1. Public indecency. Is nothing sacred anymore? Let's bring back civility to electronic media. Be nice. Don't say something on social media that you would not say in person. If you would not state the message to someone's face because of its content, then do not say it on social media. Don't hide behind social media with distasteful or mean-spirited messages. We love social media. One wonders how we ever got along without it, but be sure to follow social etiquette protocol.

Table Etiquette

Men and women enter the dining room or the meeting room together. When passing through the doorway, it is considered good manners to allow the lady to enter first, even in business. It is also good manners to hold the door for someone as they are passing through. This is true for both men and women. After all, doors are equal opportunity. Be sure to offer a sincere thank you to the one who is kind enough to hold the door for you.

Folks need to stand behind their chairs once they reach the table, until there is a person at each chair. This will allow the tables to fill up more efficiently. The men pull back chairs for the women standing on their right and seat them before taking their places.

Always enter the dining chair from left to right. Enter left. Exit right. This is the way we read and write; from left to right. Entering and exiting your chair is the same way; from left to right. This will prevent unknowing folks from bumping into one another as they attempt to find or exit their dining seats. This can be especially treacherous at a round shaped banquet table. After all, we do not want to have people as bumper cars.

This format is used if you need to leave the meal for some reason; to visit the washroom, for example. Always push your chair back to its place once you leave the table. Place your napkin to the left of your place setting, not on your chair. Once you return to the table, enter your chair on the left and replace the napkin to your lap.

It is the mark of a real gentleman to rise when a lady at the same table needs to exit the table during the meal. All of the gentlemen at the table will rise, placing their napkins to the left of their dinner plates. They stand while the gentleman closest to the lady on her left assists the lady with her chair. The lady places her napkin left of her plate, then exits right out of her chair. The gentleman on her left replaces her empty chair to its proper location.

When the lady returns to the table, all of the gentlemen at the table rise, while the same gentleman on her left pulls out her chair for her. The lady enters the chair from the left. The gentleman makes sure she is comfortable. The lady then replaces her napkin to her lap, and the meal continues in a convivial style.

In a business meeting being held in a conference-style room, all remain standing until the speaker, who may be a management person, arrives and selects their seat. If the business meeting is held in an auditorium setting, this creates a different scenario in which one may choose a seat upon entering the room.

Sit erectly in your dining chair with your feet on the floor and your chair drawn close enough to the table so that your back is supported. If your back is supported, your tendency to lean forward on the table is lessened.

Seating The Guests

It is regarded as good manners for the host to enter the dining room first with the most important female guest. The hostess then enters last with that guest's escort. If there is only a hostess, then it is mannerly for her to enter with the most important guest, male or female.

The host/hostess is seated at the head of the table, and a guest of honor sits on the right. The partner of the host/hostess sits at the opposite end of the table. Other guests are seated according to the wishes of the hostess.

Name placards may be used. Once the name placards are placed around the table, they should not be moved by any guest. The host/hostess has a reason for placing people in their chosen seats, and one needs to respect that.

Men and women should be alternated around the table. Husband and wife are usually not seated next to each other.

Saying Grace

Grace is not said at all tables, but if you know that it will be, or if you are not sure whether it will be said, be quiet and watch for the host/hostess to bow their head. Sometimes a moment of silence is taken. It is embarrassing for the hostess if she must wait for Mr. Talkety-Talk to finish.

How To Use The Napkin

Your napkin should not be touched until grace is finished, if it is said. Follow the lead of your host. You should not touch your napkin until the host(s) picks up their napkin. Once the host picks up her napkin, then you are cued to pick up your napkin and place it on your lap.

A dinner napkin is sized 20x20 inches. A luncheon napkin is sized 14x14 inches. If the napkin is a large-sized dinner napkin, unfold it in half and lay it lengthwise across your lap with the fold closest to your waist. The napkin can be folded in a rectangular shape or a triangular shape. This allows protection for your clothing, and you may lift up the top section of the napkin to keep your fingers clean. A small napkin used for luncheon or informal meals should be unfolded completely.

Use your napkin frequently if you are eating foods that are especially moist, for none of the food should ever show on the lips or face. Do not rub or wipe the lips with the napkin; merely press the napkin against the lips. Taking small enough bites so that each bite can easily be taken into the mouth is a help in keeping the lips free of food.

When To Begin Eating

A general rule of thumb is to wait for the host to begin eating first. If one meal is taking longer to arrive at the table, the host may give permission for guests to commence eating once the host gets permission from the guest who is waiting. For cold foods or a buffet, wait for the host to announce dinner and continue to wait until the head guest begins.

At a seated table, the host or hostess is the first person at the table to take up a piece of silver and begin eating. They will do this as soon as everyone at the table has been served. The other guests follow their movements so quickly that all apparently begin eating at one time.

Follow Your Host

If the host is serving, he should never remark, "You go ahead while I pour the tea." Such a statement forces his guests to be inconsiderate of him. The host should seat himself and begin eating immediately after serving, even though he must soon excuse himself from the table to serve the tea.

If you are in doubt about how to eat a food served at a dinner party, glance at the hostess and see how they are eating it. If you are in doubt about which piece of silver to use, again follow the lead of your host.

Outside, In

It is very easy to remember which eating utensil to use. Start from the outside of the place setting and work in toward the service plate or the main meal plate. On the right side of the plate, fish fork first, then soupspoon, then service knife. This is the silver used for the main meal. On the left side of the plate, it will be the salad fork, the shorter fork first and then the dinner fork.

You may think of the old "b" and "d" trick to remember your utensils. Form a small "b" with you left hand by curling your index finger to your thumb and holding your other three fingers straight up, forming the letter "b." With your right hand, do the same thing, and your fingers form a "d." Bread and butter plate on your left. Drink on your right.

You can also think of the fancy car: BMW. In your table setting, the "B" is always on your left: the bread and butter plate. The "M" is in the middle. This is the service plate or main dinner plate. On the right is the "W" or the water glass and other glasses. BMW. Ta-da.

1. Salad Fork
2. Vegetable Fork
3. Service Fork
4. Service Plate
5. Napkin & Napkin Ring
6. Service Knife
7. Vegetable Knife
8. Teaspoon
9. Soup Spoon

10. Fish Fork
11. Bread & Butter Plate
12. Butter Knife
13. Dessert Spoon
14. Cake Fork
15. Water
16. White Wine
17. Red Wine
18. Champagne

The silver that is placed on the table will give clues as to what you will be eating. If there is no fish fork in your place setting, but rather a soupspoon, this means you will be enjoying soup rather than fish for your first course.

The dessertspoon and cake fork are placed on the table above the service plate, to be at the ready for dessert. The dessertspoon and cake fork should not be touched until it is time to have dessert at the end of the meal.

If you notice only a dessertspoon and no cake fork, this is a clue that your dessert is something requiring a spoon, such as ice cream. On the other hand, if you notice only a cake fork and no dessertspoon, then this means your dessert is something that requires only a fork, such as cake. Generally speaking, if your dessert arrives on a plate, it will require a fork. If your dessert arrives in bowl, then it will require a spoon.

It is truly a bonus if you notice both a dessertspoon and a cake fork, for you may have hit the ultimate dessert: cake with ice cream. Should you hit the dessert jackpot of cake and ice cream, you may choose whether to use your dessertspoon or the cake fork to enjoy. When you are finished with your dessert, the utensils used need to be placed in the finished position of 5 o'clock on your plate.

If you are having a dessert that usually requires a fork, but you are given only a spoon, it is fine. Sometimes catering departments do not have dessert forks. Use the spoon, even though it feels a bit awkward.

Silver Habits

How you hold your silver while you are using it and where you lay it is as important as whether you use the correct piece. When a cocktail appetizer such as shrimp cocktail is eaten with a fish fork, the fork is never left in the cocktail glass between bites or after you finish the appetizer. When you are not holding the spoon in your hand, lay it on the plate on which the cocktail glass stands. If a small plate is not provided with your shrimp cocktail, use an extra napkin on which to place your utensil.

How To Hold Silver

Always hold the handle of the fork with the thumb and forefinger. Never grasp the fork in the palm of the hand. Food is usually conveyed to the mouth with the fork held in either the left or the right hand depending on which is your dominant. When the fork and knife are not in use, lay both at the side of the plate in the resting position. When you are finished with the meal, the fork and the knife should be laid across the plate at the 5 o'clock position. The tines of the fork should be placed downward.

This position signals to the server you are finished and allows them to retrieve your place without the fear of a piece of silver falling to the floor. It is all about efficiency.

The Dinner Knife

Your dinner knife is used only for cutting foods such as meats and coarse salads that cannot be cut with a fork. Cut off single bites just before putting them into your mouth; never cut several bites at once. Try to resist scraping your dinner knife against your fork to clean off food.

Once you have used your knife to cut the food, place the knife in a T-position at the top of the dinner plate, and then use the fork to transport the food to your mouth. Grasp the dinner knife by the handle with two fingers and your thumb. Do not let your forefinger reach lower than the top of the blade even though you may be using a short-handled knife. Do not grasp your knife in such a way that it appears you are gripping the handle of a wheelbarrow.

When the knife is not in use, lay it with the blade turned in across the upper right side of the plate in the resting position. Do not make a bridge of your knife, that is, stretching it from the plate to the table. If one were having a picnic, the ants would surely think this a bridge to paradise.

The handle of the knife never touches the table after you have first picked it up. The knife either needs to be in a resting position or a finished position.

The Dinner Fork

The dinner fork is used more than any other piece of silver on the table:
1. To hold foods firm while they are being cut with a knife.
2. To cut foods that do not need to be cut with a knife.
3. To convey all foods to the mouth unless they are so soft they must be eaten with a spoon.
4. To spread jellies and fruit butters on bread if a spoon or knife are not available.
5. To eat the salad when no salad fork is provided.
6. To enjoy the dessert in case no dessert fork is provided.

Always grasp your dinner fork with your thumb and let it lay horizontally across your thumb to be guided by your forefinger. It should never be held like the handle of an ax. After all, you are not preparing to fell a tree. The tines of the fork should be facing up as you transport the food to your mouth.

If you are dining European style, the fork tines face down, and the fork is always held in the left hand with the knife held in the right hand simultaneously.

The knife continues to be held as the food is taken to your mouth. When you take a break in eating, both the knife and the fork are laid down on either side of the plate in the resting position to be at the ready when you resume eating.

If you find the salad fork closer to the plate than your dinner fork, you are most likely in France, where the salad is often served after the main meal.

The Salad Fork

If a salad fork is provided, it should be placed to the left of the dinner fork. The salad fork is to be used for eating the salad and is left on the salad plate when the salad is finished. If the salad is eaten with the dinner fork, the fork is never left on the salad plate. Once you have completed your salad, the salad fork needs to be placed in the finished position: turned over with tines down and placed at the 5 o'clock position.

The Butter Spreader

A butter spreader is used only for spreading butter on bread. It is never removed from the bread and butter plate. If no butter spreader is provided, the butter should be spread with the dinner knife. Once you use your butter spreader, place it back on the plate, sharper side facing you and at the back of the plate.

A bread and butter plate is not used in France, but at Windsor Castle, there are bread and butter plates at all state banquets.

The Teaspoon (one word)

A teaspoon is used to stir beverages and, if you wish, to take a single sip to test the heat. The spoon is then laid on the saucer. Hold the spoon with the thumb and forefinger of the hand of which you are most comfortable.

The Tea Spoon (two words)

The tea spoon is a smaller spoon. Think of the collections of spoons Grandma used to have hanging on her wall all in a row. This small, dainty spoon is used to stir tea in a bone china teacup. The spoon then rests nicely on the teacup's saucer, which, of course, has done its duty by holding the teacup. Since teacups are not considered musical instruments, you should never clink the spoon on the edges of the cup as you are stirring.

As well, you should not use the tea spoon to squeeze the living daylights out of a tea sachet teabag as it finishes brewing the tea. Rather, use the tea spoon to gently lift the very hot tea sachet out of the cup. Place the used tea sachet on a tea caddy.

Alas! Many Americans really do not understand tea. If you are not provided a tea caddy, then smile gently and use the vessel which is provided for empty sweetener packets and used stir sticks to dispose of your tea sachet.

Second Helpings

The host asks his guests from time to time during a meal if they would like more of this or that. Be moderate with this courtesy or the guests will be so bothered with frequent passing of foods they will not enjoy the meal.

A host should never insist his guests to take a second helping. If the guest says, "Thank you, but no," the host should not press the moment by making a remark such as, "Oh, don't disappoint me. I worked hard on this." If the issue is forced in this way, the guest may leave the food untouched with the feeling they are being rude.

If the dinner is served in a home or where people know each other well, it is correct to ask for a second helping if one is desired.

Passing Food

When eating family style, the question often comes regarding which way to pass the food. At a traditional meal, where food is served in large bowls placed in the center of the table, the host always begins by picking up a serving bowl of food. The host then holds the bowl while offering it to the person on his left. The guest on the host's left takes the food they want. A serving utensil should be placed in the food bowl. The host then helps themselves to the helping they want. The food is then passed to the right.

Offer left, pass right. The scenario of offering left, passing right is true for the first go-round. Once everyone has filled their plates, any second helpings are simply passed right.

State Your Preference

If the host asks you which piece of meat you prefer when he is carving, or if the hostess asks you when your plate is being filled in the kitchen, tell her. If they are thoughtful enough to ask you, do not reply, "I don't care" or "It doesn't matter." Even though you may have no choice, it is courteous to name your preference.

If you wish a smaller portion, it is permissible to ask for it. It is better to do this if you are a light eater, or if you are dieting, than to accept a large portion and leave most of it on your plate. If a vegetable is served that you do not eat, ask that it be omitted from your plate, unless it is the only vegetable served. If that is the case, take it and eat a little of it or do not eat any of it.

Fingerbowls

Fingerbowls are not as widely used as they once were, alas, but they are still in some clubs and dining rooms. Their use needs to be understood.

The fingerbowl usually is served at the end of a meal. Lightly dip the ends of the fingers never beyond the tips, one hand at a time, into the water. Dry the fingertips on each hand immediately after you dip them. Often a warm, dry towel is offered for this use.

Never dampen your mouth with your wet fingertips and never dip an edge of a napkin into the water and use it on the lips or other part of the face.

Manners At The Table

Dining room etiquette includes more than the use of silver. What one says and does is important. The following are suggestions:

- Do not blow on your food to cool it.
- Do not pour hot drinks into saucers to cool them.
- Hold a bone on both ends with the fingertips on both hands when it is necessary to pick it up.
- When eating a roasting ear of corn, hold it on both ends with the fingertips of both hands.
- Do not let crumbs or liquids cling to the lips.
- Do not lick the lips conspicuously.
- For the ladies, do not leave lipstick rings on cups.

- Do not stack dishes at the close of a course in an effort to assist the person serving. The servers are trained and have their system to follow.
- Do not ask for something on another person's plate, or offer something from your plate. If you want to share food, ask for an extra plate and divide the food before you begin to eat.
- Do not give someone food from your hands.
- Do not fill your fork or spoon full and take only part of the food into the mouth with the first bite.
- Do not dunk your food in public.
- Do not make gestures with the hands while holding silver.
- Do not leave your spoon in your cup or beverage during the meal or at the close of a meal.
- Do not use your handkerchief or tissue vigorously at the table. Leave the table if this is necessary.
- Do not use your dinner napkin for anything except a dinner napkin.
- Do not use your knife to convey food to your mouth.
- Do not leave a portion of the food served you on your plate for manner's sake. This is not necessary. Never scrape or wipe your plate.
- Do not discuss reducing or gaining issues at the table. Never say, "It makes me fat," or anything similar, or refer to foods by saying, "I like it, but it doesn't like me."
- Do not talk about possible human allergies or other bodily functions at the table.
- Do not remark about how full you are when you quit eating, as "I am ready to burst." Merely state that you do not care for anything more.
- Hold your napkin over your mouth if it is necessary to remove particles of food from the teeth during a meal. It is better to excuse yourself to the washroom to engage in this type of personal hygiene.
- Wait until everyone is served before you start eating.
- Avoid taking large bites. Cut your food into pieces of convenient size and eat each piece when you have it ready. Never cut off several bites before starting to eat.

- Never reach across the table or across your neighbor's plate for food.
- Never remove food from your mouth unless it is spoiled. Swallow it under any condition even though it may be distasteful. If food is too hot, drink some water quickly.
- If you have the unfortunate circumstance of getting a tough piece of meat that is not chewable, use your index finger and thumb to remove the piece. Have your napkin readily available. Quickly place the piece of food into the napkin. Call for the server to kindly bring you a fresh napkin.
- Unless you are using the fork and knife, keep your hands in your lap.
- There is no room for elbows on the table, or forearms.

Good Gastronomy!

How to Deal With Soda and Water Bottles

If soda pop in cans or bottles is served, take care to open the tab at the top of the can away from you, so as not to spray your newly starched shirt with sugar water. Glasses should always be provided for soda. Pour the soda over the ice and drink from the glass rather than the can.

If the soda or water is contained in a bottle, the cap needs to be replaced after pouring. Though cans and bottles on the business table are unsightly, alas, time does not always allow you to properly dispose of the container. Do the best you can and if time allows it before the start of the meeting, dispose of your cans and bottles in a proper manner. Resist the temptation to carry a water bottle with you at all times.

How to Eat Bread

Do not cut individual slices of bread or rolls; always break it. When bread is being passed, take them with the fingers unless a pair of tongs is provided for the purpose.

Break off a small piece of bread, butter it and eat it before breaking off another piece. Hold the piece of bread lightly on the bread and butter plate instead of in the hand when buttering bread. Use the small knife provided for the purpose. Once you have used the butter knife, replace it across the top of the small bread plate with the blade side turned in.

Eat thick sandwiches, or those meals that contain fillings that are hard to bite or break, with a knife and fork. It is also appropriate to take smaller bites of the thicker sandwiches, if you feel more comfortable that way. The key is smaller. Small, dryer sandwiches may be eaten with the fingers. Break or cut a sandwich of any size before starting to eat it.

How to Eat Desserts

If the dessert is thick or very moist such as puddings or soufflés, consume with a spoon. For cakes, pies and bars, use a fork. A knife may be handy to cut the dessert before it is conveyed to your mouth with the fork. A well-mannered person will break the cookie in half, then take a bite at a time to consume. Then break off another piece, until the cookie is gone.

How to Eat Seafood

Spear oysters and clams served on the half shell with the oyster fork. They are too slippery to hold on the fork in any other way. Never cut them. Eat each one as a single bite. Do not drink the liquid.

Eat seafood cocktails, including oyster, shrimp, lobster and crabmeat with an oyster fork. When finished, the oyster fork should be laid on the plate on which the cocktail is sitting.

A full bib is often used for lobster. It looks a bit unsightly, but for those of us who love to eat lobster, it is functional and wonderful.

Foods to Retrieve With Hands

Bread: Break slices of bread, rolls, muffins and croissants into half or into smaller pieces before buttering and eating.

Bacon: Bacon with fat on it requires a knife and fork. If the bacon is crispy and crumbly, eat it with your fingers.

Finger foods: For small foods such as finger sandwiches, small quiche, etc., watch the cues of your host. If the finger foods are offered on a platter, always place them on your plate before eating them.

Hot dogs, hamburgers, potato chips and other assorted picnic-type foods are proudly eaten while being held in your hand. Be cautious the yummy condiments — ketchup, mustard, pickles, onions — are not lost on the way to your mouth. If the sandwich is too big to bite into, feel free to cut it into halves or fourths to make it easier to eat.

Is there any hot dog as good as one eaten at your favorite baseball park?

Other foods meant to be eaten by hand: corn on the cob, lobster, clams, oysters on the half shell, spareribs, chicken wings in informal situations, sandwiches, olives, raw vegetables such as carrots and celery, some fruits, brownies and cookies.

How to Eat Soup

Eat soup from the side of the spoon, not from the tip. Dip your spoon on the side away from you, fill it about half full and sip slowly and quietly.

Sip, not slurp. This is a good way to also test and see how hot the soup may be. Taking a small amount from the edge of the bowl will allow you to check the temperature of the soup.

If the soup is thin and there is danger of a drop falling from the bottom of the spoon, rest the spoon on the rim of the soup plate for a moment before lifting it to the mouth. Do not put the spoon completely into your mouth, or tip the plate to get the final drop.

Bouillon or consommé often is served in cups. Take two or three sips from the edge of the cup with the round-bowled bouillon spoon to test the heat. Then lay the spoon beside the cup on the plate and drink the liquid slowly. Raise the bouillon cup to the lips with a hand on each handle.

When cream soup is served in a cream soup cup, which is similar to a bouillon cup except larger, the soup is eaten with a round-bowled soupspoon.

Never break bread or crackers into soup. When small round oyster crackers are served with soup, they are floated on the surface, a few at a time, and eaten while they are still crisp.

How to Eat Relishes

Radishes, celery and other crisp relishes are eaten with the fingers. Hold olives with the fingertips and nibble the meat off the pit. Deposit the pit on the bread and butter plate. Never put a whole olive in the mouth and then expel the seed. Rather, use your fingers to remove it. Watermelon spitting contests are the exception to this rule.

How to Eat Vegetables

If a salad is difficult to manage, cut it with a knife.

Asparagus is eaten with a fork.

Potatoes cooked in any manner (except French fries) are eaten with a fork. Baked potatoes may be eaten from the skin, or may be removed from the skin with the fork before butter is added.

If your baked potato is served hot from the oven still wrapped in aluminum foil, use your fingers to unwrap the foil. Careful, it will be hot. You may open the top part of the foil and leave the potato in it to consume the potato or you may completely remove the foil to enjoy your potato. Gently fold the used foil and lay it under the edge of your bread and butter plate.

If a bread and butter plate is not offered, put the foil under the edge of your dinner plate.

Eat artichokes with your fingers. Peel the leaves off one at a time, dip the end of the tip nearest the stalk into melted butter or sauce and scrape off the edible portion of the leaf between the teeth. Lay the remainder on the plate. Eat the heart with a fork after all leaves are removed.

How to Eat Fruit

Cherry tomatoes have the ability to create a fast train track on a plate as one tries to consume them. When the cherry tomato is smaller, it can be pierced with a fork to be eaten. It does not need to be cut in half. If the tomatoes are of a larger size, pierce with a fork held in the left hand and cut with a knife held in the right hand. It may be necessary to brace the fruit with a knife as it is speared with the fork.

Berries are eaten with a spoon. The exception to this rule is strawberries served with the hulls left on, on a plate that perhaps holds a mound of sugar. The berries are taken with the fingers, dipped in the sugar, and put into the mouth. The same is true for strawberries dipped in chocolate. If the berries are small enough, they can be eaten using your hands. Otherwise, use a fork.

Fresh fruits with stones or cores – plums, peaches, apricots, pears and apples – are held firmly on the plate with the fork in the left hand and pared with a fruit knife. When paring, cut the skin at the top of the fruit and draw the skin downward toward you. When the fruit is pared, cut it in halves and remove the stone or core. Using your knife and fork, cut off pieces and eat them.

For fresh fruits that are pre-cut, use a fork to spear the fruit then transfer fruit to the mouth. When eating a banana, strip off the skin, lay the fruit on the dessert plate and eat it with a fork. Never bite a banana in public. Cantaloupe is usually eaten with a spoon, although a small fork is correct if it is preferred. Melon balls are eaten with a teaspoon. Sliced oranges are eaten with a knife and fork. Grapefruit is eaten with a spoon. A grapefruit spoon is preferable, but a regular teaspoon will work as long as the grapefruit is pre-cut. Cherries, grapes, raisins and nuts are eaten with the fingers.

Watermelon is most easily eaten by cutting off a convenient bite with a fork, removing all seeds that you see and transferring the piece to the mouth. If you take a seed into your mouth, remove it with the thumb and first finger.

Removing Items from Your Mouth

There may be times when you need to remove a food item from your mouth such as olive pits, chicken bones, fish bones, etc. To remove the item from your mouth, very carefully, with two fingers, grasp the item from your mouth and lay it on the edge of your bread and butter plate. If the piece of food is very large, you may use your napkin to retrieve the food from your mouth. You will then need to ask the server for a fresh napkin.

What to do if your meal companion has food on their face

It is an unfortunate side effect of enjoying a meal – sometimes a bit of food will lodge itself onto your meal companion's face, without them realizing it. Should you say something?

"Yes." The best way: get your companion's attention discretely. Use your index finger to point on your face where the offending food is located. You can also use your napkin to show the placement of the food. The companion will be grateful you helped them correct a situation before it became embarrassing to them.

All Things Liquid

Wine connoisseurs generally agree that each type of wine needs a particular type of glass vessel to bring out the distinctive characteristics of the wine. A robust burgundy, for example, needs a glass that allows enough room for the burgundy to be swirled, which brings out its bouquet. The glass also needs to taper properly at the top so the bouquet can be captured and sipped.

Generally speaking, the stem of a wine glass should be long enough to keep your hands from touching the bowl, which can affect the wine's temperature and hence its bouquet.

A primer on glasses:

1. Water: full body glass with a shorter stem. You may hold the water glass by its bowl. If the stem is long enough, hold the glass by the stem to preserve its chill.

2. Brandy: brandy snifter. Roll the snifter between both hands and then cup it in one hand. Warming the glass brings out the flavor of brandy.

3. White wine: slightly smaller stemmed glass with a wider bowl to seize the bouquet. Hold the glass by its stem to sustain the wine's chill.

4. Burgundy reds/pinot noirs: a wide bowl stemmed glass. The wide bowl enhances the complexity of the beverage. The glass will be slightly taller and larger than the white wine glass. Hold the glass at the bottom of the bowl where it meets the stem.

5. Champagne: a narrow fluted stemmed glass, which minimizes the wine's surface area and keep the bubbles from dissipating.

Wine is presented in tinted bottles because wine will eventually spoil if exposed to light. The indentation at the bottom of the bottle helps to strengthen the structure of the bottle, but is also intended to capture the sediments.

The order of the glasses for a formal table setting:
Water-Brandy-White Wine-Pinot Noir/Burgundy-Champagne/Sparkling
Wine-Red wine

Note: At a formal table setting, you may see up to five glasses placed at each individual place. No, you will not use all of them. The purpose of this is to be at the ready when the guests arrive. Once a guest is seated and has selected their choice of wine, the waitstaff will then remove the unnecessary glasses. Only the water glass and the guest's choice of wine glass will remain.

Bon appetit! (I wish you a hearty appetite.) Bonhomie! (good natured, easy friendliness; geniality).

Technical Manners

Smartphones which answer questions for us and give us directions. Electronic messages on the computer. Computers that can be in our pockets without a cord. Personal handheld devices. Clocks that are now ubiquitous. They are strapped to our wrists and glow from our microwave ovens, dashboards, computers and the smartphone. Even when the entire house is turned off, they still glow.

All are inventions of our modern world intended to make life easier and more manageable for all of us. So why do so many of us feel overscheduled, overwhelmed, sleep deprived and darn near appointment crazy?

The answer is simple. The onslaught of new technology, which promised to set us free, has instead padlocked us to the rhythms of everyday life. The smartphones, e-mails, laptop computers and so on instill in us expectations of instantaneous actions. Now. Right Now.

In our rush to account for every minute, we have become slovenly in our electronic manners and general protocol with regard to our fellow human beings. People will often say things on social media sites they would never say in person. Be true to yourself and be consistently well-mannered and civilized. Take a break from your smartphone and consider the following suggestions in coping with our modern electronic world.

A few years ago, I did a two-and-a-half-hour manners dinner with 35 teenagers from a leadership group. Conversation flowed, glasses clinked and a good time was had by all. The laughter was amazing. The teens' jaws dropped in amazement when I reminded them at end of our time together that they had just gone two-and-a-half hours without looking at their smartphones. They loved it.

Smartphones

What is the emotional attachment that so many of us have about our smartphones? Is it really necessary to carry one's telephone constantly and lay it on the boardroom table in front of us?

Cellular phones have their proper place and time. Review where the off switch is located and use it with discretion, especially when in a business meeting. While in public, no one is interested in listening to your private conversation, even as important as you think it may be.

Once, while in the driver's license renewal station, a woman while waiting was talking into her smartphone. In very clear enunciation, she recited her Social Security number in front of a room full of astounded people. Not sure the listener heard it correctly, the woman repeated the number again. The woman didn't seem to realize there were even people around her. Amazing.

As an added note: It is considered ill-mannered of the group if the announcing speaker feels the need to remind everyone that "Smartphones are not allowed. Please disengage all smartphones now." Stay ahead of your business game. Shut down your smartphone before having to be reminded to do so or if the smartphone is slated to be used as part and parcel of the business presentation, stay focused on the business at hand and don't surf the net or check personal e-mail messages.

Voicemail Messaging

The bane of voicemail messages these days is that too many voicemails come off as fast speed gibberish or something akin to hieroglyphics, as in, "Thisissusiesoandsofromabccompanyandiwanttotalktoyouimat1234567." And the caller id number does not match the number left on the message. Being the dutiful worker, you listen to the voicemail again and again and again. Even then, you may not be sure of the person's name or telephone number or the request of the call.

The proper way to leave a voicemail is following:

"Hello, this is Susie Brown from ABC Company. Hope you are doing well today. I am calling to inquire about your services. Please give me a call at 1-2-3-1-2-3-4-5-6-7. Again, this is Susie Brown. I can be reached at 123-123-4567. Thank you. Goodbye."

When ending your call or voicemail, always say "Goodbye" rather than "Bye" or "Buh-bye."

Electronic Messages

It is neither impolite nor inefficient to wait or to simply say, "Let me get back to you on that tomorrow" or "Let's check in tomorrow and see if it still works for both of us."

Of all the different forms of electronic media, it is important to acknowledge that you have received the message, even if you are unable to do the request at that moment. A quick message back to the sender using the same media format stating: "I'm on it. Will get back to you soon." is the gold standard for communication within business professionals.

A general rule of thumb is 24 hours. If you can return the message within 24 hours, it is still considered good manners. Do not sabotage your business career by not returning a difficult message, whether it be e-mail or a phone call. Tackle the hardest calls when you are fresh and rested. It will make them seem easier, and they may not be as bad as you anticipate. Don't be someone who annoys others with inconsiderate e-mail protocol.

- Choose an appropriate e-mail address. You may want to rethink addresses like partygirl@gmail.com.
- Spellcheck your e-mail and use proper spelling.
- Pay close attention to your lists and how you use them. Distribution lists are great for some things, but be mindful to not spam your recipients. If you have the same people on multiple lists, they may receive several copies of your e-mail.
- Use salutations: Dear Sally or Joe, Dear Admissions Officer, etc.
- Be as polite and respectful in an e-mail as you would in a face-to-face meeting or telephone conversation.
- Do not use all lowercase or all uppercase letters in an e-mail.

Lowercase is difficult to read and uppercase feels as though you are shouting.

- Do not use "IMPORTANT INFORMATION!!!!!" OR "PLEASE READ!" as subjects for your e-mails. These are commonly used for junk e-mail or viruses.
- "Reply All" is a very good tool, but it is widely misused. If you have four or five recipients, then Reply All is a good thing, but only if all recipients need to have the information.
- Receiving an email with a few names on it precludes that all names listed need the information (unless stated otherwise in the e-mail). When you reply, be sure to include all names from the original email.
- The out of office message is a very good thing. If you are going to be away from the office, it can be a major timesaver for folks who are trying to reach you. The out of office system response only goes out once per sender and not as a reply to all. See above.
- Message recall doesn't work. Except in a few corporate e-mail systems, once you press "send," your message is gone. By broadcasting "Sally Smith would like to recall this message," you are telling your recipients that, not only do you not know how to compose an e-mail, but you also may not know how e-mail works. Also, message recall is confusing to your recipients.
- The proper thing to do is to send another immediately with the message, "Please delete. Sent in error. Thank you."
- Another take: A message announcing that a sender wants to recall their e-mail is probably the quickest way to ensure it gets read right away by recipients.
- Do not post inappropriate or offensive messages about anyone on any website. What goes around will come back around to bite you.
- Forget not the power of the pen: Anyone can dash off an e-mail as a thank you. It takes a special person to pick up the pen to send a simple thank you note or a handwritten greeting. Taking the time to handwrite a note and put an attractive postage stamp on it speaks volumes about your good class and style, and it will set you apart from the masses in the eyes of the receiver.

A word about type and font for your electronic messages. Just because you are typing rather than writing, that does not give you the right to shout your words or practice alphabetic purgatory. Properly punctuate your messages. All capital letters send the signal that you are shouting to your intended recipient. This is considered rude and disrespectful. Stop littering the information superhighway with these sorts of things. Your family and friends may be too polite to call you on it. But don't call a grammatical time-out by writingwithoutproperspacingspellingandpunctuation. English is English. Practice it on your computer. Better yet, write a handwritten note. Your recipient will be grateful.

Laptops and Notebooks

Be cautious of using a laptop computer in your business meeting. Are they handy? Yes. Couldn't live without yours? Probably not. Just be aware that even as quiet as they are, they still make clicking noises that can be distracting to the speaker or the business at hand. Use your good judgment about using or not using your faithful laptop. Engage the mute button. Your notebook computer can be equally obtrusive if you use your fingernails (rather than finger pads) to type.

Automated Teller Machines

Automated teller machines are a marvelous invention. How did we ever get on without them? Discreetly use the following tips for safe use of your favorite ATM:

- Be alert and aware of your surroundings.
- Use ATMs in populated, well-lighted areas.
- Avoid going to an ATM alone if possible.
- Space is needed: If someone is in front of you, give them three to five feet of space for their comfort and safety and yours.
- Remove your ATM receipt from the machine and keep it in a safe place.
- Have your ATM card ready before your approach the ATM.
- Never record your ATM PIN on anything in your purse or wallet.
- Cancel your transaction and leave if your see anyone or anything

that looks suspicious.

- If you are followed after making an ATM transaction, go immediately to a safe location and call the police.
- Consider signing up for an electronic media safety system to ensure your information stays safe.

Drive-Up ATMs
- Keep your auto running while operating the ATM.
- Pull up close to the ATM.
- Remain in the car with the doors locked.

Protect Your Identity

- Place your Social Security number only on official documents that require it. Do not record the number on anything in your wallet, briefcase or purse. Store the original in a bank safety box.
- Never leave your purse or wallet in view in an unattended, unlocked or locked, car.
- Do not give out financial information over the telephone or electronic media unless you initiated the call and you know the recipient.
- Be cautious when sending financial information via the Internet. Use only secure sites.
- Promptly remove mail from your mailboxes and deposit outgoing mail that contains account numbers in secured mail drops or at the post office.
- When you are ready to discard them, shred all documents such as checks, applications and statements that contain account information.
- Check bank and credit card statements every month for accuracy.
- Review your credit report diligently. Many banks and credit card companies now have fraud alert folks who will contact you immediately should there be suspicious activity on your account.

A few years back, radical Brazilian educator Paulo Freire was attending a conference of Midwestern political activists and heard over and over about how overwhelmed people felt about the duties they faced each day. Finally, he stood up, and in slow, heavily accented English he declared, "We are bigger than our schedules." The audience roared with applause.

Decorum in a Digital Age

"Change in etiquette usually comes slowly, just as changes come slowly in the dictionary," wrote Amy Vanderbilt in her seminal book on manners published more than half a century ago. Change usually comes slowly, but in looking at the etiquette of public spaces today, one finds everywhere great change occurring at breakneck speed.

Technology has snarled the lines between public and private spaces. Cellphones make our most intimate conversations available to anyone within earshot, while bright colored headphones create an oasis of pure solitude even in the midst of the most dynamic crowd.

The social state of equal rights for all things electronic has led to a revolution of sorts for art lovers. The desire to make art more accessible has also profoundly changed how we expect people to behave in social spaces once governed by complex, elaborate rules. The rules are in place so the art can be preserved yet enjoyed, but are the rules changing? Perhaps we are entering a new age of extreme individualism, in which the very idea of enjoying public space together is giving way to something more chaotic.

Silence and reverence was once prized in many public spaces, including libraries, museums and concert halls. Today, the vibrancy of many of those spaces today is measured by voices, laughter and general hullabaloo.

Etiquette and manners are also remarkably resilient, reforming in new ways in an ebb and flow kind of way, to adjust to the pattern of life we live today. Since the beginning of time, people have stepped out of the way when they witness someone taking a photograph with a camera. We don't want to disrupt the photograph so is taking a selfie in a museum any different?

We have significant forces shaping our planet today. We are living in increasingly crowded spaces and a growing collection of electronic devices.

Some have said there is no world without art. For our theaters, museums, as well as in nightclubs, buses and commuter trains and libraries and all of the spaces we share as a public, are there any "should's" or "have to's" that govern our behavior when we are in public? Maybe not but there are a few themes.

The correlation between the intensity and rarity of the artistic experience deserves our respect. Dance and live music cannot be reproduced in our homes, on the stereo or on the television. There is something different about seeing it in person. When we witness dance or music in all of its raw glory in the flesh, it changes us. We are completely absorbed. There is something fundamental about paying homage to the art form by honoring it through reverence of silence and gratitude.

As a member of the audience of any art experience, we are duty bound to respect the artistic form being presented to us. We also have an obligation to respect the individual rights of those around us in the theatre to not take away from their experience by lighting up the dark with our electronic device.

ELECTRO**NICE**TIQUETTE

Notice the important four letter word in the middle of "electro**nice**tiquette."

Let's be nice. Because, in the end, empathy and a light-hearted spirit will always yield a better art experience for everyone.

People first, then technology.

Telephone Manners

Presenting a professional and polished image, both in person and on the telephone, is important in the business world. Talking to customers over the telephone and helping them feel well informed and appreciated is essential.

The telephone is often the first point of contact a potential customer may have with a company so it is important the initial call make a good impression with them. In specific telephone-related positions such as sales, marketing, customer service, etc., you need to adapt to different styles and techniques, such as being able to handle a difficult customer or a complaint call, or be persuasive enough to encourage people to buy a product or service from you.

In general, if you are friendly, courteous, helpful and well-mannered, answering the telephone should not be an issue at all. Whether you are the executive, farmer, front-office receptionist or executive secretary, the following telephone tips should always be followed.

1. Speak clearly and slowly. State your name at the beginning. Ask a

pleasantry: How are you? Has spring arrived yet at your place? etc. Then state the reason for your call. Pause briefly between sentences. Don't speak so quickly that the listener asks you to repeat yourself. The listener cannot see your face or body language, therefore, taking the time to speak clearly, slowly and in a cheerful, professional voice is important.

2. Use your normal tone of voice when answering a call. If you have a tendency to speak loud or shout, avoid doing so on the telephone. Sometimes, when we are excited or nervous, our voice may get louder or faster. Take a deep breath and get your nerves under control.

3. Do not eat or drink when you are talking on the telephone. Break time or lunchtime is the time to drink and eat.

4. Do not use slang words, vulgarity or misuse your verb tenses.

5. Respond clearly with "yes" or "no" when speaking. Never use curse words. Finish each word you say: "going" rather than "goin'" Avoid saying words such as "yeah," "whatever," "no problem," etc.

6. Address the caller by their title i.e., "Good morning Mr. Jones," "Good afternoon Ms. White." Never address an unfamiliar caller by their first name, unless the caller gives you permission to do so. See the Names Manners section for further information.

7. Listen carefully to what the caller has to say. The ability to listen is a learned skill. Even if the caller is upset or angry, still listen. When the caller is finished speaking, say, "Is there anything else I need to know? I'm sorry you are upset. I am here to help. Let me make sure I understand what is going on." Repeat back to the caller what has just been said to verify that you heard everything correctly.

8. It is always a good habit to repeat the information back to the customer when you are taking a message. Verify that you have heard and transcribed the message accurately.

9. Be patient and helpful. Make the caller a priority. Listen to what they have to say. If needed, refer them to the appropriate resource.

10. Always ask permission of the caller before putting them on hold. If you are responsible for answering multiple calls at once, always ask the caller politely if you may put them on hold. People dislike being

put on hold, but sometimes the nature of the work is just that way.

11. After putting someone on hold, you may find that it is going to take longer to rectify the situation than anticipated. You then need to go back to the caller every minute or so and keep them updated. It might sound something like, "We are working on this, but it is taking a bit longer than we thought it would. Would you like to still hold on?" Repeat this every few minutes until the situation is resolved or the customer decides to call back at another time. Offer to call the customer back once the problem has been resolved.

12. The caller could have already waited several minutes before getting through to you and may become annoyed should you try to pass them on to someone else. Make every effort to not leave someone hanging on hold for more than a few minutes.

13. Give 100 percent to each call. Do not get distracted by people around you. If someone tries to interrupt you while you are on a call, politely remind them that you are on a customer call and that you will be with them as soon as you can.

14. Be prepared. Always have a pen and pad handy should you need to take down notes from the call. Do not make a caller wait for you to get your things in order. Have them ready and beside the telephone.

15. Take notes on a computer.

16. I find it handy to have a spiral notebook next to the telephone, always at the ready if I need or want to make notes on a call. Keep the notebook once it is filled. You can then refer back to it if needed to refresh your memory on the details of a recent call.

Making Telephone Calls

We all have days when we feel a bit off, crabby, too busy, too stressed or simply not in the mood for the work ahead of us. However, when a customer calls, the last thing they need to hear is someone complaining or using a surly voice. They also do not want to get the feeling they have become a bother by calling.

It is important to be upbeat and positive when answering the telephone. Always greet the caller with a smile in your voice. Use the time of day and your organization's name along with your name when you answer the phone. An example might be, "Good morning, Agri Manners, Patricia speaking. How may I help you?" Then stop and let the caller speak. Use your name unless your organization has a policy of not using names.

Here are some additional tips when you initiate a call:

1. Always identify yourself properly by stating your name. When calling a customer, whether in person or when leaving a message, always identify yourself by providing your name, company name and contact telephone number.

   For example, "Good afternoon. This is Tom from Agri Manners. Could you give me a call please? My telephone number is 123-456-1212. Again, this is Tom from Agri Manners. My telephone number is 1-2-3-4-5-6-1-2-1-2. Thank you."

   Note that a space is given between each number when you repeat it the final time. It is much easier for the person on the other end when they have to write down the phone number.

   How many times have we listened to voicemails that have sounded garbled or are spoken so quickly the message is unintelligible? Perhaps the caller speaks in a very soft voice. Don't go there. Slow down and be more methodical about leaving your voicemail. It does not take much more time, and the receiving person will be grateful for your clear and courteous voicemail.

2. Do not give any other information on the voicemail. Spouting off invoice or order numbers tends to take too long and makes it difficult for the person receiving the voicemail to get everything written down properly. Keep it simple and just give your telephone number and extension, if needed. You can always refer to the invoice numbers, etc. when you are talking with the person on the telephone.

3. Be mindful of confidential information when leaving messages. Also, be aware of people around you while talking on the phone. Practice discretion. You don't want to share information with some unscrupulous person who might take down personal information.

4. If you need to leave the message for another colleague, do so as soon as possible while the call is still fresh in your mind.

Good manners can make the difference in building a business, and great manners will set you apart. If you are stressed or hurried, it is easy to have everything pile up, causing you to not observe the basics of telephone etiquette. Take each message in the order in which it was received and work your way through them. If you take a deep breath before you make the call, good manners and patience can get you the results you want in an easier and quicker way.

Some quick tips to brush up on your telephone manners:

Telephone strategy
- Treat the call as if it were a meeting. Have a purpose, and an agenda.
- At the beginning ask the other person if it is okay to talk now.
- Write out a script if needed.
- Be prompt when answering the telephone. Generally speaking, answer the phone before five rings.
- Decide what to do if someone answers other than the person you are calling. Would you prefer to leave a message, go to voicemail, or call back later? Decide this before you make the call.
- Speak more slowly when making a call or leaving a voice message, especially if you have a pronounced regional accent. Important details can be overlooked when you speak too quickly. Slow down.
- If you're on a scheduled call, be at your desk at least five minutes before the appointed time. Have all of the necessary paperwork ready.
- Learn the first names of the people who answer the phones at the numbers you call often. Speak in a friendly way to them. Over time, you may be become acquainted enough to send them a card or gift on their birthday or over the holidays.
- The person who initiated the call is the person who is responsible for ending it. Be respective of other people's time.
- Always end the call in a pleasant way. Recap what has been discussed. Review next steps to be taken. It is always a good practice to let the caller say good bye before you do.

Do's and don'ts for Telephone Calls

- Don't type or shuffle papers while you're on the phone. It suggests you have something to do that is more important than the caller to whom you are talking. This is disrespectful to the caller. Plus, it is annoying for the caller to hear.
- If you need to put the telephone down, do it gently to spare your caller's ear. Let the caller know you are going to put the phone down.
- Whatever you do, do not chew gum. Rid your mouth of food, gum, cough drops, or candy before talking on the phone. The receiver amplifies your noise.
- If you feel a sneeze or cough coming on, say, "Pardon me," then turn your head and cover your mouth and the receiver.
- Ask their permission before putting them on speaker phone.
- Speak directly into the receiver. Don't entomb it in your shoulder.
- Mind the time of day. If you are a business that has customers from coast to coast, be mindful of the differences in time zones. 4 p.m. for you might be 5 p.m. for someone else.
- If you dial the wrong number, explain yourself and verify the phone number so you don't repeat the mistake. Use a kind voice when doing so. Apologize for disturbing the person by calling. Don't just hang up. That is sophomoric and rude.
- If you are the caller, and the telephone rings at least five times with no one answering, chances are the person is not available to talk.
- Cut down on the background noise when taking or making a call. Radios, TVs and computer noises can be distracting over the phone.
- Never make outgoing calls of a personal nature from your organization's phone unless your employer has given you permission you may do so. Make sure you dissuade relatives and friends from calling you at work. After all, you are at work to work.

Taking telephone messages

- Record the time and date the call came in.
- Verify the caller's name, organization name and telephone number.
- Initial the message, so if the person who received the message has any

questions, they can contact you.

- Get a short statement about the caller's intent.
- Make sure you deliver the completed telephone message to the proper person for whom it is intended.

Time Manners: Fashionably Late or Strict Time?

What are time manners?

My father never used an alarm clock. Ever. It was the most amazing thing. He would arise at 5 a.m., year-round, to start his day. Though his career was that of an agricultural banker, the farmer in him never left. "If you haven't got half a day's work done by 9 a.m., then the day is wasted," he would declare.

I remember one particularly snowy winter's day when he was dressed and out the door by 5 a.m. I found out later that he had gone to the bank to shovel the snow away from all the sidewalks surrounding the bank. He then returned home, showered, ate breakfast and was back at his bank desk by 7:05 a.m.

Shoveling the snow was not necessarily in his job description. He was an officer in the bank. When I inquired after this, he simply stated, "It is the right thing to do. One doesn't want people to get hurt by falling." I not only was given Dad's sense of timeliness, but also his ironclad work ethic. It is both a blessing and a curse at times, but mostly a blessing.

Running Late

All across the country, people are running late. They are meeting friends, hosting a party, tailgating at the game, or going to dinner at someone's home, and they are perpetually late. Ad infinitum.

If you are the host, how do you handle it if guests are late? In the old days, if you were late, the meal started without you. People who had servants were even afraid to come late to dinner in their own homes. In addition, the old days dictated that the equipment of one's kitchen not be shown to the guests. This meaning the pan, bowl and beaters used to smash the mashed potatoes.

These days, we entertain in our kitchens and take pride in our gleaming, up-to-date gadgets. We want our guests to see them. Today, we pretend as though it doesn't matter if our guests are late, but deep down, we are offended and hurt. Yet we cannot find the courage to say anything to the latecomer.

- Be decisive at the invitation stage. Make the time be the center part of the invite. "Could you please be here at 7 p.m. sharp, as so-and-so has an early flight tomorrow?" "Dinner will be served at 7 p.m." In other words, be specific.
- At the point of invitation, assign guests a task to do once they arrive at the party. "I really need some help with the carving of the turkey. Could you be here at 6 p.m. to assist?"
- If you are meeting up somewhere with friends, be on time. With some folks, lateness is a symptom of unreliability and overall selfishness. Think twice if you want to spend your time waiting on someone who is perpetually late.
- If people are coming to your house and they are late, start without them. Why not? It is up to you whether or not you offer to recap any missed courses.
- Don't be afraid to talk about the lateness during the course of conversation. You've heard of the elephant in the room. Amazingly, even when it is the point of conversation, people still may not get it. Be patient with them. Remember that you have the option of not inviting them again.

If you are truly running late because the baby got sick or your boss had you working on a project later than usual these are legitimate reasons. Running late because you are getting your nails done is not a legitimate reason. There are times when all of us may be running late. There is an easy solution.

Call someone to let them know that you will be late, or send a text message. Give an approximate time of when you may arrive. People are generally okay if they know that you are okay and on your way.

With nearly every soul in America in the possession of a cellphone these days, there really is no reason why you cannot call or text. It takes two minutes and saves hours of heartache and distress on the part of your host. Not to mention friendships.

Late Guests
- If the invitation says 7 to 9 a.m. or 6 to 10 p.m., that is what it means.

If you cannot stay the entire time, you need to stay for at least an hour. Otherwise, your hosts will think you ambivalent at best.

- If you are double-booked for a particular evening, let your hosts know ahead of time that you will need to leave early. Give an approximate time of when you will need to leave.
- Don't feel guilty about leaving. It is not unreasonable to go home at, say, 10 p.m. on a weeknight or 11 p.m. on a Saturday. Say your good-byes, say your thank yous and leave.

Late Hosts

Sometimes it is the hosts that are late. I discovered this when, some years ago, upon arriving at my friend Sue's house for a dinner party, she declared, "I've just arrived home from the market."

Sigh.

- On weekdays, the host needs to have dinner ready by 7:30 or 8 p.m. at the latest so that guests may leave by 10 or 10:30 p.m. On Saturdays, it should be 8:30 or 9 p.m. at the latest. Of course, the time frame is up to the hosts.
- Prepare as much as you can the day before.
- If you are desperate or even not, utilize those fancy prepare at home dinners. My friend, Mary, has been known to purchase these gourmet meals, then carefully scoop them into her own serving dishes and take the credit. Serving dishes I am okay with, taking the credit, well, perhaps not so much.
- People with children or work commitments the next day cannot be kept late. Remember, those folks will arise, bleary-eyed, at 5 a.m. whether they choose to or not.

Lateness in Business

- Being late for anything in business is a no-no. By your being late, you are stealing time from someone else. Don't do it.
- Never, ever be late for an interview. Under any circumstances. For an interview, you need to arrive between 10 and 15 minutes before the start of the interview.

- It is always better to arrive early than late. Always.

Time manners will be with us always. Get used to it. If need be, set your clocks ahead by 15 minutes. This will ensure that you will be on time.

"Punctuality is not only a duty, but is also a part of good manners;
it is favorable to fortune, reputation, influence, and usefulness; a little attention and
energy will form the habit, so as to make it easy and delightful."
—Charles Simmons, Author

Tipping Manners

In the United States, tipping was not prevalent until after the Civil War. Even then, it was considered a holdover from Europe and was not overly popular. People would put out a few coins at the beginning of the meal.

The precise origin of tipping is uncertain, but it is commonly traced to Tudor England. By the 17th century, overnight guests staying in private homes would offer a sum of money to the hosts' servants. Not long after, customers began tipping in London coffee and tea houses and other establishments.

Samuel Johnson was an English writer who made lasting contributions to English literature as a poet, essayist, moralist, literary critic, biographer, editor and lexicographer. Johnson's "A Dictionary of the English Language" was published in 1755. One institution frequented by Johnson had a coin bowl printed with the words "To insure promptitude." The word "tip" is thought to be an acronym for this phrase.

Tipping began as a practice of the aristocrats and it quickly spread among the upper classes of Europe. From the beginning, tipping has brought about feelings of anxiety and resentment. In the mid 1800s, the Scottish writer Thomas Carlyle, after leaving the Bell Inn, complained, "The dirty scrub of a waiter grumbled about his allowance, which I reckoned liberal. I added sixpence to it, and [he] produced a bow which I was near rewarding with a kick."

Following the Civil War, Americans began traveling to Europe in large numbers. They brought home with them the tipping phenomenon to show their sophistication. As tipping spread, book publisher William Scott wrote his 1916 anti-tipping screed, "The Itching Palm." "Tipping, and the aristocratic idea is exemplifies, is what we left Europe to escape," Scott wrote. Another periodical of the same era condemned tipping for creating a class of workers who relied on "fawning for favors."

In 1904, the Anti-Tipping Society of America was founded in Georgia. Its 100,000 members signed pledges not to tip for one year. Traveling salesman opposed the tipping practice, as did many labor unions. In 1909, Washington state became the first of six states to pass anti-tipping laws, but tipping persisted. The new laws were rarely enforced and, when they were, they did not hold up in court. By 1926, every anti-tipping law had been repealed.

As many international travelers know, one doesn't tip servers in many other countries around the world, where the servers are more likely to be paid a living wage. This has led some U.S. restaurants to adopt a similar practice.

The average tip has increased over the decades. The 10 percent tip that was the average in the 1940s has increased to a standard 15 percent. Most Americans — 80 percent — say they prefer tipping to paying a service fee, primarily because they believe tipping provides an incentive for good service according to a recent Zagat survey. Michael Lynn, a Cornell University professor of consumer behavior and marketing, says the Zagat survey showed there is little correlation between good tipping and good service.

Economists have struggled to explain the phenomenon of tipping. Why do we tip at all since the bill is presented at the end of a meal and cannot retroactively improve the service received? In practice, most people do tip because of social expectations, even when they've had less than stellar service.

The need to pay a tip, psychologically, is for the guilt encompassed in the unequal relationship we have between patron and waiter. We cannot ignore it. Ego also plays a part, especially when it comes to over tipping. It makes us feel good to help out someone by giving them a tip.

The single most important factor in determining the amount of a tip is the size of the final bill. Diners will generally give a similar percentage of tip no matter the quality of service or the setting. They do so largely because it is expected and people dislike social disapproval. It is somewhat embarrassing to have another individual wait on us, so we tend to want to give a tip to help ourselves feel better about this unequal relationship.

Most Americans prefer that waiters be paid higher wages instead of tips. This has already been shown to be true at fast-food restaurants and private clubs where tipping is not allowed. Some full-service restaurants add on a full-service charge for groups of six or more diners.

Since more people are contributing to the check, the responsibilities of the waiter are divided among them. In some cases, if diners take offense at the service charge, then the management may remove the charge. In most cases, the customers' issues are not about the lack of service, but more about the loss of control they feel at not being able to pay a tip.

If you do not tip a waiter because of bad service, you might be penalizing them for something they had no control over, such as a backed-up kitchen. Many restaurants pool tips, and servers give a share of their tips to busboys and bartenders, and sometimes even the dishwashers and hosts. Some restaurants chains electronically track and report tips for tax purposes and employees may be taxed on the full amount of the night's tips, even though they have to distribute a portion of it to other staff members.

The Motivational Effect

Recently, this author dined in a restaurant in Kansas City where, upon receiving the check for the meal, noted a new phrase printed on the final bill. "Staff fairly compensated." This was a new thing. I gently inquired of my waiter if his was a salaried position. "Why, yes," he said. "How did you know?" I pointed to the new phrase. He smiled. I signed the bill, then handed him a $5 bill, so I ended up tipping him anyway.

As more restaurants eliminate tipping and budget instead for salaries, the tipping issues will continue to surface. Tips don't necessarily motivate waiters to perform better. Tipping is too ingrained in the human psyche for us to do away with it completely. It helps us as patrons feel better.

General Guidelines for Holiday Tipping

The holiday season is the traditional time to say, "Thank you" and "I appreciate the work you do for me" to those who have provided services to you throughout the year. One of the best ways to express appreciation is through a handwritten note, which needs to accompany the tip.

Whether and how much to tip varies widely, depending upon:

- The quality and frequency of the service

- Your relationship with the service provider
- Where you live (amounts are usually higher in larger cities)
- How long you have worked together
- Your budget
- Regional customs and social expectations

If you tip regularly at the time of service, then you may forgo or give a more modest holiday tip. Always include your child in gift decisions for teachers, day care providers, nannies and babysitters.

Every situation is different, but following are some general guidelines. Remember to let common sense, individual circumstances and the holiday spirit be your guide. What to give is always an individual decision.

Babysitter, regular: One evening's pay, plus a small gift from your child.

Child's teacher: Check your school's policy first. Give a gift, not cash. Consider gift certificates to a bookstore, restaurant or a gourmet food item.

Day care provider: $25-$70 each and/or a small gift from your child for the providers who give direct care to your child(ren).

Nail/hair stylist: The cost of one regular salon visit.

Dog walker: An extra week's pay and/or a gift.

Fitness trainer: Up to the cost of one session.

Housekeeper/cleaner: Up to an extra week's pay and/or a gift.

Letter carriers: U.S. government regulations permit carriers to accept gifts worth up to $20 per occasion but not cash.

Live-in help e.g., nanny, housekeeper, and butler: One week's to one month's salary based on tenure and customs in your area, plus a personal gift.

Newspaper carrier: $10-$30.

Pet groomer: If the same person grooms your pet all year, up to one session's fee and/or a gift.

Yard and garden worker: $20-$50.

Rudeness in Traveling and Moving Around Life

There are many things that go on in and around airports, train stations and other domains where people congregate out of necessity. Usually, a few people have taken it upon themselves to make it more difficult for the rest of us decent, regular folks by doing something harmful or potentially harmful.

As a result, airports and other travel hubs are, unfortunately, not the pleasant places they used to be.

Consider the following examples of rudeness in traveling and moving:

- People who block the baggage claim area in the airport.
- People who bring stinky food on the airplane and usually any fast food is stinky.
- Rushing off the plane without waiting for the person(s) in front of you to move first.
- People who block the aisles during flights.
- Loud people: adults and/or children.
- Crying babies on an airplane.
- People who don't understand the rules of moving walkways: stand right and walk left.
- Overpriced food courts in airports.
- Snoring adults.
- People who do personal grooming in a public traveling place.
- People who charge toward the lavatory door as soon as it opens, blocking the person who is exiting.
- Flight attendants with bad breath or bad manners.
- People who recline their seats so much that it bumps into your leg.
- People who get up and walk around after the pilot tells them not to.
- People who disrupt the flow of folks moving off the airplane because they stop to attend to their children, baggage, etc.
- People who tailgate your automobile as you are driving the speed limit.
- Automobile drivers who do not stop when the stop arm is out on a school bus. This is more than just rude, it's also against the law.
- People who do not pull over for police or emergency vehicles.
- People who do not take responsibility for the car accident they cause.
- People who are not respectful of slower moving farm equipment.

17 Tips to Help You Navigate from Point A to Point B
1. Be on time. Show up at the airport on time. Even better, be there early.

It is a much better scenario for you if you can wait at the appropriate gate to board your flight. It never works to try to hurry through rush-hour traffic at the last minute. Every stoplight will seem longer than usual.

2. **Be prepared.** Have your photo ID and ticket/boarding pass ready to present to the luggage handlers and security officers. If possible, print out your boarding pass ahead of time. You can also pull up your boarding pass on your smartphone. This is excellent. If you have a carry-on bag, make sure you are ready to put it on the security conveyor belt. Put your liquids in a see-through bag in a convenient place so you can remove it.

3. **Say hello to the TSA folks and other airline folks.** Presenting yourself as a friendly and likeable person always helps. There are enough cranky people in the world. Stand out from the crowd and say hello and thank them for their service. A smile back is guaranteed.

4. **Dress well.** I always dress up a bit to travel. I've noticed I receive more respect from the service providers and fellow passengers. A nice skirt and blazer, and nice shoes. A sportcoat and trousers with a starched shirt. There are enough people who dress down to travel. Dressing up a bit always helps. It shows that you are a caring and respectful person to yourself and, chances are, you are that way to others as well. People will notice.

5. **Don't complain (part 1).** There are enough people complaining. Traveling is not easy, and it takes a toll on all of us, but we are all in the same scenario. If you have a legitimate complaint, then follow the proper channels to register your complaint.

6. **Don't complain (part 2).** Standing in line is usually not a pleasant experience, but it doesn't help any to grumble and grouse about it. It certainly doesn't help the people around you. Stay aware of what is going on around you, and move forward in the line as the space becomes available.

7. **Don't crowd others.** Be respectful of others' personal spaces when standing in line or anywhere else at the airport.

8. **Pay attention.** Be aware of everything going on around you at all times. This is not only important for etiquette purposes, but it is a safety measure as well. When the security officer says something, listen carefully, answer all questions to the best of your ability and follow instructions.

9. **Never be contemptuous or arrogant.** Always respect airline and

airport personnel. They have important jobs to do and that shouldn't include having to deal with a disrespectful passenger. You might have heard about a TSA person doing something wrong, but that is probably not the norm. Most of them are doing the best job they can.

10. **Stay close to your belongings.** If you leave an item while going to the washroom or grabbing a sandwich, you're likely to have it confiscated by security. Given the world we live in today, have your belongings at your side at all times.

11. **Be polite at all times.** Planes are often booked at maximum capacity, which means airports are often crowded, especially the bigger airports. There is no reason to speak to anyone in harsh tones or with foul language. Always use good manners when interacting with other passengers and the people who are there to serve you. Kind words will make your trip much more pleasant than harsh words.

12. **Bring earplugs, ear buds or headphones** to block out noise.

13. **Make your child behave.** Before you leave home, review your expectations with your children. They need to be on their best behavior at all times when traveling by air, bus, train etc.

14. **Be careful about cellphone calls.** Because many airports are very busy, talking on your telephone means that everyone around you will be a part of the call. If you have an important call, find as private a place as possible to take/make the call.

15. **Don't get personal.** Chances are you won't know many folks around you. Save personal chatter for another time. Most people are nice, law-abiding citizens but all it takes is one person to mess up your life and make it difficult for everyone else. Don't be the person who stands in the middle of the airport talking loudly on their phone for all to hear. This is annoying for those around you.

16. **Be ready to board.** Keep an eye on the clock so you're ready to go when called. If you need to use the washroom, do it early. Have your boarding pass out or smartphone with your boarding pass showing and ready to hand to the gate agent.

17. **Cover your mouth when you cough or sneeze.**

Chapter Eighteen

Rudeness in Everyday Life and Everyday Manners

The word bacon dates back to the 1500's. In Middle English, Bacoun referred to all pork. During the 17th century, bacon referred only to cured pork. The average American eats 17.9lbs of bacon per year.
Source: www.bacontoday.com

Most people realize that etiquette and good manners are essential to any civilized society. The basis of etiquette is to behave and act in a way that is accepted as gracious and polite in social situations. Good manners can mean the difference between success and failure in many aspects of personal and business life.

Consider the following list of everyday rudeness:

- People who let their dogs bark all day outdoors while they are away.
- Trash thrown out on public or private roads.
- Grabbing a parking spot on which someone else is waiting.
- Crabby clerks.
- Surly clerks not saying "Thank you."
- Clerks saying "Have a nice day" instead of "Thank you." Say "Thank you" first, then "Have a nice day."
- People saying "No problem" instead of "You're welcome."
- People driving too fast through mall parking lots.
- Fans who boo the opposing team in athletic stadiums.
- Drivers who tailgate.
- People who don't pull over for emergency vehicles.
- Folks who do not respect farm equipment being driven on the road.
- Folks who are critical of anything because they don't understand it.
- People who do not clean up after themselves.
- People who don't respect animals.
- Not helping an elderly person or any person when help is needed.
- Servers who are not well groomed.
- Narcissistic co-workers.
- Shrill and loud telephone rings.
- People who don't return calls.
- Unsupervised children in nice restaurants.
- Infants in formal restaurants.
- Offensive, anonymous Internet messages.
- People who misrepresent themselves.
- Blaring stereos.
- Bullying in any form.

- Fireworks at night being set off in residential areas where fireworks are illegal.
- Disrespect for law enforcement officers.
- People who think the laws are not made for them.
- Nosy neighbors.
- People who are not neighborly.
- Customers who do not show appreciation.
- People who misrepresent the authority they've been given.
- Criminals who disrespect the law.
- People who don't bathe or shower often enough.
- Stressed-out parents reprimanding their children in public.
- Partners who are not honest.
- People who spew out profanity and poisonous words.
- Dishonesty in general.
- Electronic thievery.
- People who take advantage of other people.
- Bosses who have forgotten how to be caring human beings.
- People who promise to do something, then don't.
- People who don't return their grocery cart to the proper location.
- Belching out loud.
- Coughing without covering your mouth.
- Using your sleeve as a napkin.
- Wearing a cap or hat inside a church, restaurant or public places of decorum and honor.
- Talking on your cellphone while checking out at the cashier's desk.
- Talking loudly on a cellphone while in a public place.
- Using a cellphone in your hand while driving.
- Texting while driving, which can be unlawful.
- Using words in a text message or electronic message that you would not use in person.
- The list goes on and on…

The place to start with manners and etiquette is in your home with family. Your spouse, children, in-laws and other extended family members will all respond better when you have consistent good manners on a daily basis.

Family members also respond better when "please" and "thank you" are used, than when orders are barked out in a cross voice that creates tension. Cooperation, give and take, and mutual respect all come easier when the practice of manners has a permanent place in the home. Children who are taught to respect their parents and have good manners take those lessons with them as they move into adulthood and into their own independent lives.

General etiquette rules for family members:
- Respect each other's personal space.
- Respect each other's belongings.
- Don't interrupt when someone else is talking.
- Be on time for dinner.
- Never open a family member's mail.
- Say "Please" and "Thank you" consistently and genuinely.
- Don't text or talk on your cellphone during a family meal.
- Practice good conversational skills in the presence of family and friends.
- Be interested in family member's activities. Ask questions. Listen.
- Do not call family members by disrespectful names, even in an attempt at humor.
- Chew with your mouth closed.
- If you make a mess, clean it up.
- Ask before you borrow something.
- If you borrow something, return it in better shape than when you initially borrowed it.
- Pick up after yourself.
- Respect Mom and Dad and do what they ask.

Social Etiquette

Social etiquette involves how you behave while in public with friends and strangers, whether you are at someone's home or in a public restaurant. Treat your friends and neighbors with respect, and you are more likely to remain on their lists of people they trust, care about and invite to parties. It is the neighborly thing to do.

Basic social etiquette rules:
- Always be on time for dates and get-togethers. Showing up late is rude and shows a lack of respect for other people's time.
- Make eye contact when you are speaking with someone.
- Never interrupt the other person.
- Give and receive compliments graciously.
- Honor thyself. Treat yourself with respect and honor.
- Refuse to gossip with and about friends. After all, if you share gossip with someone, that person will wonder what you are saying behind their back.
- Hold doors for everyone, including the elderly, physically challenged and parents with young children.
- When you are invited to a party, don't show up empty handed. Bring a host or hostess gift.
- If you are sick and contagious, let the other person know. It is generally best to postpone your plans and reschedule after you are better, since it is rude to knowingly expose your friends to illness.
- Pay your fair share when you are with a friend or group. If you take advantage of your friends, they may not invite you again, or want to be your friend any more.
- Show kindness to someone who needs a friend.

Do the right thing, even/especially when you think others aren't looking.

"Don't worry when you are not recognized, but strive to be worthy of recognition."
—Abraham Lincoln

Everyday Manners

There are times in daily living when you need to make a choice of whether to use good manners or be a boorish clod. When one chooses to be boorish, it implies rudeness of manner due to insensitivity to others' feelings.

A close sister to boorish is churlish, which means surliness, unresponsiveness and ungraciousness, along with stupidity. Surely you do not want to be known as a boorish, churlish individual?

For the sake of humanity and good civility, always take the high road and be a respectful lady or gentleman. There will be situations that will be very trying and difficult. Don't cave in and let your emotions get the best of you. Take a step back. Be honorable to yourself and to others, and do the right thing by being respectful and dignified with your response.

Keep in mind that if you are weary, tired or hungry, it is going to be harder for you to be strong and respectful. Take good care of yourself and know when it is time to rest and nourish yourself. When you lay your head on the pillow at night, you want to be able to say, "I did the best I could today given the circumstances I had."

For everyday manners, here are some tips:
1. Notice people.

If you step outside your house during the day, you're likely to encounter people, so try to be friendly. Pay attention. Say hello.

Even on dark days when everything seems to be going miserably wrong, sharing a smile has the potential to lift your mood as well as the mood of the person you are greeting. Offer a greeting, and you might brighten someone's day as well as your own.

Certain words carry a remarkable amount of power when you take the time and care enough to be polite and courteous to others. Add "hello," "please," "thank you," "you're welcome" and "excuse me" or "pardon me" to your daily vocabulary. Make these words and the actions that go with them so much a part of your life that it seems to come natural to you. As a result, you may find others responding with a shared kindness and respect in return.

2. Always be mindful of the clock.

There is an old saying that goes something like, "He was born late." It is tongue-in-cheek, but sometimes one wonders if it isn't true. There are few things more annoying in life than someone who is always late: late to church, late to work, late to appointments, etc.

The reality of it is that, by being late, you are stealing time from someone else and that is not fair to them. When someone has gone to the work and effort of preparing a meeting, planning an event, etc., you need to respect the people and the work involved enough to show up on time or a bit early. We are not talking about the times in life when something unexpected makes you late. If something unfortunate happens to you, then make a phone call to them or send a text you are running late. For regular day-to-day activities, you need to be on time.

Unlike my Dad, I do need an alarm clock sometimes, but I set it to what I call "Bud Time." My Dad's nickname was "Bud." The actual time of the clock is set 15 minutes ahead of what the actual time is. When the alarm goes off, I am up 15 minutes ahead of time, which often works to keep me moving so I won't be late. You may want to give "Bud Time" a try.

3. Be the first to help.

The daily rhythm of life provides many everyday opportunities for you to help someone else out. Often, it is all a matter of paying attention and being aware. If you see someone whose arms are overloaded with packages, or someone who is struggling to carry something, help them out. Open the door for them. Step back if a parent with a baby carriage is coming through the door. If you accidentally bump into someone, say "Excuse me." When you see someone cleaning up following a meeting, be the first to offer help.

4. Help in Unexpected Ways

Practice "random acts of helping" on a daily basis. Be aware of what is going on around you as you run your daily errands. Watch for a purposeful way to help someone out.

One way I practice random acts of helping (RAH) is this. I keep an eye out for who is following me as I proceed through checkout lane of the supermarket. Once my items are bagged and paid for, I turn to the person next in line and ask if I can help. I then begin lifting their grocery items from the shopping cart onto the conveyor belt. I do this especially if I see an elderly person or a young mom or dad with children. Without exception, I hear, "Oh, my!" "How nice!" "Thank you so much. That really helps." People are pleasantly surprised and grateful. The altruistic feeling stays with me, which is wonderful. I don't do it because I have to. I do it because I choose to. Help in unexpected ways often and RAH, RAH for you.

5. Show Consideration and Respect To Others

When interacting with other people, show them consideration and respect. Allow others to express their opinions without being argumentative with them. People are entitled to their opinions. If their views differ from yours, that is okay. Such is the nature of life. You can still respect the individual, but differ on issues. Agree to disagree as it were.

Sometimes the differences become great enough that you may need to take a break from them and not interact as much as in the past. This is a decision you will need to make. People grow and change and sometimes outgrow each other.

Respect people's personal space as you would want others to respect yours. This means if you are in line at the ATM, leave enough space between you and the person in front of you so the person feels safe entering their personal codes. There are many common tasks in life in which personal space needs to be honored, not only for respectful reasons, but for security reasons.

When you are in the company of someone of greater authority or who is chronologically older than you, show them the proper respect. Elderly people have more life experience and need to be honored for living it well.

The old saying "If you don't have anything nice to say, then don't say anything" is wise and should be followed in most social situations. This is also true in families. Don't put yourself in a position of having to backtrack or apologize for something that you should not have said in the first place.

6. Tell the truth.

You will rarely go wrong by telling the truth. The world is filled with half-truths, watered-down truths and every variation between. We are not talking about interpretations of the truth here. Rather, we are talking about the sincerity in action, character and deed from you. You cannot control other people and how they react to things. You can only control yourself.

If you always tell the truth, it will be much easier for you in the long run. If you do not tell the truth, then you will have to constantly remember the stories you told to cover the truth. We all learned as children to not do that. It makes too much work and energy to remember accurately. It is much easier to just tell the truth.

Sometimes the truth is difficult to tell because we realize we have done the wrong thing, or we have made a mistake. The key is whether or not your mistake was unintended or malicious. If it is the latter, then this is a different scenario.

Most times, when a nice, respectful person makes a mistake, it is unintentional. An accident. You didn't intend to do it. Because of the difference in intent, it may be a bit harder to tell the truth. But say the hard thing called the truth. Then apologize for your mistake.

7. Let Others Go First

If you can let others go first without uneasiness and discomfort, then do so. This includes walking, standing in line and driving.

A mother with small children will appreciate getting through the checkout lane quickly, particularly if her children are hungry or restless. If a driver needs to move into your lane, and you can let them in without the person behind you rear-ending you, then gesture for the driver to go ahead.

The key is to be cooperative and nice about it. It doesn't help anyone if one driver is tailgating or driving in an erratic way on the interstate. We are all in this together. Let others go first sometimes. It is the nice thing to do.

8. Hold Down the Noise

We live in a world that has become too noisy. It feels like sensory overload most days. Our car locks chirp to notify us they have done their job. Our home appliances have their own musical tune that is played once the cycle is complete. Our gigantic television sets play advertisements at a higher volume than the regular programming. We all have cellphones with enough varied ringtones to make a symphony.

Enough already. Please rethink your auditory footprint.

Keep your cellphone ringer volume as low as possible. Do not be the person who has to be reminded to silence their cellphone in a performance setting. If you have a tendency to speak in a loud voice, take the volume down a few notches. If you work in an office cubicle, be considerate of your fellow officemates by keeping your voice low while talking on the telephone. Don't play your radio too loudly so it bothers your officemates. Don't honk at other drivers unless it's to avoid an accident. Use your automobile turn signals; they make a nice sound. You know where you're going but the other drivers don't.

9. Eat Politely

Whether you brown bag your lunch or you're eating in a restaurant, everyone appreciates good table manners that, hopefully, your parents taught you. Do not place both elbows on the table, then proceed to shovel food into your mouth while you are wearing your cap. Do not talk with your mouth full or partially full. Do not reach in front of people to grab items. Use your napkin. Push your chair back under the table and clean up after yourself.

Formal dinners have more elaborate etiquette rules. If you will be attending a formal dinner, brush up on your table manners. See the section entitled "Table Manners."

10. Remove Your Hat

Everything old is new again. Removing your hat when indoors still holds true. If you have been in the field working or have dirtied your hat because of your job duties, it makes it even more imperative to remove the hat indoors. Who wants to sit next to a table in a restaurant where dirty hats are being worn? Hats should not be worn in restaurants, houses of worship or other public places where it may be offensive to others.

If your hat is large and could obstruct someone's view when at church, theater or other performance, remove it. If you are on a business call or job interview, don't risk being seen as impolite by leaving your hat on. Ladies may wear hats in church and other places, but still be aware that you may be blocking someone's view.

For the gentlemen, when the national anthem is played, it is a sign of respect and honor to stand and remove your hat. Place it over your heart. Do not replace the hat to your head until the national anthem has completed playing.

11. Stand Up Straight

Every day, we are bombarded with work duties, family activities and personal things to do. The list is never ending. Despite the demands of our daily lives, practice good posture throughout the day. This includes standing and sitting. Our shoulders can creep up as the day goes on as a result of the stressors we face. Make a conscious effort to loosen your shoulders and stretch them out occasionally. Readjust your body so you are practicing good posture. You don't want your body to turn into a question mark from having bad posture. See the section on Posture Manners and Good Posture Matters.

12. Send a Thank You Note

Showing gratefulness will always be in style. When someone does something nice for you, or sends you a gift, make the time to thank the person with a handwritten note. Place a pretty stamp on the note. People love to receive thank you notes that have come from thoughtfulness and gratefulness. It's the least you can do for a person who has taken the time to think of you in a kind and respectful way.

13. Send a Birthday Card

There are few things nicer than receiving a birthday card in the mail. It is not a bill. It does not require anything of you other than to enjoy it. What a cheerful and wonderful way to recognize someone you care about. Keep a listing of people who are important to you. Remember them with a birthday card. It will uphold the notion of you as a kind, caring and considerate person.

If you forget to send a card, send an e-mail or text wishing Happy Birthday!

14. Introduce People

When you are in a social situation where you are the only person who knows the other people, take the time to introduce them. It becomes uncomfortable if introductions are not made, especially if you are at a formal dining table. Take the time. People will appreciate it.

15. Tell Someone: You Have Made A Difference in My Life

The older I get, the more I recognize all the people who have made a difference in my life. There are many of them, and I am so grateful to have had them be a part of my life. They have made me into the person I am today. I have made it a point to tell people either in writing or in person they have made a difference in my life and why. This is a wonderful gesture and is altruistic enough to enrich your life and someone else's.

Hello
Please
Thank You
You're Welcome
I'm grateful for you in my life.

Chapter Nineteen

Grammar Manners

"Think what a better world it would be if we all, the whole world, had cookies and milk about three o'clock every afternoon and then lay down on our blankets for a nap."- Senator Barbara Jordan
Source: www.funny-quotes-life.com

The Most Common Mispronounced and Misspelled Words

We communicate through oral and written language. Our written work, whether it be business proposals, correspondence, etc., is a direct reflection on how we are perceived as an agricultural business professional. Every piece of correspondence that goes out with your name on it needs to be well- written, error free and the best you can possibly do as a professional person. Grammar manners is a resource for your use in written language.

Oxford Dictionaries are continually monitoring and researching how language is evolving and changing. The Oxford English Corpus is key to this process and provides evidence on which to base current language usage.

According to the Oxford English Corpus, proper use of the English language is fundamental to how a person communicates with the world. In the seven seconds it takes for us to meet and form an impression of a person, assessments are made based not only on our level of confidence, but also the manner and words we use in our speaking and writing.

English is a global language, and the Oxford English Corpus contains language from all parts of the world, not only from the United Kingdom and the U.S. but also the other English-speaking countries of Ireland, Australia, New Zealand, the Caribbean, Canada, India, Singapore and South Africa.

A "corpus" is a collection of texts of written or spoken languages presented in electronic form. It provides evidence of how language is used in real life situations, The Oxford English Corpus tracks and records the very latest developments in language today. By analyzing the Corpus and using special software, words can be seen in context, as well as new words that are emerging, as well as noticing other trends in usage, spelling and so on.

The Oxford English Corpus is based mainly on material collected from pages on the internet although some printed texts, such as academic journals, have been used to supplement certain subject areas. It represents all types of English, from literary novels and specialist journals to everyday newspapers and magazines to the language of blogs, e-mails and social media.

As the Corpus develops and more text is added, it becomes possible to trace how language changes over time: words becoming more or less common, features spreading from one region to another and the emergence of new meanings. In this case, The Oxford English Corpus, an electronic collection of more than 2.5 billion words, shows the words that are most often misspelled.

Here are the 100 most commonly misspelled words listed in alphabetical order and are spelled correctly.

1. Accommodate	26. Disappear
2. Achieve	27. Disappoint
3. Across	28. Ecstasy
4. Aggressive	29. Embarrass
5. Apparently	30. Environment
6. Appearance	31. Existence
7. Argument	32. Fahrenheit
8. Assassination	33. Familiar
9. Basically	34. Finally
10. Beginning	35. Fluorescent
11. Believe	36. Foreign
12. Bizarre	37. Foreseeable
13. Business	38. Forty
14. Calendar	39. Forward
15. Caribbean	40. Friend
16. Cemetery	41. Further
17. Chauffer	42. Gist
18. Colleague	43. Glamorous
19. Coming	44. Government
20. Committee	45. Guard
21. Completely	46. Happened
22. Conscious	47. Harass
23. Curiosity	48. Honorary
24. Definitely	49. Humorous
25. Dilemma	50. Idiosyncrasy

51. Immediately	76. Really
52. Incidentally	77. Receive
53. Independent	78. Referred
54. Interrupt	79. Religious
55. Irresistible	80. Remember
56. Knowledge	81. Resistance
57. Liaison	82. Sense
58. Lollipop	83. Separate
59. Millennium	84. Siege
60. Neanderthal	85. Successful
61. Necessary	86. Supersede
62. Noticeable	87. Surprise
63. Occasion	88. Tattoo
64. Occurred	89. Tendency
65. Occurrence	90. Therefore
66. Pavilion	91. Threshold
67. Persistent	92. Tomorrow
68. Pharaoh	93. Tongue
69. Piece	94. Truly
70. Politician	95. Unforeseen
71. Portuguese	96. Unfortunately
72. Possession	97. Until
73. Preferred	98. Weird
74. Propaganda	99. Wherever
75. Publicity	100. Which

The Top Ten Most Commonly Mispronounced Words

clothes – The e is silent.

February – You must pronounce both r's: Feb-roo-a-ree, not Feb-yoo-a-ree.

athlete – Make sure there are only two syllables: ath-leet, not ath-a-leet.

probably – This must have three syllables: prob-a-blee, not pra-lee or prob-lee.

colleague – Don't pronounce the final ue.

espresso – There is no x sound: e-spres-o, not ex-pres-o.

Wednesday – The d is silent.

escape – There is no x sound: es-cape not ex-cape.

library – The word has three syllables: li-bra-ry, not li-bary.

picture – This is the most commonly mispronounced word. It is pronounced pik-cher, not pit-cher.

How we present ourselves on a daily basis through the language we speak is central to how people will perceive us. If you want to be known as a person who is respectful, courteous and successful, then refrain from vulgarity and swear words. There is no place in a civilized life for curse words or other language that is offensive and rude.

Proper Verb Tenses and Good Grammar

My grandfather used to have a saying, "Who woulda thunk it? It's purt-near unbelievable." Of course, he was saying the phrase a bit tongue-in-cheek, but he was also speaking that way to make his point: Don't act or talk like a knucklehead. People tend to write in the same way as they speak. Our syntax or our writing voice will be consistent in the way we put words onto a paper, electronically or otherwise.

Here are some hints for you to make your grammar and verb tenses be up to par and sound marvelous. A well-mannered and respectful person will always speak with words that fit the civilized person they are meant to be.

What is simple past tense and how do I use it?

You will use simple past tense when you talk about actions that have already happened at some time in the past.

Present tense	Past tense
see	saw
go	went
swim	swam
fly	flew
catch	caught
drink	drank
eat	ate
ring	rang
mean	meant
wake	has woken

Examples of simple past tense.
1. I see a balloon in the air. Present tense.
2. I saw a balloon in the air. Past tense.
3. I need a drink of water. Present tense.
4. I drank the water. Past tense

Regular verbs can be altered using –ed –d and –ied
1. Add –ed to the basic form of the verb
   Example: work + -ed = worked   Present tense: work. Past tense: worked
2. Verbs that end in -e take –d
   Example: live + –d = lived Present tense: live. Past tense: lived
3. Verbs that end with the consonant + y take –ied
   Example:- study + –ied = studied Present tense: study. Past tense: studied

Irregular verbs cannot be altered using -ed –d and –ied. They need to be learned on their own.

A small list of irregular verbs
buy	bought
drink	drank
get (up)	got (up)
have	had

sleep	slept
come	came
drive	drove
give	gave
read	read
swim	swam
do	did
eat	ate
go	went
see	saw
take	took

Examples of how to use regular and irregular verbs in sentences

Affirmative	Negative
I cleaned the house.	I didn't clean the house.
You washed the clothes.	You didn't wash the clothes.
He lived in England.	He didn't live in England.
She studied French.	She didn't study French.
It ate its food.	It didn't eat its food.
We had a good time.	We didn't have a good time.
You went to the mall.	You didn't go to the mall.
They saw a good movie.	They didn't see a good movie.

Examples of simple past tense used in a sentence.

- Mr. Bean was born in London August 4, 1970.
- He worked as a secret agent for many years.
- Yesterday, Mrs. Bean woke at 7 a.m.
- Mr. Bean didn't work last week because he was on holiday with Mrs. Bean.
- When I was younger, I didn't like to go shopping with my sister as she went to too many shops.
- The rain has stopped after it soaked my garden.

Hint

The past tense form of do = did.

I didn't have any money last month.

Didn't is a contraction form of a word with the apostrophe indicating a letter has been left out.

Remember did + not = didn't

A contraction can be context and audience dependent, so depending on its use, it may be more effective to spell out the words rather than use a contraction.

First Person, Third Person

First person: I am on a team with six members who do not get along.

Third person: The team consists of six members. There is some internal conflict among the members.

Did you know:
• Stewardesses is the longest word typed with only the left hand.
• Lollipop is the longest word typed with only the right hand.
• No word in the English language rhymes with: month, orange or purple.
• The sentence: "The quick brown fox jumps over the lazy dog" uses every letter of the alphabet.
• The words: racecar, kayak and level are the same whether they are read left to right or right to left.

Language can be so much fun.

Speak the English language with all of its beauty. Finish the ends of your words and use correct verb tense daily.

Chapter Twenty

Moving Forward with Grace, Strength, Honor and Manners

A dairy cow eats about 100 pounds each day of feed, which is a combination of hay, grain, silage and proteins (such as soybean meal), plus vitamins and minerals. U.S. dairies are producing almost three times more milk with about half the number of cows compared to 1960. On average, a cow will produce 8 gallons of milk today—that's the equivalent of 128 glasses.
Source: www.midwestdairy.com

Photo courtesy of AgriLife Studios, www.agrilifestudios.com

For those of us involved in the nation's largest industry—the production, processing and distribution of food, it is imperative we represent ourselves in the most respectful way possible on a daily basis. American agriculture, from farmers to vendors to the consumer is one of our nation's most valuable assets.

Farming has become (at one end of the spectrum) more diverse with smaller operations and, at the other end, more concentrated with huge livestock and cropping enterprises. A new generation of farmers, many of whom are women and minorities, are stepping in to take on the monumental task of feeding an ever growing population.

In today's new world, appropriate contemporary manners and civility means practicing a duty and respect to agriculture and its related businesses that approach the balance between privilege, duty and responsibility.

Following are some thoughts for you to consider as you continue your journey. Carry them with you as a reminder of moving forward with grace, strength, honor and manners:

What Steps Would You Take If You Knew You Could Not Fail?

1. Discover the awesome power of a vision.
2. Allow your dream to sit in the driver's seat of your life.
3. Never surrender leadership to negative assumptions.
4. Become a good manager of positive assumptions.
5. Empower your ego, but keep it in check and balance.
6. Become option oriented. Always ask: What are the options?
7. Alternate conscientiousness and awareness.
8. Fashion a fruitful flexibility.
9. Get into the habit of listening and listening well.
10. Never give up the core of your dream.

Life, According to You

We become sons and daughters, then we become soldiers of life. Are you making the most of your life? What are you building?

- It's nice to be important, but it is more important to be nice.
- Every task in the world starts with the first step. Take the first step.
- Walk tall.

- Stand tall.
- Fear not.
- Live your faith consistently.
- Character is what you are when no one is looking.
- Never be bitter, always be better.
- There is a blessing in every battle.
- Suffering will happen, but remember to grow from it.
- You are writing the story of your life. A chapter each day.
- People read what you write, either faithful or true.

We need to learn from our past, not live in our past. The future will be frozen for us if we are stumbling into our futures. What are the lessons you have learned?

Calibrate your past. Move forward with strength and essential good manners.

The VIP Principle

V – Value – What are the values you live?

I – Identity – Is your identity consistent with your values and the growth the new YOU is taking?

P – Purpose – What is your purpose in life? What are you building?

A well-mannered person is also a person who is grounded. You know what you want out of life and are moving toward it. A person who is respectful and civil to all will also understand how to receive.

The Joy of Receiving

1. Learn how to receive compliments.
2. Learn how to receive criticism.
3. Learn how to chart your course.
4. Learn how to face a crisis. Manage the plan to manage the crisis whether it's medical, financial, career etc.
5. Learn how to handle conflict and disagreements.
6. Ask questions.

You will learn through it all; the good, the bad and the ugly. People need to learn how to be more receptive to the inevitable ebb and flow of life. There will be ups and downs.

You have to open yourself up to be vulnerable sometimes. It takes a humble and honest person to be open and to admit when a mistake was made, then to start the healing process by offering an apology.

When you are at your best, go for brilliance. If it's a great idea, say *how*, not no.

There might be a time in your life when you have to treat some bad people nicely, and they won't deserve it, but treat them nicely. Not because they are nice, but because you are nice. We tend to grow the most in those situations where we are most outside of our comfort zone.

Maintain a Good Sense of Humor

A neighbor had owned a large farm for several years. He had a large pond in the back forty, and had it fixed up with nice picnic tables, horseshoe courts, basketball court, etc. The pond was constructed for swimming when it was built.

One evening, the old farmer decided to go down to the pond as he hadn't been there for a while. As he neared the pond, he heard voices shouting and laughing with glee. As he came closer, he saw it was a group of young women skinny-dipping in his pond. He made the women aware of his presence, and they all went to the middle of the pond.

One of the women shouted to him, "We're not coming out until you leave!"

The old farmer replied, "I didn't come down here to watch you ladies swim or get out of the pond. I only came to feed my alligators."

- Be the helper.
- Be the first to help.
- Make space for someone else.
- Keep and maintain a healthy sense of humor.
- Have a one-sentence mission statement for you.
- If it's a great idea, embrace it.
- What are you building?
- It's about relationships; building, maintaining, nurturing, growing, healthy, respectful relationships.
- Be an honorable woman or man.
- Having everything you love is not as important as loving everything you have.

- Become your word.
- Grace means having just enough.
- Never underestimate the power of the human mind and spirit.
- Say please and thank you.

The Beauty of Simple Words – 5, 4, 3, 2, 1

Words can help. Words can calm. Words can thank and show appreciation. Often, the most powerful words are the simplest words.

I call this "5, 4, 3, 2, 1". Use my words and add your own. Let me know if you have any additions. I would love to add them to my repertoire.

Five Words:

- You are a neat person.
- I love working with you.
- Would you like another helping?
- You have earned a raise.
- They want to see you.
- Taking care of the land.
- It's a dream come true.
- You've helped me so much.
- It was a terrific harvest.
- You're invited to a wedding.
- Spring is on the way.
- Farm prices are all up.

Four Words:

- Would you like help?
- Happy to see you.
- They are feeling better.
- Come be with me.
- Spring planting is underway.
- Let there be light.
- The stars are aligned.
- In God we trust.
- It fits just right.
- (Name) has come home.
- 10 fingers, 10 toes.
- Are you coming home?
- Will you marry me?
- Thank you for coming.
- Speak from the heart.
- You've made a difference.
- The stars are aligned.
- Gas prices are lower.
- Pitchers and catchers report.
- You're back in business.
- The date is set.
- I can't believe it.
- You are a star.
- Princess Charlotte Elizabeth Diana

Three Words:

- May I help?
- You were marvelous.
- See you later.
- I miss you.
- Thinking of you.
- Paid in full.
- I'm so thankful.
- I love you.
- You're in remission.
- Really, I can?
- Come again soon.
- I can't wait.
- Veni, Vidi, Vici (Julius Caesar: "I came, I saw, I conquered.")
- Think about it.
- Dreams come true.
- Dinner is served.
- It's a girl.
- It's a boy.
- He is pleasant.
- Cultivating the land.

- It's an opportunity.
- Feeding the world.
- Happy New Year.
- My best friend.
- The big day.
- Treasure the moment.
- Say something special.
- Just for you.
- Celebrate life's gifts.
- He is healthy.
- She is healthy.
- I'm coming home.
- Say something nice.
- I own it.
- Our new home.
- High school sweetheart.
- No more snow.
- You're all set.
- Yes I will.
- Enjoying the weather.
- What a win.

Two Words:

- Thank you.
- Much obliged.
- Oh my!
- You're welcome.
- Take care.
- Welcome home.
- Happy birthday.
- I do.

- I will.
- Remember Winston (Marble plaque inside the door of Westminster Abbey in London).
- Snow day.
- Happy Hanukkah.
- Merry Christmas.
- Happy Easter.

- That's it.
- Warm cookies.
- Good posture.
- Notice people.
- Good stewardship.
- Hard work.
- My hometown.
- Family traditions.
- Forever remembered.
- Fond memories.
- College sweetheart.
- It's raining.
- Farm wife.
- You're hired.
- No rain.
- Thank heavens.
- It's working.
- Agricultural Professional.

One Word:

- Please.
- Farmer.
- Rancher.
- Brilliant.
- Magical.
- Congratulations.
- Respectful.
- Hello.
- Peace.
- Santa.
- Awesome.
- Grateful.
- Sweet.
- Trust.
- Promoted.
- Respect.
- Integrity.
- Mannerly.
- Responsibility.
- Honored.
- Served.
- Confidence.
- Success.
- Agriculture.
- Kitten.
- Puppy.
- Calf.
- Lamb.
- Ewe.
- Appreciate.
- Yes.
- No.
- Remembered.
- Celebrate.
- Free.
- Graduated.
- Commencement.
- Smile.
- Friend.
- Rain.

Initials
- TGIF – Thank Goodness It's Friday
- R.S.V.P. – Respondes s'il vous plait
- LOL – Laugh Out Loud
- XXOO – Kisses and Hugs
- BFF – Best Friends Forever
- FYI – For Your Information

There is a rhythm to life, an ebb and a flow. We have days where we are "on" and other days when we may feel a little "off." Be gentle with yourself. Take good care of yourself.

As an ag professional, you are the heartbeat of our nation because the cultivation of the earth is the most important labor of all.

We are all connected to a much bigger thrill. Consider when you experience a gooseflesh, more commonly known as a goose bump. You can't talk yourself out of goosebumps. A tiny muscle on the follicle of each hair connects you to something else. You can be a glorious individual who is always well mannered and honorable. It can give you goosebumps when you know you have built a life you love.

The following characteristics represent the foundation for your life and for the infrastructure surrounding the remarkable person called you.

Resilient Attributes

- A strong flexible sense of self-esteem.
- Independence of thought and action without fear of relying on others.
- The ability to give and take in one's interactions with others.
- A well-established network of personal friends, including one or more confidants.
- A high level of personal discipline and a sense of responsibility.
- Recognition and development of one's special gifts and talents.
- Open-mindedness and receptivity to new ideas.
- A willingness to dream.
- A wide range of interests.
- A keen sense of humor.

- Insight into one's own feelings and those of others and appropriate communication of feelings.
- A high tolerance of distress.
- Focus, a commitment to life, and a philosophical framework within which personal experiences can be interpreted with meaning and hope, even in seemingly hopeless moments of life.
- Grace, humility, respect, manners.

Resilient Surroundings

- Coherent but flexible structures.
- A human network.
- Respectfulness.
- Recognition.
- Assurance of privacy.
- Tolerance of change.
- Acceptance.
- Defined, realistic limits on behavior.
- Open communications.
- Responsiveness to new ideas.
- Tolerance of conflict.
- Promotion of reconciliation.
- Hopefulness.
- A sense of community.
- Constructive human values.
- Empathy.
- Love.
- Trust.
- Honor.
- Respect.

Be Grateful

- Be grateful for a loving God, who shows himself in so many ways we don't even realize.
- Be grateful for those who love you.

- Be grateful for being a citizen in a free world country.
- Be grateful you are making a difference in this world.
- Be grateful for the display of a good deed.
- Be grateful for the gifts we are given daily: faith, health, shelter, food and family.
- Be grateful to those who give, even when they may have nothing to give.
- Be grateful for the power of prayer.
- Be grateful for giving thanks. Always give thanks.

As we express our gratitude, we must never forget that the highest appreciation is not to utter words, but to live by them.

—*John Fitzgerald Kennedy*

Reference List

Accountemps study, May, 2015.

Alexander, G.M., & Hines, M. (2002). Sex differences in response to children's toys in nonhuman primates *(Cercopithecus aethiops sabaeus)*. *Evolution and Human Behavior,* 23, 467-479.

Allik, J., & McCrae, R.R. (2004). Toward a geography of personality traits: Patterns of profiles across 36 cultures. *Journal of Cross-Cultural Psychology,* 35, 13-28.

Argyle, Michael. (1990). *The Social Psychology of Work.* London, England: Penguin Books.

Ashton, M.C., Lee, K., Perugini, M., Szarota, P., de Vries, R.E., Di Blas, L., et al. (2004). A six-factor structure of personality–descriptive adjectives: Solutions from psycholexical studies in seven languages. *Journal of Personality and Social Psychology,* 86, 356-366.

Autry, James A. *Love & Profit. The Art of Caring Leadership.* (1991). New York: William Morrow and Company, Inc.

Bandura, A. (1965). Influence of a model's reinforcement contingencies on the acquisition of imitative responses. *Journal of Personality and Social Psychology,* 1, 589-595.

Bandura, A. (1983). Psychological mechanisms of aggression. In R.G. Green & C. I. Donnerstein (Eds.), *Aggression: Theoretical and empirical reviews* (Vol. 1, pp. 1-40). New York: Academic Press.

Bandura, A., (1999). Social cognitive theory of personality. In L. Pervin & O. John (Eds.), *Handbook of personality: theory and research* (2nd ed., pp. 154-198). New York: Guilford.

Bandura, A. & Walters, R.H. (1963). *Social learning and personality development.* New York: Holt, Rinehart & Winston.

Bernstein, D.A., Penner, L.A., Clark-Stewart, A., Roy, E.J. (2006). *Psychology* (7th ed.). New York: Houghton Mifflin Company.

Blaikie, Thomas. (2005). *To the Manner Born. A Most Proper Guide to Modern Civility.* New York: Villard Books, an imprint of The Random House Publishing Group.

Carver, C.S., & Scheier, M.F. (2004). *Perspectives on personality* (5th ed.). Boston, MA: Allyn & Bacon.

Costa, P.T., & McCrae, R.R. (2002). Looking backwards: Changes in mean levels of personality traits from 80 to 12. In D. Cervone, & W. Mischel (Eds.), *Advances in personality Science* (pp. 196-217). New York: Guilford Press.

Eysenck, H.J. (1990). Biological dimensions of personality. In L. A. Pervin (Ed.), *Handbook of personality: Theory and research* (pp.244-276). New York: Guilford.

Eysenck, H.J. (1990b). Genetic and environmental contributions to individual differences: The three major dimensions of personality. *Journal of Personality,* 58, 245-261.

Eysenck, H.J.(1994). A biological theory of intelligence. In D. K. Detterman (Ed.), *Current topics in human intelligence* (Vol. 4). Norwood, NJ: Ablex.

Fagot, B.I. (1995). Psychosocial and cognitive determinants of early gender-role development. *Annual Review of Sex Research,* 6, 1-31.

Forni, P.M. (2002). *Choosing Civility.* New York: St. Martin's Press.

Forni, P.M. (2008). *The Civility Solution.* New York: St. Martin's Press.

Geary, D. C. (1999). Evolution and developmental sex differences. *Current Directions in Psychological Science,* 8, 115-120.

Law, D. J., Pellegrino, J.W., & Hunt, E.B. (1993). Comparing the tortoise and the hare: Gender differences and experience in dynamic spatial reasoning tasks. *Psychological Science,* 4, 35-40.

Luisa Capetillo. (2015, May 3). In Wikipedia, The Free Encyclopedia. Retrieved 19:24, June 2, 2015, from http://en.wikipedia.org/w/index.php?title=Luisa_Capetillo&oldid=660656917

Levy, G.D., Taylor, M.G., & Gelman, S.A. (1995). Traditional and evaluative aspects of flexibility in gender roles, social conventions, moral rules, and physical laws. *Child Development,* 66, 515-531.

Madison, Dolley. (1886). *Memoirs and Letters of Dolly Madison.* Boston: Houghton-Mifflin.

Martin, C.L., and Fabes, R.A. (2001). The stability and consequences of young children's same sex peer interactions. *Developmental Psychology,* 37, 431-446.

Martin, C.L., & Ruble, D. (2004). Children's search for gender cues. *Current Directions in Psychological Science,* 13, 67-70.

Maslow, A. H. (1943). A theory of human motivation. *Psychological Review,* 50, 370-396.

Maslow, A. H. (1954). *Motivation and personality.* New York: Harper.

Maslow, A. H. (1970). *Motivation and personality* (2nd ed.). New York: Harper & Row.

Maslow, A. H. (1971). *The farther reaches of human nature.* New York: McGraw-Hill.

McCrae, R.R., & Costa, P.T., Jr. (2004). A contemplated revision of the NEO Five-Factor Inventory. *Personality and Individual Differences.* 36, 587-596.

McCrae, R.R., Costa, P.T., Jr., Martin, T.A., Oryol, V.E., Rukavishnikov, A.A., et al. (2004). Consensual validation of personality traits across cultures. *Journal of Research in Personality,* 38, 179-201.

McCrae, R.R., & John, O. (1992). An introduction to the five-factor model and its applications. *Journal of Personality,* 60, 175-215.

Mischel, W. (2002). *Introduction to personality* (7th ed.). Fort Worth, Texas: Harcourt Brace.

Mischel, W. (2004). Toward an integrative science of the person. *Annual Review of Psychology,* 55, 1-22.

Mischel, W., Shoda, Y., & Smith, R. (2004). *Introduction to personality: Toward an integration* (7th ed.) New York: Wiley.

Null, Christopher. Chrisnull.com. Retrieved 19 September, 2014.

Patrick, Bethanne. (2011). *An Uncommon History of Common Courtesy.* Washington, D.C. : National Geographic Society.

Pervin, L.A., & John, O.P. (2001). *Personality: Theory and research* (8th ed.). Oxford, England: Wiley.

Peterson, C.; Maier, S. F.; Seligman, M. E. P. (1995). *Learned Helplessness: A Theory for the Age of Personal Control.* New York: Oxford University Press.

Pomerantz, E.M., Altermatt, E.R., & Saxon, J.L. (2002). Making the grade but feeling distressed: Gender differences in academic performance and internal distress. *Journal of Educational Psychology,* 94, 396-404.

Ross, Josephine. (2006). *Jane Austen's Guide to Good Manners. Compliments, Charades and Horrible Blunders.* New York: Bloomsbury USA.

Roth, S. (1980). "A revised model of learned helplessness in humans." *Journal of Personality* 48: 103–33.

Ruble, D.N., & Martin, C.L., (1998). Gender development. In W. Damon & N. Eisenberg (Eds.), *Handbook of child psychology: Vol. 3. Social, Emotional, and personality development* (5th ed., pp. 933-1016). New York: Wiley.

Schlesinger, Arthur M. (1968). *Learning How to Behave: A Historical Study of American Etiquette Books.* New York: Cooper Square Publishers, Inc.

Seale, William. (1986). *The President's House.* Washington, D.C.: White House Historical Association.

Seligman, M. E. P. (1975). *Helplessness: On Depression, Development, and Death.* San Francisco: W. H. Freeman.

Simpson-Giles, Candace. (2001). *How to Be A Lady. A Contemporary Guide to Common Courtesy.* Nashville, Tennessee: Rutledge Hill Press.

Simpson, J.A., & Kenrick, D.T. (1997). *Evolutionary social psychology.* Mahwah, NJ: Erlbaum.

Skinner, B.F. (1961). *Cumulative record* (3rd ed.). Englewood Cliffs, NJ: Prentice-Hall.

Taylor, S.E., Klein, L.C., Lewis, B.P., Gruenewald, T. L., Gurung, R. A. R., & Updegraff, J.A. (2000). Biobehavioral responses to stress in females: Tend-and-befriend, not fight-or-flight. *Psychological Review,* 107, 411-429.

Tenenbaum, H.R. & Leaper, C. (2003). Parent-child conversations about science: The socialization of gender inequities? *Developmental Psychology,* 39, 34-47.

http://www.washingtonpost.com/blogs/wonkblog/wp/2015/02/10/your-lifetime-earnings-are-probably-determined-in-your-twenties/

http://www.washingtonpost.com/news/grade-point/wp/2015/04/28/ after-george-washington-died-his-wife-burned-her-letters-except- these/?postshare=201430254840849

http://www.gallup.com/poll/181289/majority-employees-not-engaged- despite-gains-2014.aspx

Whitcomb, John and Claire. (2000). *Real Life at the White House.* London: Routledge.

http://www.loc.gov Library of Congress.

http://oxforddictionaries.com/words

http://www.oxforddictionaries.com/us/words/the-oxford-english-corpus

Wortman, C.B. & Brehm, J.W. (1975). Response to uncontrollable outcomes: An integration of reactance theory and the learned helplessness model. In *Advances in experimental social psychology,* L. Berkowitz, (ed.). Vol. 8. New York: Academic Press.

Zatzick, C. D., Deery, S. J. and Iverson, R. D. (2015), Understanding the Determinants of Who Gets Laid Off: Does Affective Organizational Commitment Matter?. Hum. Resour. Manage. doi: 10.1002/hrm.21641

http://www.huffingtonpost.com/zagat/how-to-tip_b_2293902.html Retrieved 31 May 2015.